HINDU INFANTICIDE

HINDU INFANTICIDE

AN

ACCOUNT

OF THE

MEASURES ADOPTED FOR SUPPRESSING THE PRACTICE

OF THE

SYSTEMATIC MURDER

BY

THEIR PARENTS

OF

FEMALE INFANTS;

WITH

INCIDENTAL REMARKS ON OTHER CUSTOMS PECULIAR TO THE NATIVES OF INDIA.

EDITED

BY

EDWARD MOOR

GYAN

Published by

GYAN

Gyan Publishing House
5, Ansari Road
Daryaganj, New Delhi-110002
Phone: 011-47034999, 9811692060
E-mail: books@gyanbooks.com

Distribution Network
gyanbooks.com
India, USA, Canada, UK, Australia, France

ISBN: 978-81-212-8696-1 (PB)
First Published, 1811

2nd Impression 2023

Printed at: Gyan Press, Delhi.

HINDU INFANTICIDE
Editor: Edward Moor

HINDU INFANTICIDE.

AN

ACCOUNT

OF THE

MEASURES ADOPTED FOR SUPPRESSING THE PRACTICE

OF THE

SYSTEMATIC MURDER

BY

THEIR PARENTS

OF

FEMALE INFANTS;

WITH

INCIDENTAL REMARKS ON OTHER CUSTOMS PECULIAR TO THE NATIVES OF INDIA.

EDITED,

WITH NOTES AND ILLUSTRATIONS,

BY

EDWARD MOOR, F.R.S.

AUTHOR OF THE HINDU PANTHEON.

LONDON:

PRINTED FOR J. JOHNSON AND CO.

ST. PAUL'S CHURCH YARD.

1811.

TO

LIEUT.-COL. ALEXANDER WALKER,

Late Political Resident in GUZERAT.

THE course of Dedication for this Volume, deemed by you more obvious than this which I have adopted, being already doubly occupied, there can remain no difficulty in determining to whom its inscription ought to be secondarily directed.

Were you a stranger to me, the important part which you have borne in effecting the abolition of the sad practice of INFANTICIDE, now, happily, as far as refers to the extensive limit of the British Influence in *India*, to be spoken of as one that *was* of lamentable prevalence, would have prompted me to this prefixture of your name; but when a sense of propriety is strongly seconded by that feeling of Friendship that hath for so many years subsisted between us, it becomes a pleasing duty; and you will receive this Address as a tribute willingly offered to the remembrance and to the continuance of long-lived and uninterrupted Respect and Esteem.

When I, farther, call to mind the confidential Regard, originating perhaps in official intercourse, but strengthened by a congeniality of disposition in the promotion of public and private good, that so cordially subsists between our common and highly-respected friend Mr. DUNCAN and you, I am additionally impelled to this measure, thinking that it will not be unpleasing to either: while associating my own name so honourably, and in such a Cause, must be an object to me of laudable ambition.

Wishing that all desired good may await your arrival, and prosper your abode, in your native country, after an absence of thirty years spent most zealously and usefully in its foreign service in *India*, I heartily, My Dear WALKER, bid you FAREWELL.

EDWARD MOOR.

Bealings, Suffolk,
March 1, 1811.

PREFACE.

Although it may not be very interesting to the Public, it will not, I hope, be entirely otherwise, and will be satisfactory to me, if I be allowed the liberty of stating the sources whence I have derived the materials for this little Volume.

In the Dedication of my *Hindu Pantheon*, as well as in the body of that work, I have adverted to the general subject of the present; and noticed a manuscript on *Indian Infanticide* being in the best hands, hoping it would be submitted to the *Public*.

I had not at that time any idea that it would be so submitted in its present form. The manuscript was in the possession of Sir Joseph Banks, to whom it had been transmitted by the Honourable Mr. Duncan, Governor of *Bombay*, and I was authorized to avail myself of it as I pleased in my *Hindu Pantheon*, then, as was known in *India*, in the press: but I was too far advanced to admit conveniently of my benefiting by this kind attention; and I thought, moreover, that the subject so handled, demanded a more respectful introduction to the Literary Public, than in an episode, as it were, in a larger work. Nor when Sir Joseph Banks put the manuscript into my hands, had I any expectation of the subject assuming its present shape. I, however, copied and arranged it for the press; and soon after I had so done Colonel Walker arrived in *England*; and on being made acquainted with my intention, he furnished me with the original papers, among others, whence a considerable portion of Mr. DUNCAN's manuscript, in the form of a summary, or abridged memoir, had been drawn up.

Deeming the subject sufficiently curious and interesting to warrant its separate publication, and not being straitened for room or time, as was the case in respect to the *Hindu Pantheon*, I resolved on submitting to the Public the entire papers, part of which only were condensed in Mr. DUNCAN's admirable summary. Several letters and reports, posterior in point of time to the termination of that summary, were among the materials with which Colonel WALKER furnished me. None of these had been written with any view to publication.

My enlarged project was now communicated to Sir JOSEPH BANKS. It is bespeaking the good opinion of the Public to say that he warmly approved it; and but repeating what is known to all, that he was, as ever, prompt in forwarding by his assistance and advice, this, like every other, effort, having in view a public good: and such, it is hoped, may, through however humble an instrumentality as the Editor of this Volume, be hereby promoted.

Thus assisted and encouraged, I recast my materials; dividing them into the convenient arrangement of Chapters; and retaining for the two first the commencement of Mr. DUNCAN's Memoir; which, as far as those Chapters extend, comprises a portion of time anterior to Colonel WALKER's co-operation in the holy cause of extirpating Infanticide from among the *Hindus;* and refers to a part of *India* distant from the scene of those operations. To a time and country, indeed, wherein no *European* but Mr. DUNCAN knew of the existence of the crime, and when consequently no one but himself laboured to eradicate it.

An outline of this interesting discovery, and of the exertions successfully made to effectuate the abolition of the sad habit so developed, was briefly published in the *Asiatic Researches:* but, to render this Tract fully comprehensive of its subject, I have, from Mr. DUNCAN's memoir, detailed the rise, progress, and happy result of that discovery; as, with other points connected with this and the preceding paragraph, will more clearly appear from my occasional notices in the course of the work.

Finding that several of my papers, from having been copied in *India* by native writers, were inaccurate; and imagining that others on the same subject, not in my possession, might probably exist among the records at the *India-house*, I, with the desire of making my Tract as worthy of the Public eye as was in my power, applied to Mr. ASTELL, the most worthy and enlightened Chairman of the respectable Court who so ably Direct the Affairs of our Indian Empire, for permission to correct from their records my defective materials, and eventually to extract others of which I was not possessed.

On unfolding my scheme of publication to Mr. ASTELL he was pleased to approve it; and to aid it by obligingly acceding to my wishes. For this ready and polite condescension, I thus return my grateful thanks.

In the commencement of Chapter VI. I have noticed my acquisition of materials from this source. It will, in a confined degree, be there seen, and may be thence extensively inferred, that this most respectable body, amid the multiplicity of important objects unremittingly pressing oh their attention, do still yield the promptest cognizance to the calls of humanity; and that any point involving the happiness or welfare of any, of the many millions, of their deserving subjects in *Hindustan*, is viewed by them with interest and sympathy. The opportunity is grateful to me, and it has several times occurred, of making respectful mention of the liberality of the Honourable Court to me on literary occasions. It would look like ostentation to recapitulate them; and I therefore generally return my best thanks.

It is, I feel, necessary to notice, and apologize for the frequent references that I have, in the course of this work, found it expedient to make to the *Hindu Pantheon*. I am, indeed, almost ashamed at their frequency, although it has, in some degree, been unavoidable; for, as therein observed, Mythology is, with the *Hindus*, all-pervading. Their history, science, literature, arts, customs, conversation, and every thing, are replete with Mythological allusions. Now, as the greater part of my notes and interpolations scattered through the following pages are of that description; and as I have endeavoured in my former work to say something, however brief and superficial, on the attributes and character, and the legends most popularly connected with the history, of every deity comprehended within the vast range of the Pantheistic Idolatry of *India*, I found in my said work some notice explanatory on most points that seemed to require it, of this. And having no library, and writing where I have access to but few books, I, of course, found my own poor work easiest, and, in this case, generally sufficient, to refer to.

On a practice so universally abhorrent to every humane

breast as Infanticide, a uniformity of sentiment must prevail. Every one who thinks, speaks, or writes on it, must experience the same train of emotions, and express himself in nearly the same terms. This will sufficiently account for, and excuse, any sameness of phraseology, or repetition, observable in this volume; wherein different persons write, and the same person at distant periods, on the same subject. It will also relieve me from the necessity of any reflections, or expression of my own feelings. I could but have repeated what is already said by my worthy friends; and in saying what I have deemed necessary, I have sometimes with difficulty refrained from such reflections. It is not from deficiency of sympathy that I have so coolly edited this work on a practice, the contemplation of which must move a Stoic. I have checked mental ebullition, and erased its result when it hath heedlessly escaped me. Nor, I am confident, will my Countrymen require any stimuli to direct their feelings to a due appreciation of the enormity of the crime of Infanticide, and of the merits of those good men, to whose benevolent zeal, Humanity is indebted for one of her greatest victories. And I persuade myself that my generous Countrymen, who have so nobly and successfully exerted themselves in the abolition of the detestable traffick in their brethren of *Africa*, will not contemplate without interest the honourable efforts of the individuals of our own nation, who have without *eclat*, and without any expectation of publicity, or recompence, save the consciousness of approving Heaven, laboured, and to the extent of the *British* influence with equal success, in the same vineyard; and have, under the aid and blessing of Providence, rescued from annual destruction, thousands of our sisters in

Asia:—and that they will be prompt to bestow on them, albeit unlooked for, that cordial, though silent, tribute of approbation, so grateful to minds that thus impelled can thus labour; and though silent yet if cordial, the most desirable and only return that can be here commensurate to the importance of the service rendered to Humanity, thus triumphant over one of the most agonizing infringements of her laws that she was ever doomed to suffer.

The portion of this Volume that hath fallen to my lot to execute, is small. This "Account of the Measures adopted for the Discovery and Suppression of Infanticide among the *Hindus*," as well as the good work itself, is by the joint hands of Mr. DUNCAN and Colonel WALKER. The arrangements and editorial parts only are mine. The notes that I have interspersed through the work, sufficiently distinguished from the other matter, the Courteous Reader will receive in the good will with which they are offered. To some Readers they may not prove altogether useless; and may to others, I hope, be amusing: so that even those who are too wise to be instructed by my humble efforts, may, I trust, considering my motives, still condescend to be pleased.

Confidently, but with becoming deference, I now leave the best of causes—HUMANITY—in the best of hands—those of the BRITISH PUBLIC.

EDWARD MOOR.

1st March, 1811.

MEMORANDUM—*touching the* MAP *prefixed to this Work.*

IN page 212 I have noticed my intention of giving with this Tract, a Map of *Kattywar*, if it could be engraved in time, so as not to delay publication, which it is very desirable to avoid, in as far as sending the work to *India* by the ships of the present season is much wished; and the season is far advanced.

The Engraver has, however, hastened his work so as to finish all that I put into his hands. But had time permitted, I should have made the map more full. As it is, I have a few words to say thereon.

Every point in *Kattywar*, or the portion of *Guzerat* so named, formed by the gulfs of *Cambay* and *Kutch*, is laid down from surveys made by Lieutenant HARDY of the *Bombay* Artillery. He accompanied Colonel WALKER's detachment on different services, for that purpose; and being the only survey that I know of ever made of that province, it will be looked on I hope as a valuable addition to our published stock of Oriental Geography. Mr. HARDY is a very accurate surveyor, and a very respectable and promising officer.

The points not included within the limits above specified are taken from maps already before the public, and are filled in to give a clearer locality to *Guzerat*, in the glance of those not conversant in Eastern Geography. *Saint* JOHN'S *Point*, the southernmost position, is about a degree, nearly due north from *Bombay*.

The only alteration that I have made in Mr. HARDY'S work, save reducing it from a scale of eighteen inches to a degree, is in the orthography; in which I have taken some liberties, pursuant to the system that I have followed for Oriental words. For this I have to ask the excuse of Mr. HARDY and all parties concerned.

I regret that I had not the map to refer to occasionally in the course of the work, where mention is made of towns, &c. whose situation might, by such references, have been made clearer to the Reader: but in my uncertainty as to being able, or otherwise, to give the map at all, this was evidently unattainable.

It remains for me to say something on such features of my map as are evidently irrelevant to geographical subjects. The *Head*, is of that respectable friend of Colonel WALKER'S mentioned in page 197; there called GANGADHER PATWERDHEN SASTRI. On the map he appears more classically designated in characters appropriate to a learned *Pandit*, *Srì* GANGA-DHARA *Sastrì*, which if literally interpreted might be to many Readers unintelligible; nor much more so perhaps to those wholly unread in *Hindu* mythology, when rendered "*The Revered* GANGES-BEARER, *learned in the Sastra*." This learned person is reverently honoured with the prefixture *Sri*, of which see page 152. He being a *Saiva* is distinguished by one of the thousand names of SIVA—

"From whose red clustering locks famed GANGA springs."

And here we may, as ever, note in passing, a geographical fact veiled in a mythological fable. The *Ganges* is now known to spring from the head of a hill named after this person of the *Hindu* tritheistical divinity, who appears GANGES-BEARING, GANGA-DHARA, in many plates of the *Hindu Pantheon*.

The black letter impression is of the *Sikka*, or state seal of the *Raja* ANANDA RAO GAIKAWAR, sovereign of *Guzerat*, of whom the Reader will find lengthened notice in the following pages. It is thus read:—*Sri Raja* SAHU *Chater pati akilà prant pretap* PURANDERA, ANANDA RAO GAIKAWAR, *Sena Khas-kheyl Shamshir Behader*. And may be thus rendered:—

"Subservient to the canopied Lord *Raja* SAHU, the staunch, magnanimous, brave Prince, like unto INDRA, is ANANDA RAO GAIKAWAR—a warrior of prowess in the use of arms."

SAHU is the usual distinction of the nominal sovereign of the *Mahrattas*, kept, as noticed hereafter, a state pageant by the hereditary usurpers of his countries. PURANDERA is a name of INDRA, of whom so much occurs in the *Hindu Pantheon*. It means the *Destroyer of Towns;* which among his many names, is that likely to be remembered in the neighbourhood of *Guzerat*, from the mythological fable of his having overwhelmed *Ujayana*, or *Ogein*, the capital of SINDEA's hereditary possessions, many feet deep by a shower of sand. The historical fact is, that *Ogein*, so submerged, now lies the interesting *Herculaneum* and *Pompeia* of *India*. Both fable and fact are detailed in the *Hindu Pantheon*.

The other names and titles of this seal are sufficiently discussed in future pages.

The *Gaikawar* uses another seal which is of *secondary* or inferior importance, as implied by its name, *Mùtàlì*, a corrupt *Persian* word. The impression runs thus:—

Sri MALSARA *kànt charanì tatper* GOVIND RAO *sùt* ANANDA RAO GAIKAWAR, *Sena Khàs-kheyl Shamshìr Behader nìranter*.

And is thus translated:—

"Subservient to the holy mandates of the Lord of the Goddess MALSARA, is the son of GOVIND RAO, ANAND RAO GAIKAWAR, a warrior of eternal prowess."

This is the seal usually given to the minister, or the principal officers of the state, such as *Sùbàhs* of provinces, at a distance from the residence of the sovereign. It is not engraved, and I shall stop only to observe that the goddess MALSARA named therein is an *avatàra*, or incarnation, of PARVATI, become flesh to accompany her lord SIVA in his manifestation in the person of KANDEH RAO, or KANDUBA, as fully detailed in the *Hindu Pantheon*. This is the tutelary deity of the *Gaikawar* family; an anomaly in reference to their sectarial patronymic (ANANDA, GOVINDA, GAIKAWAR, &c.) derived from a *Vaishnava* source, that this is no place to discuss.

A third royal seal is also in use in *Guzerat*, much smaller than the preceding two, the impression of which is in *Sanskrit* characters equivalent, though corruptly written, to the *Persian* words *Mùratab shùd*, which signify *finished—performed—the end—finis*, &c. They call this the *Martabsùd* seal, and it is usually affixed to the conclusion of public letters and deeds. One of these seals is often entrusted to inferior local officers for the purpose of authenticating their reports, and giving authority to their acts. A *fac simile* of this seal is engraved on the map.

The other seal is a very curious subject—it is in *Persian* characters, of the *Raja* of *Kutch*, and is to be read thus:—

مها راو ميرزا راجه رايدهن فدوي شاه عالم پادشاه غازي
پاطني حرمن شريفين سنه 1199

Maha Rao Mirza Raja Raid'han fedwì SHAH AALAM *Padshah ghàzì—pàtnì herman sherìfìn—sanneh* 1199.

And may be thus translated:—

" The noble *Rao Mirza Ràja Ràid'han*, the devoted of the victorious King SHAH AALAM—the pilot (or guide) to both the most holy temples. Year (of the *Hejra)* 1199.

The word *pàtni* is said to mean in the language of *Sind*, one who helps to embark, or to steer or direct a vessel, and has been given to the *Raja* of *Kutch*, in consequence of the assistance he affords to pilgrims proceeding from *Hindùstàn* to *Mekka*. " Both the most holy temples," mean those of *Jerusalem* and *Mekka*.

This *Bùj* chief, as he is sometimes called, is of the sect who worship DEVI in her " *Lion-borne* " form, as she is often seen in the plates of the *Hindu Pantheon*, in which work many of her various forms are fully discussed. The *Raja* therefore denotes his faith by crowning his seal with this symbol of the might of DEVI, the consort of the Avenger SIVA.

The impressions of these seals, of which *fac similes* are

engraved on the watery degrees of the map, and their translations, were given to me by Colonel WALKER; and the following I find among some memorandums referring to them.

"It may be remarked generally of these seals, and particularly of those of the *Mahratta Rajas*, the strange intermixture of *Persian* and *Arabic* terms with those of *Sanskrit* and *Hindu* origin. The *Hindu* writings and deeds are commonly as remarkable for simplicity of language and expression, as the compositions and inscriptions of the *Mahomedans* are of a contrary character. But they naturally began to admire and soon to imitate the pompous and inflated language of those who had conquered their country, and imposed on them another government.

"The *Mahrattas* were more easily led to adopt this practice, as they were merely soldiers of fortune, and generally very ignorant and illiterate, just rising into power and consequence, when the *Moghul* empire was in its greatest splendour, and when its maxims, and all connected with its government, were objects of admiration and consequently of imitation."

Notice on the Orthography of Oriental Names and Words that occur in this Volume.

à is intended to be pronounced as in *fall*, or *fast*.
a . . . . as in *America*.
ì . . . . *ea* in *sea*, or *ee* in *see*.
ù . . . . *oo* in *fool*, or *u* in *full*.

This will generally suffice—the letters are not always accented; as it was thought sufficient to do it a few times in each word. The Reader will therefore see the same word printed *Ràja-pùtra*, for instance, and *Raja-putra*; SÌVA and SIVA.

Where practicable I have always used the K, initial and medial, in preference to C.—KALI, in preference to CALI—KRISHNA to CRISHNA—SAKA to SACA, &c.

The attentive Reader may, perhaps, observe that the same word is not always spelled uniformly. This has arisen partly from inattention, and partly from design. Whether written MAHOMMED, MAHAMMED, or MOHOMED, *Ràja*, or *Ràjah*, for instance, is of little moment. The pronunciation will be nearly the same: and near enough, even in words less known, to answer every useful purpose.

Proper names of persons are printed in small capitals—names of places, and words in foreign languages, generally in *Italics*. This is, I think, a useful practice in works wherein such names and words occur frequently.

CONTENTS.

practised there, 18, 19, 20; farther inquiries on the practice; modes of, &c. 19, 20; found to exist more and more extensively; practised by *Mahomedans*, but forbidden in the *Koran;* customs of *Ràj-pùts; Hindu* superstition, 20, 21. Families, &c. of the *Rajas* of *Kutch;* excuses for Infanticide; early marriage, &c. of *Hindus;* NANA FURNAVIS with difficulty finds a maiden young enough to be a bride, 22, 23. Women encourage the destruction of their children, 23, 25; the *Jarejahs* and other tribes in *Kutch*, 24, 25; mothers even, 25; demonstrations of the fact, 25, 26; exceptions reproachable, 26, 28; farther inquiries into the existence and extent of the crime; modes of, &c. 27, 28, 29; legendary origin of, 29; encouraged by *Brahmans*, 29, 30. Exceptions to the universality of Infanticide among the *Jarejahs*, 30, 31, 32; *Brahmanical* potency, 31; Instructions by the *Bombay* Government to Colonel WALKER to counteract the practice, 32, 33; his reply, developing its extent; distant prospect of suppressing it, &c.; geographical orthography of *India* defective; political dependence of *Guzerat;* suppression of Infanticide there, commixed with political and military arrangements; correspondence with the supreme Government thereon, 34 to 37. Farther communication from Colonel WALKER; difficulties encountered; but some encouragement to hope for eventual success, 38, 39, 40. Commendations by the *Bombay* and Supreme Governments of Colonel WALKER's exertions; conclusion of Mr. DUNCAN's summary, 41.

CHAPTER III.

Report from Lieutenant-Colonel ALEXANDER WALKER, *dated* BARODA, 15*th March* 1808, *of the measures pursued by him for the Suppression of* INFANTICIDE *in* KATTYWAR, *or* GUZERAT, page 42.

Retrospection to earlier exertions in the good cause, 42, 43. Probable and legendary origin of Infanticide among the *Jarejahs*, 43, 44, 45, &c.; the *Ràj-gùr*, or domestic preceptors, encourage it, 44, 45. The power, numbers, &c. of the *Jarejahs* more extensive formerly than at present, 47; their pride supposed to have originated Infanticide among them, 48; a brave, and generally humane tribe, 48; their character, habits, and other points connected with the main subject, farther considered, 49, 50, 51; no earlier attempt made to check their unnatural propensity, 52; strange indifference thereon, 52; various modes of perpetrating the act, 53 to 56; sometimes even by mothers! 55, 57; who, in other respects, are gentle and amiable, 56. Death of a daughter among the

Postscript, to the foregoing Report, page 103.

CHAPTER IV.

Extracts, translated from the Correspondence between Colonel WALKER, SUNDERJI SIVAJI, *Jarejah* JEHAJI, FATTEH MAHOMED, *and others, on the subject of* INFANTICIDE, *referred to in the foregoing* REPORT, page 108.

CHAPTER V.

CHAPTER VI.

ERRATA.

Page 38. The word *Bhúmia*, is not, as here surmized, a provincial pronunciation of *Brahman*; but means, among other things, a terrestrial, rather than a spiritual, guide—one particularly conversant in the affairs of the country. It is derived from *Bhú*, the *earth*, *soil*; and hence applied to the proprietors of territory; and to a *Thakúr*, or native chief, as well as to the possessors and cultivators of the land, who are considered as the original inhabitants of the country. As well as in *Guzerat* the term is used in senses not dissimilar in *Mysore*; and in other parts of *India*.

Bhudevi is the terrestrial name of Parvati, as goddess of the *earth*—as the names of Diana were varied to suit her various forms, she being Luna in heaven, and Proserpine or Hecate in hell; so her archetype, the *Hindu* Parvati, is the heavenly Bhavani, on earth Bhudevi, and Patala-devi as consort of the regent of the infernal regions. Bhu-deva, as spouse of the earthly goddess, is a name of Siva. See Index to the *Hindu Pantheon*.

Page 62. In the note, twelfth line from the bottom, the parenthesis is wrongly placed—it requires to be removed from after the word "source," to "Index." On that note, I have farther to observe that I suspect error in my strained derivation of the name of a district in *Kattywar*. *Mucho Kanta*, I am told, cannot safely be traced to my surmized source, *Matsya-kanta*.

Page 69, paragraph 144. For "procuring bastards," read "marrying bastards."

HINDU INFANTICIDE.

CHAP. I.

Summary, by the Honourable Governor DUNCAN, *of the measures adopted by him at* BENARES, *for the suppression of* FEMALE INFANTICIDE, *practised in that neighbourhood, by the tribe of* Ràj-kumàr, *and others.*

Extract of a Letter from Mr. JONATHAN DUNCAN, when Resident at *Benares*, to the Governor-General in Council, dated 26th April, 1789.

..............."THE first class is the tribe of [a] *Ràj-kumàr*, who deduce their descent from *Raja* [b] PIT'HAURA, in whom ended, about 600 years ago, the *Chauhan* dynasty of the princes of *Dehli*, and from whose stock the present race of the *Ràj-kumàr* (who then also assumed this new family denomination) is believed to be sprung. Their number, it is said, doth not altogether exceed forty thousand; most of whom inhabit, in nearly one society, the opposite line of our boundary in the dominions of his excellency the *Vizier*; but unfortunately for the quiet of both countries, they possess lands that pay about 20,000 rupees revenue in the districts of *Anglee* and *Kereeat-*

[a] Or *Raja-kumara, royal children*, or princes of the blood royal. E. M.

[b] Some notice is taken of this personage in a note at the end of this chapter. E. M.

Mehera on our side. They are originally [c] *Raja-Putras;* and even exceed that tribe in the wildness of their notions, and peculiarity of their manners; scarcely owning any allegiance, either to the *Vizier's* or to our Government; and always ready to betake themselves to arms, to which they are from infancy inured, in resentment either of public or private wrongs, real or imaginary. At the same time they have, I am assured, a sense of honour from which they do not deviate; and are noted for faithfully adhering to such engagements as they may contract."

Extract, from the same to the same, dated 2d October, 1789.

" The necessity of using Sepoys in the general business of the collections will, I have every reason to believe, rapidly diminish. The parts of the country now the most disorderly are on the *Juanpore* frontiers, and these disorders, as already detailed,

[c] Offspring of the royal race: in the MS. written *Rauje Poot,* as it is generally pronounced in conversation. The tribe of *Raja-putra,* or *Raj-put,* is a subdivision of the grand class *Kshetriya,* commonly pronounced *Kehtri,* the second of the four grand divisions of the *Hindus.* The *Kehtri,* or *Kshetri,* is the military class, out of which kings and soldiers are, or ought to be, exclusively taken. The tribe of *Rajput* is again variously subdivided; there being, it is said, not less than a thousand sects or tribes comprehended in it; itself being but one of five hundred sectarial varieties of the class of *Kshetri.* These round numbers are not, I judge, presumed to be very exact. See *Ayin Akbery,* Vol. III. p. 87, *Calcutta* Ed.—" The natural duties of the *Kshetri* are, bravery, glory, fortitude, rectitude; not to flee from the field; generosity, and princely conduct." WILKINS' *Bhagavat Gita,* p. 130. See also *Gentoo Laws,* Introd. p. c. and *Hindu Pantheon,* p. 380.

In the mythological origin of the *Hindu* race, the *Kshetri* is fabled to have sprung from the *arm* of BRAHMA; and the word means *protection.* It would perhaps be impossible, and useless probably if otherwise, to trace with any accuracy the sectarial variations among any grand division of the *Hindus*; differing from each other, as they generally do, in degrees varying from trivial to important; from social and domestic habits, up to moral and theological conduct and speculation. E. M.

arise chiefly from the *Ràjkumàrs*, concerning whom I am in daily expectation of receiving the instructions with which your Lordship (Earl CORNWALLIS) has signified it to be the intention of Government to favor me; till when I have deferred proceeding to that quarter, and to the adoption of the measures, that I have had the honor of submitting to your *Lordship's* consideration, for maintaining as much peace among that obdurate and extraordinary race of men, as they seem capable of enjoying—but that portion appears not to be great; for two of them, *viz.* ZALEM[d] SING (before mentioned in my address of the 26th of April) and [e]GURDAT having lately levied their forces with a design to fight each other on our borders, I have been obliged to warn the commanding-officer at *Juanpore* to be on his guard against their possible inroads. The appearance of peace between these men has since increased, but we must not yet relax our caution against what may happen, for I cannot rely on their moderation; and, besides, what can be ex-

[d] Some of the warlike tribes of *Raja-putra* so generally affect the nominal termination of *Sing*, that it has become almost universal among them as a proper name. *Singh* or *Singa*, in *Sanskrit*, is the lion; an apt symbol of the ferocious courage of this race of warriors. *Zalem* may have a like signification in *Sanskrit* as in *Arabic*; in the latter, it is a derivative from ظلم, *zulm*; meaning power, tyranny, or oppression: the latter is its most general sense. ZALEM SING, hence designates the mighty or irresistible lion. E. M.

[e] Or GOORDUT, as in the MS. It might perhaps be more correctly written *Gurdata*, or *Gurudata*, that is, the gift or boon of a *guru*, or spiritual preceptor; as having been yielded to an unfruitful bed by the generative deity from the efficacious intercessions of a pious pastor. This is not unusual. BRAHMA-DATA, the gift of BRAHMA-DEVA-DATA, the boon of the lord, literally *deodand*, &c. Thus may be found the origin of some western names. MITHRA-DATA, for instance, slightly altered to MITHRIDATES, or MITHRADATES; in *Sanskrit*, meaning the gift of the sun; similar to SURYA-DATA, or HELI-DATA: HELI is a name of the sun both in Greek and *Sanskrit*. See *Hindu Pantheon*, pp. 192. 287. 322. E.M.

pected of men inured as they are from their birth and by education to the most atrocious deeds? I am well assured, and it is indeed here generally believed (and being so it is my duty not to keep such enormities, however sanctioned by usage, from the knowledge of Government) that it is no unfrequent practice among the tribe of *Ràjkumàr* to destroy their daughters, by causing the mothers to refuse them nurture; whence this race of men do often from necessity marry into other *Raj-put* families. The greatest exception that I can find to this melancholy truth is, that now and then, the more wealthy *Rajkumars* will sometimes spare, and bring up their female issue; especially where they happen to have none of the male line. This horrid custom is said to exist also among some other tribes, more especially in the *Vizier's* dominions, and is thought to be founded in the extravagant desire of independency entertained by this race of men; joined, perhaps, to the supposed necessity of procuring a suitable settlement in marriage for these devoted females were they allowed to grow up; and the disgrace which would ensue from any omission in that respect. Nor is this species of atrocity of recent institution: for a similar prejudice, as existing among the *Indians*, was known by the ancient *Greeks* and *Romans*, as is found in the relations they have left of this quarter of the world."

From the same to the same, dated from Gherwarah, in the province of Benares, 26th December, 1789.

..........." I cannot conclude this address without mentioning, that having been lately through that part of the country where those of the *Ràj-kumàr* tribe reside, I have conversed with several of them; and having, from their own confession, found that the custom of female child-murder has long been, and still continues very prevalent among them, as noticed in my address of the 2d October, I have prevailed on those situated within our frontier, to agree to renounce in future this horrid practice: to which effect they have entered into the engagement which will be found translated in the accompanying extract of my proceedings. As there remain a few names to be yet affixed to this covenant, it is still circulating among the parties, and I shall hereafter mention the number of the names of the subscribers; to increase which, and farther to promote the salutary object in view, I have written concerning it to *Lucknow* (the capital of the *Nawab Vizier's* territories, within which, as already noticed, the greatest number of the *Ràj-kumàrs* reside). And as this baneful habit is not confined to the *Ràj-kumars*, but extends, though not in a degree so prevalent, to the tribe called [f] *Raghuvansa*, who reside in our [g] *Pergunna* of *Mongra*, and *Talook* of *Chandwack*, and in other parts, I have taken measures for their signing a separate similar engagement, from which I have very sanguine hopes that this system of Infanticide will be put a stop to, or

[f] *Raghuvansa,* means the offspring, or descendants of RAGHU. It is sometimes written *Ragvunsy,* and so commonly pronounced; or *Rugbunsie,* as in the MS. The title of *Raghuvansa* may have been assumed by a sect affecting to be descendants of RAGHU, a great hero, ancestor to RAMA CHANDRA, who is hence called RAGHUVA, and was also a great warrior. A sect of *Baudhas* may also be so called; BUDHA being the mythological father of a RAGHU. *Vansa* is farther applied by *Hindu* mythologists to the fabled descendants of the sun and moon; these great races being respectively called *Surya-vansa,* and *Chandra vansa;*——*va,* I imagine, as in RAGHUVA, to be an abbreviation of *vansa.* See *Hindu Pantheon,* Index, under the names and words that occur in this note. E. M.

[g] The division *Pergannah* may be compared with the *hundreds*; the *Talook,* or *Taluka,* to a *village,* in England. The *Taluk* is written *Chundwuck* in the MS. I should write it *Chandvaka,* and imagine it is classically spelled, if of sufficient importance to be so dignified, *Chandravaka*; bearing some lunar allusion. E. M.

be, at least, greatly lessened; as all the *Ràj-kumàrs* with whom I conversed, did, while they admitted the fact, fully acknowledge its atrocity; in extenuation of which, they pleaded the great expense of procuring suitable matches for their daughters, if allowed to grow up. It yet appears, and ought in vindication of humanity to be here noticed, that in several cases, natural affection has induced the father of *Ràj-kumàr* families to rear one or more of their female issue; though the instances where more than one daughter has been spared are (as far as I can judge from sundry questions put to these people during my few days halt among them) but very rare; and I heard only of one general exception of a whole village, the inhabitants of which, who are all of this tribe, had, as my *Ràj-kumàr* informant observed, sworn, as he supposed, or, at least solemnly pledged themselves to each other, to bring up their females: as a proof of which, he added, that there were now to be seen several *Ràj-kumàr* old maids in the village in question; since, from the great expense hitherto usually incurred by this tribe in their marriages, the parents had been unable to dispose of those women in that way, by procuring husbands for them.

" P. S. Since writing the above, the *Ràj-kumàr* renunciation of letting their daughters perish has been received, and it is subscribed by all those of that tribe in this part of the country, including ZALEM-SING and GURDAT-SING; the latter of whom is the only one of the subscribers who disallows by the words of his signature, of his having been guilty of this crime. I have sent a copy of this original engagement to the [1] *Amil* of

[1] The head man of a district.

Judnpoor, with directions to him to see it enforced, and to apprehend and send into *Benares*, to take his trial, any *Ràj-kumàr* who shall hereafter be guilty of a breach thereof: of all of which I have duly apprized that body of men.

" I have also circulated a similar subscription in this *Pergannah* of *Ghurwarah*; for I find that its inhabitants, who are all [k] *Durga-vansas*, or descendants of one common ancestor, [l] DURGA, are addicted, more or less, to the same practice of destroying their female infants."

Engagement entered into by the Ràj-kumàrs.

" Whereas it hath become known to the Government of the Honourable English East India Company, that we of the tribe of *Ràj-kumàr*, do not suffer our female children to live; and whereas this is a great crime, as mentioned in the [l] *Brehma Bywant Purana*, where it is said, that ' killing even a fœtus is as criminal as killing a *Brahman*; and that for killing a female or woman, the punishment is to suffer in the *Naraka*, or Hell,

[k] In the MS. written DOORG, and *Doorgbunsies*. This sect may have been thus distinguished from the goddess DURGA, the terrific consort of the avenging deity SIVA. See *Hindu Pantheon*, under those words in the Index; also under Sects. Although a sectarial distinction, her worshippers may figuratively style themselves *Durga vansa*, the children or descendants of DURGA; as we find was not unusual among the ancient Europeans. " Priests and votaries (says BRYANT), were often styled the sons and the daughters of the deity whom they served." *Analysis*, Vol. III. p. 123. And in the conclusion of Mr. WILFORD's fourth essay, in Vol. IX. of the *As. Res.* he has the same remark on *Raja-vansa* and *Raja-kumara*. " In the east, and also in the west, the followers of a deity, or some legislator or institutor, are often called his offspring." E. M.

[l] I have here retained nearly the spelling of the MS. *(Brehma Bywant Pooran)*, not being certain which of the eighteen sacred mythological poems, each bearing the common denomination of *Purana*, is here meant; it is that perhaps called the *Brahmanda* (or the mundane egg), which generally ranks as the third: or, it may be that called *Brahma vaiverte*. See *Hindu Pantheon*, p. 437, for a brief notice of the eighteen *Puranas*. E. M.

called [m] *Kat Shutala*, for as many years as there are hairs on that female's body; and that afterwards, such person shall be born again, and successively become a leper, and afflicted with the [n] *jakhima'*; and whereas the British Government in *India*, whose subjects we are, hold in detestation such murderous practices, and we do ourselves acknowledge, that although customary among us, they are highly sinful; we do therefore hereby agree, not to commit any longer such detestable acts; and any among us who shall (which God forbid!) be hereafter guilty thereof, or who shall not bring up and get our daughters married to the best of our abilities among those of our own cast, shall be expelled from our tribe, and shall neither eat, nor keep society with us; beides suffering hereafter the punishments denounced in the above *Purana* and [o] *Sastra*. We have therefore entered into this engagement."

Dated 17th December, 1789.

Here ends Mr. DUNCAN's summary of the measures successfully adopted by him in the province of *Benares*, for the suppression of Infanticide in that, then the only discovered quarter. The next chapter is extracted also from Mr. DUNCAN's summary, which is throughout written in the third

[m] *Naraka* (in conversation called *Nerka*, or *Nerk*, as it is written in the MS.) is a general name of the hell of the *Hindus*; who have, however, twenty-one receptacles for sinners, one of which is also specifically named *Naraka*, or the *region of serpents*. In the *Hindu Pantheon*, page 297, is a list of the names of the hells; but that mentioned in the text, where in the MS. it is written *Kat Shootul*, is not among them. It may perhaps be a translation from some provincial dialect of the significant classical name. E. M.

[n] Or leprosy.

[o] *Sastra*, formerly written *Shaster*, means generally an ordinance; more particularly a sacred ordinance delivered by inspiration, and is strictly applicable only to sacred literature. See *Hindu Pantheon*, under *Sastra* in the Index. E. M.

person, of the measures pursued in the western parts of *India*. I shall, however, previously quote, from the xxii article of the fourth volume of the Asiatic Researches, some observations by Sir JOHN SHORE, now Lord TEIGNMOUTH, in which he introduced his brief notice of the discovery and suppression of Infanticide in the eastern parts of *India;* as above detailed more at length by the discoverer and suppressor, Mr. DUNCAN himself.

"That the practice of Infanticide should ever be so general, as to become a custom with any sect or race of people, requires" (the Right Honourable author justly observes) "the most unexceptionable evidence to gain belief: and I am sorry to say, that the general practice, as far as regards female infants, is fully substantiated with respect to a particular tribe on the frontiers of *Juanpore*, a district of the province of *Benares*, adjoining to the country of *Oude*. A race of *Hindus*, called *Rajekoomars*, reside here; and it was discovered, in 1789 only, that the custom of putting to death their female offspring, by causing their mothers to starve them, had long subsisted, and did actually then very generally prevail amongst them. The Resident at *Benares*, in a circuit which he made through the country where the *Rajekoomars* dwell, had an opportunity of authenticating the existence of the custom from their own confessions: he conversed with several; all unequivocally admitted it, but all did not fully acknowledge its atrocity; and the only reason which they assigned for the inhuman practice, was the great expence of procuring suitable matches for their daughters, if they allowed them to grow up. It is some satisfaction to add, that the custom, though general, was not universal; as natural affection, or some other motive, had induced the father of some *Rajekoomar* females to bring up one or more of their female issue; but the instances where more than one daughter had been spared were very rare. One village only furnished a complete exception to the general custom; and the *Rajekoomar* informant, who noticed it, supposed that the inhabitants had sworn, or solemnly pledged themselves to each other, to bring up their females. In proof of his assertion in favour of the village in question, he added, that several old maids of the *Rajekoomar* tribe then actually existed there; and that their celibacy proceeded from the difficulty of procuring husbands for them, in consequence of the great expenses attending the marriages of this class of people.

" It will naturally occur to the Society to ask, by what mode a race of men could be continued, under the existence of the horrid custom which I have described? To this my documents enable me to reply—partly from the exceptions to the general custom, which were occasionally admitted by the more wealthy *Rajekoomars*, more particularly those who happened to have no male issue; but chiefly by intermarriages with other *Rajpoot* families, to which the *Rajekoomars* were compelled by necessity.

" A *prohibition*" (continues his Lordship) " enforced by the denunciation of the severest temporal penalties, would have little efficacy in abolishing a custom which existed in opposition to the feelings of humanity and natural affection; and the sanction of that religion which the *Rajekoomars* professed, was appealed to in aid of the ordinances of civil authority. Upon this principle, an engagement, binding themselves to desist in future from the barbarous practice of causing the death of their female children, was prepared, and circulated amongst the *Rajekoomars* for their signature; and as it was also discovered that the same custom prevailed, though in a less degree, among a smaller tribe of people also within the province of *Benares*, called *Rajebunsies*, measures were adopted at the same time to make them sensible of its iniquity, and to procure from them a subscription similar to that exacted from the *Rajekoomars*."

The Right Honourable President of the Asiatic Society, concludes his communication by a copy of the engagement entered into by the Infanticides, as given in a preceding page. I observe, that the name of the tribe, that, in page 5, is written *Ragvunsy*, or *Rugbunsie*, is in the latter part of the above quotation spelled *Rajebunsie*: if this, or, as I should be disposed to amend it, *Rajavansa*, be the true pronunciation, my etymological conjecture, in page 5, deducing it from RAGHU, falls to the ground; and I am disposed to think *Rajavánsa* the true reading, for it has the same, or very nearly the same meaning, as *Raja putra*, or *Rajakumara*. The epithet is sometimes transposed, and we hear of *Vansa Raja*, and *Putra Raja*; the former meaning the royal offspring, the latter royal children. See As. Res. Vol. IX. Mr. WILFORD's fourth essay; at the conclusion of which the learned gentleman says, that he has " but lately become acquainted with the singular tribe of *Raja-kumaras*, who do not differ from other *Hindus* of the same class, and have now lost every vestige of their ancient religion, except the name of their institutor." This religion appears to have been *Christianity*, if the deplorable heresy of the *Manicheans* may be so termed; and the name and character that the founder of this sect assumed in *India* was BUDDHA; at another time, CHRIST, or SAKA. His followers styled themselves *Saka-Raja-vansa*, or *Saka-Raja-kumara*, the royal offspring of SAKA. E. M.

Note referred to in page 1.

Raja PIT'HAURA. Not wishing to break, in so early a page, the thread of the narrative, by the insertion of a long foot note, I there referred to this place for what I have to say respecting this personage, and his dynasty.

His name is derived from PRIT'HU, or PRIT'HVI, forms of VISHNU and LAKSHMI, as detailed in the *Hindu Pantheon*; it is otherwise written PRIT'HWI, PRIT'HAVI, PET'HOWRA, PIT'HORA; and PRIT'HWI-PALA, or protected by PRIT'HWI; and his dynasty, *Chohan*, and *Chauhana*; sometimes indeed *Chowtar:* but this may refer rather to another dynasty still extant in *Guzerat*, otherwise called *Chauda*, the same, perhaps, as the *Chaitura*, whence the *Serkar*, or province of *Chaitore*, is named.

The country over which this *Chauhan* dynasty reigned was *Sambhala*, to the north of *Kanouge*, then the imperial city of *India*.

In Vol. IX. of the Asiatic Researches, Mr. WILFORD has given a curious article (III), in which are many passages relating to the history and dynasty of *Raja* PIT'HAURA; and I shall thence chiefly, and from the second volume of the *Ayin Akbery*, extract the materials for what I have to offer concerning them.

The *Chauhan*, shortly before its extinction, mixed itself with the *Tomara*, or *Towara* dynasty, of which the genealogies run thus:

The *Tomara* family.

RAMA CHANDRA, a powerful *Zemindar* of *Gauda*, in *Malwa*.

CHAITRA-PALA, his son, was chosen Emperor of *India*, in A.D. 998, in default of a proper successor to JAYA NANDA, the last of the *Pomara*, or *Powar* dynasty. CHAITRA-PALA thus introduced the *Tomara* family. After fighting several unsuccessful battles with *Sultan* MAHMUD, he put an end to his own life in 1002, leaving two sons,

1. MAHENDRA PALA, who succeeded him; but proved, unlike his father, a weak and foolish prince, whose beautiful wife was carried away by his brother,
2. RAYA SENA, called also ANANGA-PALA. He built *Dehli* in 1050.

The *Tomara* family.	The *Chauhana* family.
RANI BADI.	BAHUSALI.
	VISALAKSHA.
	SOMA DEVA.
JIDAHANA, called also PRITHWI *Raja*, was killed in battle by BALA DEVA, the *Chauhana Raja*, in 1110. He had two sons.	BALA DEVA, killed JIDAHANA in battle, in 1110.
	NAGA DEVA.
	CIRTTI PALA.
1. VIGAHANA, who, on the death of his father, withdrew to *Gauda*, the country of his ancestors.	
2. SANKA-PALA, who appears to have succeeded his father.	
CIRTTI PALA.	PITHAURA, or PRITHWI, adopted by ANANGA PALA, *Raja* or king of *Delhi*, was killed in battle in 1192.
ANANGA-PALA adopted the *Chauhan Raja* in 1170.	

To this last PIT'HAURA the *Rajkumaras* trace their ascent. He was a great warrior, and for a time successful, as well as in love affairs; and there is an epic poem still extant, part of which is in Mr. WILFORD's possession, on the subject of his wars and amours; of which some farther notice will be taken presently.

ANANGA-PALA had no male issue, and his only daughter married a *Chauhan* king; probably CIRTTI, for PIT'HAURA was her son, and was adopted by his father-in-law, ANANGA, who declared him his successor to the throne of *Delhi*, and recommended him to the protection of JAYA CHANDRA, of the *Rhatore* tribe, emperor of *India*, then residing in the imperial city of *Kanouge*, or *Kanouj*.

JAYA CHANDRA appears to have usurped the imperial throne from the *Chauhan* family: Mr. WILFORD, however, does not perceive the grounds of their claim, but it seems to have been recognized; for when JAYA CHANDRA attempted to perform a great sacrifice of that description, where (as related in the *Ayin Akbery*, II. 119), every office must be performed by kings, " even to the duties of the scullery," and at which it was requisite that all the kings of *India* should be present, JAYA CHANDRA was told that he was not qualified to preside, for that the empire and right of presiding belonged to the *Chauhan* family, and to PIT'HAURA, who had absented himself; judging the usurper would not concede so important a point.

Some time before this great event, JAYA CHANDRA, under pretence of going to worship at *Kartikya swami*, or *Ceylon*, a place much resorted to, both by orthodox *Hindus* and the followers of BUDDHA, and even by *Mussulmans*, led thither a numerous army, with the view of forcing VIRA BHADRA, king of *Ceylon*, to become his tributary; which, probably, he effected, for the latter presented him with a most beautiful and accomplished damsel. JAYA CHANDRA being stricken in years, did not espouse the maiden, but adopted her as his daughter, and betrothed her to the *Raja* next most powerful and illustrious to himself; and the ceremonies were to have been performed at the above sacrifice.

JAYA CHANDRA was disposed to the immediate resentment of the absence of PIT'HAURA, but was persuaded to postpone it; and to render the sacrifice as little incomplete as possible, he caused a golden effigy of PIT'HAURA to be cast, and assigned it the office of porter at the palace gate.

PIT'HAURA, enraged at this indignity, took with him five hundred chosen men, and after great proofs of intrepidity, carried off the effigy of gold. The betrothed damsel, hearing of the valour and achievements of PIT'HAURA, became violently enamoured with him, and refused the choice of her adopted father; who, enraged at her contumacy, and the interruption of the ceremonies, for which he had made such vast preparations, expelled her from his *haram*, and confined her in a separate palace.

PIT'HAURA hearing this, determined to rescue her; and by the contrivance of CHANDA, a most celebrated bard at his court, found means to acquaint her with his determination, and to keep in agitation the flame that the reputation of his master had kindled in the heart of the princess: the lover himself had, indeed, ventured into her presence, disguised as an attendant on the minstrel.

At length the moment came; and most incredible exploits are related of the prodigious valour of PIT'HAURA's warriors in repelling the efforts of JAYA CHANDRA's army, who endeavoured to pursue the fugitives, but without effect; for PIT'HAURA, and his beauteous prize, reached *Dehli* in safety; not, however, without losing the whole of a hundred select heroes, called *Samantas*, whose names and exploits are detailed in the poem. The first that fell was GOVINDA RAJA; but not till he had killed seven thousand of the enemy!

Here ends the glory of PIT'HAURA; for although some accounts relate, that in the wars which ensued, he recovered his imperial rights, others state, that soon after he had thus obtained the princess, she engrossed the whole of his attention; and giving way to this pleasing but inglorious dalliance, the expelled JAYA CHANDRA, by entering into a league with the *Mahomedan* invader, SAHEBUDIN, or SHEBUDDIN, carried on a destructive warfare against PIT'HAURA, which, as is usual in such cases, ended in the destruction of the rival kings.

These contests, in which the *Mahomedan* armies were engaged, are called, by the *Hindu* poets, as most of their historians are, the wars of the *Mahabatadikas:* MAHABAT, meaning a great warrior, being the name they give to MAHOMED.

PIT'HAURA, being aroused by the spirit-stirring minstrelsy of CHANDA, made an effort, but fell in battle in 1192; and his wonderful *Samantas* having been before killed, no more is heard of the once potent *Raja.* The poets, indeed, keep him on the stage a little longer, by making him fall into the hands of JAYA CHANDRA, and introducing CHANDA to sing in his presence the praise of the prisoner's skill in archery: this raises the monarch's curiosity to witness such feats; and in the exhibition, PIT'HAURA, at the instigation of CHANDA, gave dreadful proof, by sending his unerring shaft through the heart of his rival.

But the more probable relation is, that JAYA CHANDRA, after the death of PIT'HAURA, quarrelled with his *Mahomedan* ally; for in the year 1194, he suffered a total defeat, and in his flight, attempting to cross the *Ganges* in a small boat, he was drowned.

Here ends the history of PIT'HAURA, and his rival; but I will detain my reader a moment longer, while I notice, that by some accounts, the sons of CHAITRA PALA, founder of the *Tomara* dynasty, are apparently called the *Balhara* kings in *Guzerat:* but kings and great men in *Indian* history, so frequently have a plurality of names and titles, assumed significantly, or bestowed, often from some accidental occurrence, that great difficulties arise in the endeavour to identify them; and *Hindu* historians sadly confound names and actions.

In the short list of *Rajas* given in this note, instances of this occur. RAYA SENA was surnamed ANANGA-PALA, or befriended by the god of love; and RETI PALA, or fostered by the laughter-loving goddess (these appellations had perhaps their rise in the king's successful intrigue, already noticed, with the wife of his brother, MAHENDRA-PALA, which name, meaning protected by the great INDRA, was ill applied to so weak a prince); and ANANGA-PALA, being also the name or surname of the last *Raja* of the *Tamara* race, who adopted PIT'HAURA, the last of the *Chohan* dynasty, the eras and actions of the two ANANGAS are confounded; and the more, from JIDAHANA (who was slain in battle by the *Chohan* king, BALA DEVA) son, or grandson, of the first surnamed ANANGA, being surnamed PIT'HAURA, or PRIT'HWI. CIRTTI-PALA being, farther, the immediate predecessor, both of the last PIT'HAURA and the last ANANGA, is an additional source of confusion.

The building of *Delhi* is sometimes ascribed to the last PIT'HAURA; but it was, in fact, founded by the first so named, or RAYA-SENA. The last PIT'HAURA built a fort there, that is, or its ruins, still to be seen.

The god of love, above-named ANANGA, is the same with KAMA, of whom, and of his consort, RETI, or affection, the reader will find due notice in the last article of the *Hindu Pantheon.* Of VIRA BHADRA also, he being a mythological, as well as an historical personage. See the Index to that work. E. M.

I shall now resume, in the next chapter, Mr. DUNCAN's summary of the measures pursued on the western side of *India,* in view to the discovery and suppression of Infanticide in that quarter.

CHAP. II.

Continuation of Mr. DUNCAN'S *Summary of the measures pursued by him at* BOMBAY *and in* GUZERAT, *for the discovery and abolition of* INFANTICIDE *among the* Rajput *tribes in that part of* INDIA.

THE information adverted to in Mr. DUNCAN'S letter of the 2d October, 1789 (p. 2) as to the knowledge possessed by the *Greeks* and *Romans*, of Infanticide having been practised in *India* at remote periods, was acquired from Captain WILFORD; and that gentleman having referred to [a] *Barygaza*, or *Baroach*, and the vicinity thereof, as the more immediate site where it had been observed, Mr. DUNCAN was thence led, on his first visit to *Surat*, in 1800, to inquire of KERPA RAMA, the minister of the *Nawab* of that place, whether any traces of such a practice yet existed in that quarter: to which he received the following written report:

Report from KERPA RAMA *of Surat.*

"Heretofore I have heard people say, that among the tribe of *Rajput*, and especially among the *Rajas* of that class,

[a] This name has been derived from BHRIGU, who is fabled to have lived at *Baroach*, whence it was called *Bhrigu-Kshetra*, or *Bhrigu-gosha*, BHRIGU'S-field, or place. This is sometimes pronounced *Bhrigu-kacha*, and *Barygacha*; and is supposed to be the origin of the Grecian *Barygaza*. See As. Res. IX. 83. 184.; and of BHRIGU, *Hindu Pantheon*, Index. E. M.

the birth of a daughter in their houses was considered as disgraceful; on which account, their women refused to let their newly-born daughters have access to their milk, and do put them in any way to death: but this practice is not general through all the subdivisions of their tribe, though in several places they do thus stony-heartedly kill them."

Mr. DUNCAN returning to *Bombay* from *Surat*, in July 1800, had no farther opportunity of prosecuting his inquiries into what foundation there might be for believing the practice of female Infanticide to obtain in any instances in the west of *India*, till the circumstance was again brought incidentally to his notice between two and three years thereafter, by GAJRA BYE, a descendant of one of the former [b]*Gaikowar Rajas* of *Guzerat*, who having, under a series of political events unnecessary here to relate, repaired to *Bombay*, delivered casually the following account of transactions in her own family:

Account from GAJRA BYE, *received on the 8th January*, 1804.

" DAMAJI GAIKAWAR carried his arms as far as to [c]*Kutch*, with the *Raja* of which a reconciliation took place,

[b] Some notice will be taken of this name and family in a future page. E. M.

[c] I retain this orthography (in the MS. written also *Cutch)*, not wishing to alter it in respect to so well known a district, although at variance with my usage, which would lead me to spell it *Katch*; a name that might be derived from the second incarnation of VISHNU, in the form of a *tortoise*, which animal is in some western dialects in *India*, called *Katch*, or *Kach*, or *Katchwa*. *Kutch* is a maritime province, lies low, and is subject to inundations, both from the sea and from the *Indus*, and may be well imagined to have been the scene of the miraculous interposition of the preserver VISHNU, for the recovery of the submerged earth: or, admitting this mythological fable to have reference to the universal deluge, it may on some occasion supposed to be similar, but partial, have been provincially applied to *Kutch*. The legends explanatory of this and the other *Avataras*, or incarnations of VISHNU, are detailed in the *Hindu Pantheon*. See the Index of that book. E. M.

on condition of one of the princesses, his daughters, being given in marriage to DAMAJI; which lady, named DANKUR [d]BYE, lived among the *Gaikawars* till after DAMAJI's death; when, at her own request, the then *Raja* [e]FATTEH SING permitted her to return to her own family in *Kutch*."

This incidental narrative from GAJRA BYE, leading to the question, whether DANKUR BYE had of this marriage any children? it was answered negatively; and GAJRA BYE immediately followed up his answer, by explaining, that among that lady's cast in *Kutch*, the daughters are not brought up, but drowned immediately, at their birth, in a vessel of milk. GAJRA BYE being next questioned, how then this cast of people upheld their families? observed, that they are only one of the numerous tribes of *Rajputs*, among the other subdivisions of which they find wives; and that DANKUR BYE was spared in consequence of her extraordinary comeliness and beauty having excited a particular affection in the breast of her mother.

In view to the farther investigation of the grounds of GAJRA BYE's information, Mr. DUNCAN entered into a correspondence on the subject with Captain SETON, then on a political mission at *Mandavi*, the chief port of the country of *Kutch*, a territory situated to the north-west of the province of

[d] DUNKOOR BYE in the MS.

[e] FATTEH (or, as in the MS. FUTTEH) SING, signifies the Victorious Lion—a *Hindu* having, I apprehend, in this instance, adopted a *Mahommedan* appellation, فتح, meaning victorious in Arabic and Persian. TIPPOO's grandfather was named FATTEH; his father, HYDER; his son, FATTEH HYDER; the latter of the same signification with FATTEH SING. E. M.

Guzerat, the gulf of the same name intervening, and constituting the line of division between the two states. The following are extracted from that correspondence.

From Mr. DUNCAN *to Captain* SETON, *at Kutch, dated* 8*th January*, 1804.

" I send you a memorandum from GAJRA BYE (the daughter of FATTEH SING, one of the *Gaikawar* princes in *Guzerat)* or rather the result of what she related to day in conversation; and request you will make every inquiry in your power into so curious a subject, as the alleged custom of your *Kutch* friends killing their female infants. I have heard Captain WILFORD of *Benares* say, that in some old *Greek* author in his possession, he has read of the same thing being a practice in his time in that quarter of *India*.

From Captain SETON *to Mr.* DUNCAN, *dated at Mandavi*, 23*d March*, 1804.

" The custom mentioned in GAJRA BYE's relation is in force to this day; every female infant born in the *Raja's* family of a *Ranni*, or lawful wife, is immediately dropped into a hole dug in the earth and filled with milk, where it is drowned.

" DANKUR BYE, who is now alive at *Booje*, the capital of *Kutch*, is the daughter of [f]RAHU LAKPAT, by a *Pater*, or *Guzerat* [g]*Kanchny* (strolling dancing girl) sister to [h]RAHI GUR, the last *Raja*, and aunt of [i]RAHI RAHI DHUN, the

[f] In the MS. ROW-LUCKPUT. [g] *Cunchinnee* in the MS.

[h] RAEE GORE, MS. [i] RAEE RAEE DHUN, in the MS.

present *Raja.* The latter has a son and a daughter by a slave of one of the *Rannis,* now ten and eleven years of age; the custom in question not extending to them, but only to the *Raja's* children by his *Rannis,* or consorts: neither does it necessarily extend to the [k] *Jarejahs,* or collateral descendants of the *Raja's* family, though most of them through choice adopt it, there being but two men of this cast of any note who have brought up their daughters; and these are VIDRAJI and NAUTHJI, who will be again noticed. VIDRAJI JAREJAH'S daughter is married to the son of the [l] *Bownagher Raja.*

"This custom of drowning female infants is not peculiar to *Kutch,* but is common among the heads of the *Kehtri,* or *Rajput* tribes. It is practised in the family of JAM of *Nagar,* in the peninsula of *Guzerat;* and in that of the *Miazeh,* or [m] *Ka-*

[k] *Jarejah* is the name of the cast of a subdivision of *Rajputs,* of which tribe and that particular denomination thereof, is the *Rajah* of *Kutch,* and many other families of that quarter. Mr. DUNCAN.

[l] *Bownagher,* or *Bownaghur,* is the capital of a province of the same name in *Guzerat,* fruitful in grain and cotton; its name may be derived from *Bhavani nagar,* the city of BHAVANI, a name of the consort of SIVA, in one of her beneficent forms. See *Hindu Pantheon,* under BHAVANI in the Index. E. M.

[m] A strong proof of the force of hereditary prejudice, since these *Kalowrees* have long been *Mahomedans,* to all of whom this practice is very strictly forbid. This *Kalowra* family have now lost the dominion of *Sind,* in the manner adverted to in the text. It seems, however, doubtful, whether the practice of Infanticide be continued in respect to the female offspring of this *Kalowra* tribe since their conversion to *Mahomedanism.* Besides Captain SETON'S information, it is attested also by the *Munshi,* or Persian writer, of SUNDERJI SIVAJI (mentioned hereafter) who is himself a native of *Sind.* But it is, on the other hand, strenuously denied by MULJI, the son of LALLA HARJIVAN, a *Hindu,* and likewise a native of the same country. Charity and candour may therefore incline us to believe that the *Kalowries* have no longer to reproach themselves with this barbarous practice; such as the doctrines of the *Koran* stand indeed directly opposed to. Note by Mr. DUNCAN: to which I will add, that of the sect called *Kalowra,* or *Kalowri,* I have no information. As *Hindus,* their adoration of KAL, or KALA, a name of SIVA, or of KALI,

lowrics, of *Sind*, and in others. The *Rajputs* of *Kutch* are originally from *Sind*, and are called *Sind Samma*, and *Sam Samra:* they fell back on *Kutch* before the *Mahommedans*, driving out the *Katties*, who had before driven out the [n]*Sat-Sing*, or *Seven Lions*. Those that remained in *Sind* were converted to *Mahommedanism*, and have been since driven out by the [o]*Talpuris*. Part of them here (i. e. in *Kutch*) form the cast of *Jamadars*, mentioned in my official correspondence as forming the third party in this government. They marry *Rajput's* daughters, but do not give their own, it being contrary to the *Mahommedan* religion. The *Rajputs* eat what is dressed by *Mahommedans*, but not from the same dish or plate; and of every thing, except beef and fowls, which latter are, in a manner, forbidden; as none, in whose family a [p]*Deo* (or incarnation) has been, are allowed to eat them; and as they all pretend to this honour, it would be an affront to make them such an offer. Game is preferred to tame animals; they drink spirits, but this does not imply an inferiority of cast,

his consort, of whom BHAVANI is, as just noticed, another name, may have given them their sectarial distinction, retained, as stated in the note, after their conversion to *Islam*. E. M.

[n] *Sapta Singha*, in more classical language. E. M.

[o] *Talpoories*, MS.

[p] As it is usually pronounced in the western parts of *India*, more correctly written DEVA, a *deity*; divers of whom, according to *Hindu* superstition, condescend to become incarnate in the persons of pious mortals, in whose families a sanctified potency is sometimes perpetuated. See " An Account of a Hereditary living Deity to whom devotion is paid by the *Brahmans* of *Poona*, &c." by the Editor of this volume, in the seventh volume of the *Asiatic Researches*. See also *Hindu Pantheon*, under *Avataras* in the Index.

Several of the tribes of *Rajputs* abstain pretty generally from eating flesh, especially families living in the southern parts of *India*. On the subject of *Hindus* commonly eating meat, see *Hindu Pantheon*, p. 348, &c. as indexed under *Hindus*. E. M.

neither does the licence extend to the women; who, in every respect, live as the highest cast of *Brahmanis.*

"The *Rajas* of *Kutch* and [q] *Nagar*, are descended of two brothers; the elder, of *Kutch*, named MAHA RAO; the younger, MAHA RAJ—the *Murvie* chieftain, within the peninsula of *Guzerat*, is of the same family; and the history of all is contained in the History of KYNGAR and RAVER, the two brothers above alluded to, which I shall get and translate. The next great man in their history is [r] *Raja* BARRA, who was driven from *Sind;* and the most powerful in *Sind*, was *Raja* ONER.

"I have already intimated, that the *Jarejahs* destroy their daughters; and though VIDRAJI and NAUTHJI had, from the fear of having no sons, and thereby wanting heirs of any sex, saved theirs, it is by no means a general practice. The *Jamadars*, whose origin has been before adverted to, take in marriage the daughters of the *Soda Rajputs* (who rear their female children for sale) and also destroy their infant female progeny. The expense, and difficulty of procuring suitable [s] husbands, is the excuse usually made: the *Raja's* pretext is,

[q] *Nagar*, or *Nuggur*, is situated on the northern coast of the peninsula of *Guzerat*, which country is generally called *Kattywar*, from being inhabited, though at present by no means exclusively, by the tribe of *Kattis*, above-mentioned in the text. Mr. DUNCAN.

[r] Or rather, perhaps, VARAHA; so surnamed from the third incarnation of VISHNU, in the form of a *boar*, usually, as well as the incarnation, called in discourse, *Varra*, or *Barra*. See on this subject *Hindu Pantheon*, under *Varaha*, and *Avatara*, in the Index. E. M.

[s] Among many sects of *Hindus*, among most of them indeed, the practice of very early marriage has obtained. The parties are perhaps but five or six years old, and they return for some years to their respective families. On the occasion of marriage, the *Hindus*, habitually avaricious, are generally more prodigal than on any other; and it is not unusual to see this propensity indulged, by the rich as well as by the poor, to a very inconvenient degree: feasting, music, dancers, alms, and presents, especially to temples and *Brahmans*,

that he considers it beneath him to match his daughter with any man."

From Captain SETON *to Mr.* DUNCAN, *written in* 1804.

" The family of [1]SAM, adverted to in my preceding letter, also take their wives from the tribe of *Soda*, who are at present living between *Sind*, *Multan*, and *Joudpore*. It might be supposed that the women would be averse to the destruction of their daughters, but from all accounts it is the reverse; as they not only assist in destroying them, but when the *Musselman* prejudices occasionally preserve them; they hold these daughters in the greatest contempt, calling them *majen*, thereby insinuating that their fathers have derogated from their military cast, and become pedlars."

constitute the items on which the chief expenditure turns. It is so very essential to the reputation of any family to marry off the daughters, that an exception is very rarely met with; and it excites no small surprize in natives little acquainted with European modes and fashions, to find so many of our men and women unmarried. So universal is marriage among the *Hindus*, that it would be a difficult thing to find an unhusbanded female of a respectable family arrived at puberty, that is, of the age of ten or eleven years. In point, I may instance a fact that came within my own notice. NANA FIRNAVEESE, the prime minister of the *Mahratta* empire, the PITT of *India*, lost his wife in 1796, when he was rather an old man; and as he was infirm withal, it was not expedient that he should marry, as is usual, a mere infant; and his *Brahmanical* brethren sought far and near, and for a long time sought in vain, for an unmarried marriageable *Brahmany* of a respectable family. At length one was found remote from the metropolis, at *Kolapore*, near *Goa*; and he married her. So little was this success calculated on, that a reason was expected, and given for it: it appeared, that this lady in her infancy had been afflicted with some personal debility, that had prevented her early betrothment; this had suddenly been removed, about the time of NANNA's predicament, and he was deemed fortunate in finding a damsel under such suitable circumstances. NANNA had had several wives, but no male issue. E. M.

[1] That is, of *Sind Samma*, and *Sam Samra*, as above specified. These are *Jarejahs*, all of whom had the practice of female Infanticide in their families. Mr. DUNCAN.

From Captain Seton *to Mr.* Duncan.

(This letter describes his progress through *Kutch* in 1808, four years after the preceding letter was written, on a mission to *Hyderabad*, the capital of *Sind*—omitting what doth not relate to the present subject, he continues,)

..............." Thus far we had passed through the *Abrassa*, being the *Pergannas* and forts given to the *Jarejahs*, or *Rao's* (i. e. the *Raja's*) relations. We received the greatest attention from them: wherever we halted, they came in person to visit the tents, and offer whatever their country afforded; and where we passed their forts, they came outside to meet us: this tribe, actuated by pride, and the barbarous policy of saving the expense of portioning their daughters, murder them at their birth; there being, in the whole of *Kutch*, but two daughters who have been reared; one by Vidraji, or Vyraji, *Takur* of [u] *Roi*, who is married to the *Raja* of *Bownagur*, and one by Nauthaji, who is married to the *Raja* of *Aramroy*. To supply the place of those destroyed, they pur-

[u] More correctly written Vijraji, of *Rahwa*, or *Rowagurh (gurh* meaning a strong hold or castle) in *Abrassa*. The daughter's name is Bajiba, and she is married to the son of the *Takur*, or chieftain of *Bawnagher*, as already noticed in a preceding paragraph. Besides these instances cited by Captain Seton, I have heard of another in the person of the daughter of Omraj, of *Birajagher*, in *Kutch*, who was given in marriage to Sultanji, the *Ranna*, or chief of *Purbunder*, the capital of a small principality on the western coast of the peninsula of *Guzerat*, into which family the custom of killing their legitimate female offspring has also, within these last hundred years, been introduced; and this, it would seem, from the contagion of example; for they are not *Jarejahs*, but of the tribe of *Jaitwa Rajputs*. A fourth instance is known in the daughter of Visaji, of the castle of *Kandakra*, in *Kutch*, who was married to the *Kalowri* ruler of *Sind*.

Besides these, there will hereafter appear to be some others. Mr. Duncan.

chase wives from a tribe called [x] *Soda*, whose riches are their daughters; and such is the barbarous inveteracy of these women, that when married to *Mahommedans*, they continue the same practice, against the inclination and religion of their husbands; destroying their own progeny without remorse, in view to the advantage of the tribe from which they are descended."

Thus far, continues Mr. DUNCAN, is the information derived from Captain SETON, up to the 7th of July, 1708, the date of the preceding communication.

The province or territory of *Kutch*, Mr. DUNCAN proceeds to relate, lying beyond the British influence, it has not hitherto been found practicable to operate any diminution in that quarter, of the lamentable practice of female child-murder; but greater success has attended the measures taken in *Kattywar;* previously to the farther mention of which, it may be proper to insert the following testimonies as to the prevalence of the evil, derived from sources altogether independent of each other; to the end, that in proportion to the strangeness, atrocity, and consequent appearance of incredibility as to the fact, may be the substantiation of its existence.

Translation of an account of the Jarejahs, *or* Jarechas, *received from* MIRZA MORTIZA, *a descendant of the stationary* Moghul *officers of the revenue for the province of* Guzerat.

" There are in the territory of *Kattywâr*, many [y] *Jarechas;*

[x] The *Soda* tribe of *Rajputs*, occupy the district of *Thir*, near to the country of *Sind.* Mr. DUNCAN.—Some notice will be taken of this people hereafter. E. M.

[y] Although the name of the tribe is here written *Jarechah*, instead of *Jarejah*, the latter is the more received and ordinary way of pronouncing it. Mr. DUNCAN.

such as JAM, *Zemindàr* of [a]*Islamnagher*, and [a]*Kunbhuji*, and DIVAJI, *Zemindars* of [b]*Goundel*; and DHURAJI belongs also to this tribe; amongst the members of which, the established practice is, that when a child is born, if it be a son, every observance of joy and gratulation is attended to; but if it be a daughter, she is immediately put to death, on the plea, that if they bring up a daughter, it behoves them, when she has obtained a fit age, to give her in marriage to some one; a concession which they consider as inferring the highest reproach: though, if it should happen, as an extraordinary exception, that any one should preserve his daughter, and rear her to maturity, her father becomes anxiously solicitous to procure her a husband of unexceptionable rank and character; but in that case, the parents of the maiden, thus exempted from the common fate, become the scorn of all others, young and old, who hold them in the greatest contempt: neither do such occasions occur but very rarely."

The Superintendant of Police for the town of *Bombay*, having been desired to collect and report such information as might be available from his opportunities of intercourse among the natives, made in consequence the following report.

[a] The same town and principality that in the preceding paragraph is called *Nagar*, or *Nuggur*. It is more generally known under the name of *Jamnagher*, from the hereditary name of its chiefs, who are said to claim this family appellation from JAMSHID, a former monarch of *Persia*. The denomination of *Islamnàgur*, as designative of their capital, is the effect of former *Mahommedan* influence during the height of the *Moghul* government. Mr. DUNCAN.

[a] KOONBHOJEE and DEWAJEE, MS.

[b] Otherwise *Gondul, Goundal, Gowndel*, &c. This province is situated nearly centrically in the peninsula of *Guzerat*. E. M.

Report from the Superintendant of Police.

" DAMAJI KUTCHERAZ, a respectable merchant from *Kutch*, informs me, that it is very true that the *Jarejah* tribe in that district, do very generally put their female children to death the instant they are born. The *Raja* of *Kutch* follows this practice in his family; as also the *Raja* of *Jamnagar*, the *Raja* of *Murvi*, and the others in general. Some, however, amongst the tribe, from a sense of the wickedness of the crime, and being good moral men, preserve their female children; but these are few in number. Their reason, as he has heard, for this abominable practice is, that the fathers, being of a bold domineering spirit, do not wish their daughters to obey their husbands. Being asked, where the men of this tribe get wives; he informs me, from the *Rajput* tribes. Being asked, how the infants are destroyed; he said, that, as he has heard, when a woman is in labour, a pot of milk is placed in the room; and if an unfortunate female is produced, the nurse immediately drowns it therein. He has frequently, he says, asked poor persons of this tribe, how they put their female children to death; and they have always answered, *by making them drink milk;* alluding to the above mode of destroying them. The midwives are the only persons accessary to this horrid deed; and this is their language. He has never known any *Jarejah* families in Bombay: they have little or no trade; seldom go abroad; and live principally by the produce of their lands, and as soldiers.

" DHUNBHOY, an old nurse from the district of *Kutch*, informs me, that she never was employed as a nurse in any of the *Jarejah* families in that district; that her grandmother was, and she has heard her often declare, that whenever a female child was born, the unfortunate infant was put, with its head undermost, into an earthen pot of milk, along with the afterbirth, and thus immediately destroyed. On the contrary, when a son was born, great rejoicings were made, by feasting their friends, &c. She declares, she knows not how this extraordinary custom arose; but has heard, that being a tribe of *Rajputs,* they do not wish their females to obey any one. Independently of this, no one likes to take a female of this tribe into their family, as it is reckoned very unlucky to have any thing to do with them; and in general it is but too often verified."

This is the result of my enquiries,
(Signed) S. HALLIDAY.

A farther account of this deplorable custom, was verbally delivered in April or May, 1805, to Mr. DUNCAN, by [c]SUNDERJI SIVAJI, a man of credit and respectability, who had been long employed in the purchase of horses within the territories of *Kutch* and *Kattywar*, for the use of the British cavalry in *India.*

Relation by SUNDERJI SIVAJI, *of the Port of* Mandevi, *in the Country of* Kutch.

" It is notoriously known to be the established practice among those of the *Jarejah* tribe, in the country of *Kutch,* and adjoining districts of *Kattywar* (the latter being the country name for the peninsula of *Guzerat)* not to bring up their

[c] SUNDERJEE SHEOJEE, MS. In the western parts of *India,* the name of SIVA, the destructive energy of the deity, is pronounced SHEO and SEU; sometimes SEV. E. M.

daughters, but to put them to death at their birth. The legend that I have heard as accounting for this strange practice, is as follows:

In former times it so happened, that to one of the head men of these *Jarejahs*, several female children were born; and as among the *Hindus*, it is incumbent to provide husbands for their daughters, whilst these latter are yet in their non-age, the *Jarejah* chieftain abovementioned, applied accordingly to his family *Brahman*, or priest, to pursue the necessary measures for getting the said *Jarejah's* female children contracted in marriage with the sons of his equals in the tribe; and of the like valour and power as he possessed.

The *Brahman*, after making every inquiry, and going about to every place in quest of suitable matches for these children, returned without effecting his object; reporting thereon to the chieftain in question, that although he had exerted all his endeavours to find proper alliances for his female children, still he, this *Brahman*, had not traced any one who was of competent qualifications to be his son-in-law; 'wherefore,' added the *Brahman*, 'since to retain these your female offspring in the family house after their arriving at the age of womanhood, is contrary to the rules of religion, I will take them with me, and will burn them in the fire; on condition, that it be stipulated on your part, to destroy at their birth all issue of the same sex, that shall hereafter be born in your family: laying hereon, as I now do, my solemn malediction, both here and hereafter, on you and yours, if you fail to perform the same, in such manner, that if you shall preserve any of your future daughters, they shall pass their lives in penury and want; nor shall good attend the father or mother of such children."

"It is farther reported," SUNDERJI continues, "that, after thus speaking, this *Brahman* took away those innocent girls, and consumed them in the flames; and that in conformity to the stipulation and denunciation aforesaid, the people of the *Jarejah* tribe dwelling in the country of *Kutch*, and in the *Perganas* of *Hallar*, and other places within the peninsula of *Guzerat*, have, to the present day, continued to adhere to the practice in question; whereby, whenever a daughter is born to them, they do forthwith put these helpless babes, without remorse or pity, to death; *placenta super nares osque incumbente*, without allowing of their surviving for the shortest space."

Question thereon put to SUNDERJI.

It has been understood, that [d]ADIBA, the daughter of RALAKAJI, a former *Raja* of *Kutch*, was married to one of the *Gaikawar Rajas*; whence it is to be concluded, that the practice of the *Jarejahs* killing their daughters is not without exception?

[d] The same person who is called DANKUR BYE, in preceding paragraphs; the term *Adibah*, meaning merely *sister*, by which she is known in her own family. In like manner, RALAKAJI is only another way of pronouncing RAO LAKPAT, the name of her father. In the *Kutch* language, *Adi* is sister; and *Adiba*, a more respectful expression of the same term of consanguinity. This lady's real name is said to have been MUTI, or MUTIBAH; but when she married into the *Mahrata* family of the *Rajas* of *Guzerat*, she obtained the appellation of DANKUR, or DANKU; and the title, as the wife of the ruling chief, of BHYE MAHARAJ. It is very difficult to write correctly the names of *Hindus* in European characters: neither do the natives pronounce them in a uniform manner. Mr. DUNCAN.

Answer. That is true; and ADIBA is still surviving at *Booje*, the capital of *Kutch*; yet there are nevertheless but few exceptions, such as in this instance, to the general rule; because, from the effect of the malediction pronounced, no good ensues from their preservation; insomuch, that if any daughters of this tribe get married into other houses, the grain of such houses becomes less [e]plentiful; nor do such women produce sons, but are the occasion of feuds arising in the families into which they are thus transplanted. Throughout all the country of *Kutch*, there may be six or eight houses wherein the *Jarejah* masters of families bring up their daughters; or otherwise the practice of killing them is general: and besides what happens within the limits of that country, the *Jarejah* chieftains of *Murvi* (written also *Murbi*), *Goundal*, or *Gowndel*, and *Jamnagar*, in the peninsula of *Guzerat*, do also kill their female infants.

There is an instance of VISAJI, the *Kakerwalla*[f] chieftain of *Kutch*, having given his daughter in wedlock to GHOLAM SHAH, one of the former *Mahommedan* rulers of *Sind*, of the *Kallowra* tribe, an event that must have happened forty years

[e] This idea is perfectly natural to a *Hindu*; necessarily, if at all pious, taught to look on the malediction of a *Brahman* as the heaviest of human calamities. In the *Ramayana* it is decreed, that "even he who cannot be slain by the ponderous arms of INDRA, nor by those of KALI, nor by the terrible *chakra* of VISHNU, shall be destroyed if a *Brahman* curse him, as if he were consumed by fire." See *Hindu Pantheon*, p. 403, where the potency, or omnipotency, of the *Brahmans* is discussed. E. M.

[f] This seems the same person who is called VISAJI of *Kandakra*, in the note in page 24. *Kakerwalla* is, I imagine, a personal or family epithet, derived from accident or contingency. *Kaka*, in *Sanskrit*, and in several spoken dialects, is a *crow*. (*Hindu Pantheon*, p. 142.) Hence *Kakerwalla*, or *Kakawalla*, may mean he (or the man, or the fellow) of the crow; which, although a bird of ill omen, individuals are sometimes named after. Females in *Malabar* are sometimes named KAKA. E. M.

years ago, but at present this *Kakerwalla* family do not bring up their female infants. Those who occasionally do so, are induced to it by the consideration of thereby acquiring the merit of having sons born to them. As, for instance, when a man have a succession of female children produced in his family, he will, at the suggestion of any one, be induced to believe, that by sparing and bringing them up, sons will also be acquired to him; whence, chiefly, *Jarejah's* daughters are sometimes met with; of which there is, within my recollection, another instance, in the case of the [5] *Roee*, chieftain of *Kutch*, by name VIJRAJI, or VEDRAJI, who has married a daughter of his to the son of ATTABYE, the *Raja* of *Bhownager*. That lady may now be about twenty, or twenty-two years of age; but I have not heard that she has yet had any male issue, but that, on the contrary, her husband and she do not agree."

Thus far SUNDERJI's verbal account to the Governor.

The Government of *Bombay* having under consideration, about the period of SUNDERJI's aforesaid narrative, the most available means of counteracting, as far as their influence extended, the barbarous practice thus ascertained to prevail in *Kattywár*, as well as in *Kutch*; instructions were, on the 27th of May, 1805, transmitted to *Major* WALKER, the Resident at the Court of the *Gaikawár*, in *Guzerat*, to which state the territory of *Kattywár* is tributary, " to communicate with the abovenamed SUNDERJI SIVAJI, then on his way from *Bombay* to *Beroda*, and to endeavour to prevail on him to take an

[5] This is the same name as is written (in page 24) by Captain SETON, *Roi*; and *Rahwa*, or *Rowa*, in the note. According to the orthography adopted in this tract, I should spell this word *Rai*, or *Rui*, instead of *Roi*, or *Rowee*. E. M.

active part as the agent of the British Government, for effecting the abrogation in that quarter, of a system so revolting and detestable."

In pursuance of that instruction, Major WALKER addressed the Government of *Bombay* as follows:

To FRANCIS WARDEN, *Esq. Secretary to Government, Bombay.*

SIR,

I HAVE the honor to enclose, for the information of the Honourable the Governor in Council, a translation of a letter received from SUNDERJI SIVAJI, of *Kutch;* communicating some particulars relative to the practice of female Infanticide among the tribe of *Jarejahs;* and some information on the state of affairs among the chieftains bordering on the gulph of *Kutch.*

The Honourable the Governor in Council will observe with regret, that so large a number of innocent children annually suffer from the prevalence of the barbarous custom of female Infanticide among the *Jarejahs;* but the custom seems limited to that tribe who inhabit *Kutch* and *Kattywar*, as I have not been able to trace its existence among any other people of *Guzerat.*

I have the honor to enclose an extract from my correspondence with SUNDERJI on the subject of this custom; but I fear the humane attempt of the Honourable the Governor in Council will not be successful, to any great extent, in restraining the superstitious and religious prejudices of a tribe so far removed from the authority of the British Government, and

and so little acquainted with the principles of improved society.

I have the honor to be, &c.

Baroda,
1st September, 1805.

(Signed) A. WALKER,
Resident.

Translation of a Letter from SUNDERJI SIVAJI, *of Kutch, to Major* WALKER, *dated 13th August*, 1805. *Enclosed in the preceding.*

" THE drowning of the daughters of the *Jarejahs* proceeds from this cause—in this country there is no one can marry into the tribe of *Jarejah;* wherefore they drown their daughters. There may be annually five or six hundred births among the *Jarejahs;* inasmuch as the chieftains of *Murbi, Hallar, Gowndel, Wagar, Kutch,* and [b] *Kalakút*, are all *Jarejahs*, and are all related; and among relatives it is not customary for *Hindus* to marry—excepting relatives, there are none of their tribe—such is the custom of the *Jarejahs.*"

From Major WALKER *to* SUNDERJI.

" I have been favored with your letter of the 13th of August, noticing some customs of the cast of *Jarejahs.*

[b] *Kulhakot*, MS. the same name perhaps that we usually spell *Calicut*, and pronounce *Kañkat*, and apply to a city in *Malabar*. It would be deemed a pedantic affectation to apply the amended orthography to cities so well known as this, and *Calcutta*—it is, however, to be regretted, that the geographical orthography of *India* is not improved. In the instances adverted to in this note, *Kalakút* probably derives its name from KALA, a name of SIVA. *Calicut* (or as I would, if I dared, spell it *Kàlikùt)* from his consort, KALI.—*Calcutta* is probably the same name; or may come from KAL, a personification of Time, or Eternity. For particulars, and pictures of which important personages, the reader is referred to their names in the Index to the *Hindu Pantheon*. E. M.

" I request that on this interesting subject, you will in your next letter be more particular; and detail every circumstance relative to the inhuman custom practised by the *Jarejahs* of putting their female children to death in their infancy.

" The prevalence of such a barbarous habit must be a subject of regret to all the friends of humanity, and is especially so to the British Government; whose views being ever directed to the promotion of the happiness of their subjects and neighbours, they cannot learn without horror, that five or six hundred innocent children are annually put to death, who, if suffered to live, would contribute so much to increase the population and happiness, and the consequent prosperity of the country in which they abide.

" This custom is the more extraordinary and reprehensible, as it is expressly forbidden by the *Hindu* law, and in the [1]*Brehma Vyvanta Purana*, is called a great crime: it being written, that killing even a fœtus, is as criminal as killing a *Brahman*—and the same *Purana* condemns the perpetrator to suffer in the hell called *Nerka*, as many years as there are hairs on the child's body.

" It would therefore be a very acceptable service to humanity, highly gratifying to Mr. DUNCAN and the British Government, and honourable to yourself, if you exert your influence to obtain the discontinuance of such a barbarous custom.

" When the Honourable Mr. DUNCAN was in charge of the province of *Benares*, he put a stop to it, for it was there practised by a cast called *Ràjkumàr*; he induced them to sign

[1] Written in the MS. as it is commonly pronounced in the west of *India*, *Brehma Bywant Pooran*. See p. 7. E. M.

an agreement, by which any one who committed this crime was to be expelled from the tribe, and neither to eat, drink, or sleep with the members of it; besides suffering the punishment denounced in the *Purana*. If such an agreement could be executed in *Kutch*, it would probably be effectual."

(Signed) A. WALKER,
Resident.

Baroda,
1st September, 1805.

(*Mr.* DUNCAN'S *Summary is now resumed, or rather continued.*)

The chieftains of the peninsula of *Guzeràt*, or *Kattywàr*, have for years past been subject to the payment of tribute to the *Mahrata* states of the *Peshwa* and *Gaikawàr*. The usual mode of its realization having been by periodical circuits, enforced by military array, one of the ameliorations proposed under the alliance of 1802, between the latter power and the Honourable Company, was to avoid the necessity for those ever-recurring and coercive progresses, by inducing these dependant local rulers in *Kattywàr*, chiefly through an appeal to their own interests, to accede to an equitable permanent accommodation; ascertaining the amount of their future pecuniary acknowledgments, without the concurrence of force for their realization. Toward the attainment of these salutary ends, it was deemed expedient that one general circuit should be made through the peninsula, assisted by the appearance of a detachment from the British subsidiary force; and it was thought a duty of humanity to aim also, on this occasion, at the suppression of female Infanticide; as will appear by the following extracts from the correspondence on these points between the *Bombay* and Supreme Government.

Extract—From the Government of Bombay *to the Supreme Government, dated* 15*th May*, 1806.

" Another object which the expedition might have in view, would be an attempt to reform the manners of several of these chieftains, who, in common with the *Jarejah* tribe in the contiguous country of *Kutch*, put their female children generally to death as soon as they are born. Of this fact we have received too many concurrent testimonies, to admit of hesitation in the belief of its prevalence. The accompaniment, marked *** will be found to contain such official proceedings as we have hitherto held, respecting a discovery so deplorable and humiliating to the human race."

From the Supreme Government in reply, dated 31*st July*, 1806.

" We cannot but contemplate with approbation, the considerations of humanity which have induced you to combine with the proposed expedition, the project of suppressing the barbarous custom of female Infanticide. But the speculative success even of that benevolent project, cannot be considered to justify the prosecution of measures which may expose to hazard the essential interests of the state; although as a collateral object, the pursuit of it would be worthy of the benevolence and humanity of the British Government."

Circumstances having shortly afterwards admitted of the proposed expedition into *Kattywar*, under the full approbation and sanction of the Government General, it was accordingly undertaken in the year 1807, under the immediate direction of Major WALKER (the Resident at the Court of the *Gaikawar;)* who proceeded in the immediate command of the British detachment, with the view of thereby avoiding, as far as possible, every approximation to hostility; the leading object of this service being, on the contrary, to remove, by healing measures, every latent cause of dissension: keeping, at the same time in view, the interesting object of the suppression of Infanticide.

The following is an Extract from the first subsequent Communication on that Subject from Major WALKER, *dated 29th June,* 1807.

.................." I was the more particularly induced to retain PENGUEL SING, conceiving, from his personal acquaintance and influence with the chieftains and [k]*Bhoomeans* of that division of *Kattywar* called *Hallar*, which is principally inhabited by the cast of *Rajputs* called *Jarejahs*, who are addicted to the abominable practice of female Infanticide, that the humane and benevolent views which the Honourable the Governor in Council entertains of rendering this practice less frequent, may be thereby considerably promoted.

" I shall hereafter have the honour to forward, for the notice of the Honourable the Governor in Council, the information collected by PENGUEL SING, relative to this custom, by which its extent and prevalence will be observed.

" PENGUEL SING describes it as an ancient and imme-

[k] This term is new to me, nor doth the context fully explain its meaning. I have not altered its orthography. It may perhaps be a provincial pronunciation of *Brahman*, which about *Bombay*, *Poonah* and other western parts of *India*, is corruptly pronounced *Bamman*, or *Bahman*, without the *r*.—But in writing and correct language, *Bràhman* is the proper term—in writing, indeed, *Brahmana*. The word in the text, I conjecture, is pronounced *Bhumia*, or *Bhomia*, and I shall take an opportunity of seeking its meaning. E. M.

morial custom, confirmed by prejudice and family pride; but that there are also many instances of parental affection overcoming this horrid propensity; and that under the influence of the Honourable Company's Government, the practice may be considerably ameliorated."

Major WALKER opened his proceedings on the subject of female Infanticide with the chieftain of *Murvi*, or *Murbi;* and although at first flattered with the promised acquiescence of this principal *Jurejah* family, was disappointed, by receiving, in September, a letter from that chieftain, together with one from his mother, entreating the Major to drop the subject, as the *Jarejahs* never brought up women. Humane considerations appeared to have no weight with those people, who possess but a very slight sense of religion; professing, indeed, but little more than nominally the *Hindu* faith, and living almost indifferent to the doctrines of any of the *Sastras.* Female Infanticide seemed with them a question of policy or expediency—rather a prerogative of family, than of religion. There occurred, indeed, a very few examples of their rearing their daughters; and these apparently more occasioned by caprice or accidental motives, than from those of natural feeling or compassion.

Major WALKER, the Resident, continuing his solicitude, obtained, in October 1807, a conditional written engagement from the chieftain of *Murvi*, to relinquish the practice of destroying his daughters, "from good will and deference to the Honourable Company;" provided a like concession were obtained from the *Raja* of *Gowndel*, or from the head of the principality of *Jamnagher*.

Through the indefatigable exertions of the Resident, the

chief of *Gowndel* was prevailed upon, in the December following, to give the consent thus required; an example which was soon afterwards followed by all the others; from whom, including the chieftain of JAM, the Major obtained, before the end of the year 1807, the most formal and solemn engagements, renouncing this extraordinary practice for themselves, their relations, their dependants, and their posterity; the force of which obligation being such, that if they ever commit, or connive at, the practice in future, they confer on the *Gaikawar* and on the Company, a regular power to punish the offending party. This gratifying success was communicated by the Resident to the Government of *Bombay* in his Report, dated from *Beroda*, 25th January, 1808, from which the following passages are extracted:

......" It would be improper to dismiss this Report, without noticing that the *Jàrejàh Ràjputs* are those who have been distinguished in this part of *India* by the practice of female Infanticide; but it is only necessary on this occasion to advert to the circumstance.

" The solemn and written engagements of the chiefs, renouncing in future, for themselves and their posterity, this horrible usage, will form the subject of a separate letter; and although the first efforts to suppress this extraordinary custom met a strenuous opposition, it is highly gratifying to me to report, that the success of the measure has been universal and complete."

In acknowledgment of this official Report, the Government of *Bombay* expressed to the Resident, under date 7th of March, 1808, " their highest approbation of the exertions that had thus effected the attainment of an object, such as must," it was observed, " constitute an era in that country of more importance to the interests of humanity, than all the occurrences of those people's otherwise sufficiently eventful history."

The Supreme Government were likewise pleased to express their satisfaction on the present occasion in the following terms; as extracted from a letter in reply to the preceding communication from their Secretary (Mr. EDMONDSTONE) dated 11th of April, 1808.

" The Right Honourable the Governor General in Council, has derived great satisfaction from the perusal of that dispatch; and especially from the success which has attended the Resident's endeavours to obtain from the *Jarejah* chiefs the renunciation of the barbarous practice of female Infanticide."

(Quitting *Mr.* DUNCAN's summary, I shall now present the reader with a detailed report from Lieutenant-Colonel WALKER to the *Bombay* Government, dated 15th March, 1808, whence, from the point at which we have now arrived, the summary is continued. To give both would be an unnecessary repetition; although in consideration of the general reflections and remarks interspersed by *Mr.* DUNCAN (some of which I shall endeavour to preserve in the form of notes) as well as the commendations and encomiums on *Colonel* WALKER's able and zealous exertions, in which he frequently indulges, I would willingly do so—and cannot quit without reluctance the lucid summary of my most worthy and respected friend. E. M.)

CHAP. III.

Report from Lieutenant-Colonel ALEXANDER WALKER, *dated* BARODA, *15th March,* 1808, *of the measures pursued by him for the Suppression of* INFANTICIDE, *in* KATTYWAR, *or* GUZERAT.

To the Honourable JONATHAN DUNCAN,
Governor, &c. &c. &c.
Bombay.

HONOURABLE SIR,

1. THE abolition of the singular custom of female Infanticide, formed an object of my early and anxious attention during the late service.

2. I have already had the honour to state[*] generally, the success which has attended this measure; but before I proceed to detail its progress and circumstances, I shall endeavour to ascertain the origin and history of a practice, the most barbarous that ever owed its existence, either to the wickedness or weakness of human nature.

3. The early customs and history of every people are obscure and fabulous.

4. The *Hindus*, with a facility proportioned to their credulity, generally ascribe their peculiar institutions to a divine

[*] Under 25th January, 1808. See p. 40.

origin; and by connecting their observance with religious duties, they have passed inviolate through many ages.

5. This, probably, more than any other cause, has maintained that great distinction which is evident between the *Hindus* and other nations, and also between their own *castes.*

The force of the same sentiment, has rendered institutions favourable to morals and humanity, equally venerable and permanent; and it has sanctioned many that are absurd and criminal.

6. The displeasure and authority of the Supreme Being is naturally, and with propriety, resorted to in support of customs or rites, which tend to the suppression of vice, and to the welfare of society.

7. When the customs and rites of any people are harmless, whatever form they assume, and from whatever source they may be derived, they are entitled to toleration and protection; but they ought to be punished or amended, when their evident tendency is to diminish population, and to alienate the natural affections of mankind. Of this description is the custom of female Infanticide, which prevails among the tribe of *Raj-puts,* denominated *Jarejahs.*

8. The traditionary and legendary accounts of the *Hindus,* although sometimes ingenious, are often the wild and extravagant fictions of a rude and superstitious people; but the oral account of the savage and atrocious custom of Infanticide, is comprised in a simple narrative, and exhibits, under a slight disguise, a remote historical event.

9. The *Jarejahs* relate, that a powerful *Rajah* of their *caste,* who had a daughter of singular beauty and accomplish-

ments, desired his [b] *Rajgur*, or family *Brahman*, to affiance her to a prince of desert and rank equal to her own.

10. The *Rajgur* travelled over many countries, without discovering a chief who possessed the requisite qualities; for where wealth and power were combined, personal accomplishments and virtue were defective: and in like manner, where the advantages of the mind and body were united, those of fortune and rank were wanting.

11. The *Rajgur* returned, and reported to the prince that his mission had not proved successful.

12. This intelligence gave the *Rajah* much affliction and concern; as the *Hindus* reckon it to be the first duty of parents to provide suitable husbands for their daughters; and it is reproachful that they should pass the age of puberty without having been affianced, and be under the necessity of living in a state of [c] celibacy.

13. The *Rajah* however rejected, and strongly reprobated, every match for his daughter, which he conceived inferior to her high rank and perfections.

14. In this dilemma, the *Rajah* consulted his *Rajgur;* and the *Brahman* advised him to avoid the censure and disgrace, which would attend the princess' remaining unmarried, by having recourse to the desperate expedient of putting her to death.

[b] The *Raj-Gur,* otherwise called *Raj-Guru,* is literally the Priest, Tutor, or Preceptor of a *Rajah*; but the term is applied to the domestic *Brahman* of any family in this country. The *Katties,* and even every individual of a caste, has a *Raj-Gur.* In the peninsula and *Kutch,* the *Raj-Gurs* are a distinct tribe. A. W.

[c] See p. 22, note.

15. The *Rajah* was long averse to this expedient, and remonstrated against the murder of a woman; which, enormous as it is represented in the *Sastra*, would be aggravated when committed on his own offspring.

16. The *Rajgur* at length removed the *Rajah's* scruples, by consenting to load himself with the guilt; and to become in his own person responsible for all the consequences of the sin. Accordingly the princess was put to death; and female Infanticide was from that time practised by the *Jarejahs*.

17. From this narrative, curiosity receives little gratification, and the mind no pleasure. It resembles the tales of infancy, rather than the grave history of a transaction, involving the fate of a numerous portion of the human race.

18. This, however, comprises all the information which the *Jarejahs* possess, of the origin of a custom so contrary to the dictates of nature; and which is justifiable on no plea, as it gratifies no reasonable passion.

19. Notwithstanding this inadequate and unsatisfactory account of the origin of Infanticide, many whimsical and absurd institutions, like this, are dependant less on reason than on particular circumstances; which in the course of many ages, give them importance and influence.

20 There is nothing too extravagant and preposterous for the human mind to believe, and for men to practise; but there were also motives and contingent circumstances, which might operate to the progress and continuation of this inhuman custom among the *Jarejahs*.

21. The forms and maxims, and all the religious tenets of the *Hindus*, are strongly opposed to the crime of Infanticide.

22. Whatever may have been the motives that led the *Jarejahs* to embrace the extraordinary practice of destroying their daughters, conveniency and policy have contributed to continue and extend it.

23. The scruples of religion and conscience were lulled and quieted, by the ideal security of another race being responsible for the crime. Opinions and habits, from which at first we have an aversion, as they grow familiar rise into consideration, and establish their ascendency.

24. The superstition of the *Jarejahs* easily reconciled them to the expedient proposed by the *Raj-Gur;* which freed them from the fear and consequences of sin, and undermined their compassion and affection for their offspring.

25. The sentiments of nature and humanity were supplanted by the passions of avarice and pride; for the right of destroying their daughters grew into a privilege, which they regarded as a distinction and honour peculiar to their *caste.*

26. The *Hindu* precepts and customs concerning marriage, are full of family distinctions, exact so many observances, and impose so many restraints, that a military tribe, like the *Jarejahs,* might not be reluctant to receive a dispensation.

27. These restraints, when their operation is strictly enforced, occasion many inconveniencies, and in some situations they may prove insurmountable.

28. All these difficulties are felt more in the cases of women than of men; and the expense attending their marriage is an obligation which the *Jarejahs* consider it for their interest and advantage to be exempted from.

29. According to the ancient history of the *Jarejahs,* their

first considerable and well ascertained establishment was in *Sind;* but by traditionary accounts, there is reason to believe, that they at one period extended under different denominations over a great part of *Persia.*

30. *Sind* was one of the earliest objects of the ambition of the fanatical *Khalifs* who succeeded to the power and authority of MAHOMED. As the conversion of infidels was the ostensible object of these conquerors, the greatest part of the inhabitants of *Persia* and *Sind,* were obliged to embrace the *Mahomedan* faith.

31. It is probable, that the custom of Infanticide amongst the *Jarejahs,* was a consequence resulting from the *Mahomedan* conquest of *Sind.*

32. By the conquest and conversion of the greater part of the inhabitants of *Sind,* who were undoubtedly *Rajaputras* before that event, the *Jarejahs* were deprived of the usual means of disposing of their daughters in marriage.

33. This event, or some occurrence of a similar kind in the history of these tribes, which interrupted their intercourse and their ancient habits, must, we may conclude, have arisen, and have been sufficiently powerful to introduce the strange custom of Infanticide.

34. At the period of the conquest of *Sind,* the *Jarejahs* were not arrived at that state of society, when the sentiments of humanity have much influence; but under the guidance of their passions and prejudices, they were capable of acutely feeling every circumstance that affected the honour of their family or *caste.*

35. The *Jarejahs* finding themselves suddenly surrounded by tribes who had embraced a new faith, and precluded

thereby from marrying their daughters to those among whom they were formerly accustomed to contract matrimonial engagements, may, under such circumstances, have preferred the expedient suggested and encouraged by superstition, of destroying their female offspring.

36. They may have adopted this dreadful expedient, in preference to the sin of rearing their daughters in a state of celibacy, or of exposing themselves to the disgrace which would be incurred by incontinency; and the policy of their chief may have either concurred in, or invented the delusive responsibility of the *Raj-Gur*.

37. The credulity and superstition of the *Jarejahs*, would not suspect the incompetency of the intervention of their *Brahmans*; and this veneration for the advice of religious preceptors is not a new sentiment, nor is it peculiar to any religion.

38. We know that the *Jarejahs* maintained their independency in *Sind* for a long period, and resisted their invaders with spirit and fortitude. It is probable that they were not completely subdued until obliged to migrate into *Kutch*, where they established themselves, and retained their own religion.[d]

39. But before this event, the insulated situation of the *Jarejahs* in *Sind*, amongst tribes of different classes from them-

[d] Mr. DUNCAN, in his summary, after noticing the various reasons, given more in detail in this Report, that have been offered in excuse or in extenuation of the practice in question, says, " that the same defenders of the practice in *Kutch*, farther allege, and with truth, the known humanity, in other respects, of its inhabitants, beyond even most other classes of *Hindus:* insomuch as to admit of their killing scarcely any thing, their own daughters, among the *Jarejahs*, excepted—a circumstance, among too many others, evincing the inconsistency of man!"

selves; and the expense and risk that would attend the sending of their daughters to countries where they might be affianced to *Rajputs* of a proper descent, had impelled the *Jarejahs* to have recourse to Infanticide. Being precluded from disposing of their daughters in their own vicinity, they were sacrificed to their pride, convenience, and superstition.

40. In subsequent times, when the emigration of the *Jarejahs* into *Kutch* and *Guzerat*, inhabited by *Rajputs*, offered abundance of husbands for their daughters, and removed the plea for their destruction, the custom had been established, and was considered as one of their unalienable rights.

41. The *Jarejahs* had also conceived many barbarous notions of their own superiority; and they undervalued, or despised, the tribes, amongst whom they had obtained a compulsory settlement.

42. The circumstance of conquest, under which they settled in *Kutch*, and *Guzerat*, confirmed this sentiment of superiority. As the *Jarejahs* came from a distant country, they had many foreign and strange habits; and their *Dewrey*, or household god, was different from the worship of the other *Rajputs*, among whom they were now established.

43. The custom of killing their daughters, we may suppose, had by this time produced its effect on the manners of the *Jarejahs;* and as their wars with the *Mussulmans* had made them more hardy and enterprising, than the inhabitants whose possessions they had conquered, the same cause would render them more arrogant and overbearing: and this is still the character of the *Jarejahs*.

45. The history of the *Jarejahs*, also, since they arrived in

Kutch and *Guzerat*, bears evidence of their incapacity for government, and of their capricious, and imprudent conduct.

46. It is necessary to mention these traits in the character of the *Jarejahs*, as they would operate to maintain the practice of Infanticide after their settlement in this country; and when the original pretence for its origin ceased to exist.

47. In what way soever the practice of Infanticide was introduced, it must be referred to the peculiar manners, and political state of the people. The sequel will disclose the circumstances, that at present maintain and preserve this barbarous custom.

48. Strangers to parental emotions and affections, the great cause for destroying their children is avarice; and that they may not be exposed to the cares and expense attending their establishment in life.

49. This was actually pleaded by the *Jarejah* chiefs in defence of the practice; which deprived them, they said, of much care, vexation, and expense; and which had been so long in existence, that the heinousness of the crime was altogether lost sight of in its antiquity.

50. The practice which prevailed in *Europe*, and chiefly amongst the principal families, of placing their daughters in nunneries, might be traced to the same motives that led the *Jarejahs* to put theirs to death; and both have originated in the desire of diminishing the cares and expense attending a numerous family.

51. They all pleaded their aversion to relinquish a custom which they conceived to attach renown to their *caste*, and to distinguish it above all the other *Rajputs*, in this quarter at least.

52. In order to explain the operation of these sentiments on the minds of the *Jarejahs*, it is necessary to anticipate a circumstance more fully noticed hereafter, and to mention that there are several instances of *Jarejahs* who have allowed their daughters to live.

53. In those instances they are instigated by their pride, and their ideal notions of superiority, to give large marriage portions with their daughters.

54. It is a maxim with them, that the daughter of a *Jarejah*, independent of her person, and the honour of their alliance, should carry wealth into the house of her husband, and be a valuable acquisition to her new connections.

55. An instance, however, occurred in the petty *Jarejah* chief of *Kallawar* saving a daughter, and aftewards contracting her in marriage to a son of Meru Khowass. This was considered as an extraordinary instance of degradation, which even the pressure of necessity and interest, could not excuse. The marriage was not consummated; and the father never permitted his daughter to repair to her husband's house.

56. These sentiments are common to the rich and the poor, and have undoubtedly contributed to perpetuate the practice of Infanticide.

57. In considering the causes which have tended to confirm and continue this practice, considerable weight must be given to the apathy and indifference, with which it has ever been viewed by the rest of the *Rajput* families, and the *Brahmans*, who are numerous in this country.

58. It does not appear that any effort has been made for the general suppression of this crime, for which they possessed a simple and effectual remedy, by refusing to affiance their

daughters to the *Jarejahs*, unless on the condition of rearing their female offspring.

59. Such an idea never seems to have occurred to the other *Rajputs*. On the contrary, they appear to have countenanced the practice of Infanticide, not only by intermarrying their daughters with the *Jarejahs*, but by allowing them to become the instruments of murdering their own offspring.

60. These *Rajputs* were led to this unnatural compliance, from the ease and facility with which their acquiescence enabled them to marry their daughters. To this interested motive, they appear to have sacrificed the sentiments of religion and humanity, without any repugnance.

61. They excused, however, to me, and endeavoured to palliate, their want of sensibility, by pleading the immutable usages of *caste*, and the impropriety of interfering in those of the *Jarejahs*.

62. Curiosity will naturally be excited to learn the forms, and methods, observed in committing these Infanticides; and whether they were attended by any compunction and ceremony.

63. The common expressions for Infanticide are, "*Dikri marnè chàl;*" or "the custom of killing daughters:" and "*Nani dikri marnè chàl;*" or "the custom of killing young daughters."

In conversation, and in discussing the subject with the *Jarejahs*, the term used was "*Dikri bàbut;*" or "the article or subject of girls."

64. The subject is disgusting, and I shall endeavour to state briefly the result of my inquiries. Although the *Jarejahs* spoke freely of the custom of putting their daughters to

death, and without delicacy, and without any pain, they were more reserved on the mode of their execution; and appeared at first unwilling to be questioned on the subject.

65. They usually replied, that " it was an affair of the women;"—" it belonged to the nursery, and made no part of the business of men." They at last, however, threw off this reserve.

66. The following is the translate of a memorandum from WASSONJI ESWARJI, a *Nagar Brahman*, who attended the camp in the quality of * *Vakil* from the *Gondal* chief.

" When the wives of the *Jarejah Rajputs* are delivered of " daughters, the women who may be with the mother, repair " to the oldest man in the house—this person desires them to " go to him who is father of the infant, and do as he directs.

" On this the women go to the father, who desires them " to do as is customary, and so to inform the mother.

" The women then repair to the mother, and tell her how " to act in conformity to their usage. The mother next puts " opium on the nipple of her breast, which the child inhaling " with its milk, dies.

" The above is one custom, and the following is another. " When the child is born, they place the navel-string on its " mouth, when it expires."

67. From the conversations of the *Jarejahs*, it appears that the opium is put into the mouth of the child; but the mode of administering this drug described by WASSONJI, may have given rise to the opinion, that the *Jarejahs* drown their daughters, by throwing them as soon as they are born, into a vessel of milk.

* Agent, or deputy, or envoy.

68. From every inquiry, I could not understand that the *Jarejahs* ever put their daughters to death after this manner; but the story may have had its origin in the idea of the infant imbibing poisoned milk, or from an expression which is ascribed to the father, who, when the birth of a daughter is announced, with brutal equivocation, says to the attendant, "*Dhood Pelauna;*" or "cause it to drink milk"—or "to suck."

69. This is but a popular story, and independent of the circumstance of few infants sucking immediately on the birth, the placing of opium on the nipple would probably prevent it.

70. The true manner by which the *Jarejahs* kill their daughters, as received from the chieftains of *Ràjkut* and *Jàllia*, is subsequently related.[f]

71. There is apparently neither merit nor demerit attached to the saving of their daughters; but although the act is optional and voluntary, it seems more reputable to destroy them. The few instances that have been traced to the contrary would establish, that the practice of Infanticide was considered more honorable; for, although the motive may be gross and selfish, it is the natural disposition of men to ascribe

[f] Mr. DUNCAN, after noticing several methods stated to be in use for the perpetration of the sad act, remarks in his Summary, that "the difference of these modes, from those learned through other channels, as previously related, are of little moment; and, were evidence wanting, rather add to, than abstract from, the indubitable existence and local notoriety, of the general fact. It is admitted, that some of these infants are left to the inevitable result of neglect; and the *Jarejahs* are reported to be indeed altogether indifferent as to the manner of putting their female offspring to death, provided the inhuman deed be performed."

their actions, especially when they are deviations from natural principles, to illustrious and generous sources.

72. If a father wish to preserve a daughter, he previously apprises his wife and family, and his commands are obeyed. If a mother entertain the wish of preserving a daughter, and her husband be averse to it, the infant must be put to death.

73. There are, however, instances wherein the blandishments and influence of the mother have succeeded in saving the infant, by obtaining the revocation of the decree for its destruction; but these instances of maternal solicitude are either unfrequent, or but seldom successful.

74. The father sometimes expressly orders the infant to be put to death, probably when he suspects some tendency or intention of the mother to preserve it; but in general, this sanguinary intimation is unnecessary; as silence on the part of the husband is considered to imply his resolution, that the child, if a female, should perish.

75. To render this deed, if possible, more horrible, the mother is commonly the executioner of her own offspring.

Women of rank may have their slaves and attendants who perform this office, but the far greater number execute it with their own hands.

76. This compliance of the women must appear the more extraordinary, as they belong to casts who rear their females, and are brought up in families where their own existence is evidence against this unnatural practice; but as they are betrothed at an early age, they imbibe the superstition of their husbands, and some of them appeared even as advocates for the custom.

77. They have been known to pride themselves, like the

Jarejahs,[g] on the destruction of their daughters, and to consider their murder as an act of duty; an act, which these females, who are mild, modest, and affectionate, would, if married into any other cast, hold in detestation.

78. They appear to have several methods of destroying the infant, but two are prevalent.

79. Immediately after the birth of a female they put into its mouth some opium; or draw the umbilical cord over its face, which prevents respiration. But the destruction of so tender and young a subject is not difficult; and it is effected without causing a struggle, and probably without pain.

80. The natural weakness and debility of the infant, when neglected and left uncleaned, sometimes causes its death, without the necessity of actual violence; and sometimes it is laid on the ground, or on a plank, and left to expire.

81. These accounts I learned in conversation with *Jarejahs*, and prefer them to the information of the translated memorandum.

82. The infant after it is destroyed, is placed naked in a small basket, and carried out and interred. In *Kattawār* any of the female attendants of the family perform this office; but in *Kutch* it is done by the domestic *Raj-Gur*.

83. The *Raj-Gurs* who bury the infants that perish, receive a fee of one *kori*, which is a coin equivalent in value

[g] "But," as Mr. DUNCAN observes in his Summary, "it is impossible to conceive that such a departure from all natural sentiment can be general; and it was, in accordance, reported to him, that when, in 1789, the *Rajkumars* had been induced to renounce this barbarous habitude, their wives were, during his visit to their country, ready to burst from the concealment of their houses, for the purpose of throwing themselves at his feet, in expression of gratitude, for being exonerated from an office every way so abhorrent to the maternal character."

to one third of a *rupee*, or about ten-pence sterling; and a meal.

84. In *Kutch*, the female *Raj-Gurs* are sometimes the executioners of the infant instead of the mother, and this seems to approach nearer to the origin of the custom.

85. The birth of a daughter is considered by the *Hindus* of every description as an inferior event, and they rarely make it the subject of congratulation or festivity; while the birth of a son is celebrated with every ostentation and hilarity.

86. It is not therefore surprising, that on the birth of a daughter, which they may have even preserved, and predetermined to bring up, a *Jarejah* family should discover no demonstration of joy. The event is allowed to pass over in silence, as if they were ashamed of it.

87. Should any inquisitive person ask a *Jarejah* the result of the pregnancy of his wife, if it were a female, he would answer—" *nothing.*" This expression in the idiom of the country, is sufficiently significant.

88. The infant is invariably put to death immediately on its birth; and it would be considered a cruel and barbarous action, to deprive it of life, after it had been allowed to live a day or two.

89. Although instances of this cool and deliberate murder may be very rare, yet from the examination of a [h] *Jarejah* who was reported to me as having been guilty of this deed, I have reason to believe that they sometimes occur.

90. The immediate death of a daughter is generally viewed by a *Jarejah* as an infallible consequence of its birth, and it is considered to be an event of such insignificance, that

[h] See note A of Chap. V.

he is seldom apprised of it. The occurrence excites neither surprise nor inquiry, and is never made a subject even of conversation.

91. The *Jarejahs* spoke of it with the utmost levity, and are wholly indifferent with respect to the mode of putting their female offspring to death, provided the inhuman deed be performed.

92. JUSSAJI of *Jallia* has had three daughters. They were all put to death at the time of their birth. JUSSAJI attended the camp, is a man of intelligence, and served the detachment as a guide. The character and disposition of JUSSAJI, both for humanity and propriety, is favourable; but he has not the least compunction for the murder of these children, and considers the deed to be in every respect justifiable.

93. The practice of Infanticide appears to have been discontinued by the descendants of the *Jarejahs* who inhabit *Sind*, and who have become converts to the *Mahomedan* religion.

94. I was told, however, of an exception; and that one of these converted tribes, or families, still follow the custom of their ancestors.[i]

95. A few of the *Jarejah* tribes of *Kutch*, have also discontinued Infanticide, or practise it but occasionally; for my information was not very clear and positive on this point.

96. The following *Jarejah* families in that country, were mentioned to me as systematically refraining from Infanticide;

[i] "Whether this be true or not," says Mr. DUNCAN on this passage, in his Summary, "the praise is no doubt due to the *Mahomedan* doctrines, which utterly discountenance, and severely prohibit so abominable a practice."

and their names deserve to be recorded. The families of *Bulak*, *Battan*, *Sar Kabar*, *Hoti*, *Ubra*, *Jarria*, *Gafan*, *Murasi*, *Mokara*, *Kaya*, *Retreka*, *Mor*, *Rao*, *Jessa*, *Dessa*, *Danrar*, *Dettia*, *Joria*, *Adria*, *Verai*, *Kunerdé*, and *Vim*, are enumerated as rearing their daughters.

97. Some of these families are of respectability in *Kutch;* but by far the greater part of the inhabitants follow the practice without the least remorse.

98. In the peninsula, although some individuals have occasionally preserved their daughters, it appears to have been the result of accidental circumstances and impressions; and not the effect of any steady resolution, or principle.

99. The origin of Infanticide among the *Jarejahs*, is not supposed to be more remote than 500 years.

100. As no disgrace or stigma is attached to the omission of this act, we might expect that natural affection would prevail over a barbarous custom; but this is overpowered by the influence of habits and prejudices, strengthened by little selfish views of economy, and domestic ease.

101. I endeavoured to ascertain the motives of the *Jarejahs* who preserved their daughters; and by their own confession, this act of humanity did not proceed from parental feelings.

102. It appeared to be inspired, not by motives of affection for the object, so much as by personal considerations, arising from the ideas of *Metempsychosis*, which are so universally and rigidly observed by the [k]*Sravaka Banias*, who are the followers of JINA.

[k] *Sravaka*, is the appellation by which the followers of the doctrines of JINA, or JAINA, are distinguished in *Guzerat*, *Kanara*, and in other parts of *India*. The term is, however,

103. These people consider it a sin to deprive any being or creature, however mean or noxious, of life; and their doctrines are said to have made an impression on a few of the *Jarejahs*.

104. It would be an interesting inquiry, to ascertain the number of females who perish annually from this detestable practice.

This could only be effected by a personal inspection, and a careful research amongst the *Jarejah* families, which might determine their numbers, and obtain a tolerably correct estimate of these casualties.

105. The result of my inquiries was too general, vague, and uncertain, to afford the *data* of an accurate calculation; but it may be still useful to state this information, as, although defective, it may convey some determinate notion of the extent of this offence against the first laws of human nature.

106. I shall begin by stating an account which has every appearance of exaggeration.

According to a loose computation, the number of *Jarejah* families inhabiting *Kutch* and *Kattawar*, is estimated at 1,25,000, and the number of female infants yearly destroyed to amount to 20,000.

107. Being desirous, however, of reducing this inquiry to a state of greater certainty, I endeavoured to procure a particular list of the *Jarejahs* inhabiting these countries. I found it impossible to obtain this information of *Kutch;* but the following is an account of the names and the number of *Jarejah*

strictly applicable to the laity only; the priests being called *Yati,* or *Jati.* People of the *Jaina* persuasion are very numerous in *Guzerat,* and some curious particulars are related of them by Colonel WALKER in note F of Chap. V. E. M.

families inhabiting *Hallar* and [1]*Matsyu Kanta,* furnished by an intelligent native, and well acquainted with that extraordinary race.

108. A list of the families of the different tribes of *Jarejahs* who inhabit *Hallar* and *Matsyu Kanta.*

Family	Number
“ *Jam Zadeh,* or the descendants of the JAMS	40
“ *Hurdols*	500
“ *Dungarani*	500
“ *Sissangia*	100
“ *Kubber*	100
“ *Rewani*	100
“ *Wibani*	500
“ *Lakani*	100
“ *Morani*	500
“ *Kanderya*	100
“ *Ammer*	100
“ *Bharani*	100
“ *Bhanani*	50
“ *Amran*	500
“ *Dil*	600
“ *Halla*	100
“ *Hapa*	100
“ *Kumani*	100
“ *Kana*	200
“ *Rao*	400
“ *Batach*	100
and other casts	500
	5,390

[1] This is written *Muchoo Kaunta,* or *Khanta,* in the MS. I conjecture that it would be more correctly written *Matsya kanta,* meaning in *Sanskrit,* as well as in some current dia-

109. It is supposed that the annual number of Infanticides in the peninsula of *Guzerat* amounts to 5000.

110. The number of *Jarejahs* in *Kutch*, on the authority of the natives, is ten times as many as those of *Hallar* and *Matsyu Kantha*, and this would give us a population of 150,000 men; for all these calculations are exclusive of women and

lects, the fishes throat, or fish throated, or it may have some allusion to a boney or prickly fish; *kanta* having these meanings; likewise pointed, or more especially *pronged.* NILA KANTHA, the blue throated, is a name of SIVA; for the origin of which, see *Hindu Pantheon*, p. 58. 65.

There is, I doubt not, a popular legend grounded on some mythological fable, accounting for this significant appellative. The first incarnation (if that usual *fleshy* term may in this instance be admitted) of VISHNU, was in the form of a fish; and these provinces of *Kattywàr* and *Kutch*, having been the immediate theatre of many of the poetical exploits of the preserving power, especially in his *Avatara* in the person of KRISHNA, we may expect to find many names of places, and persons, and things, thence derived. The city of *Dwarka*, built by command of KRISHNA, on the western shore of *Guzerat* (see *Hindu Pantheon*, p. 114) was his favorite retreat, after his exodus from *Matra*; and is the scene of many poetical effusions. A good account of this classical city and neighbourhood is much wanted.

The *Gaikawar* dynasty, now reigning in *Guzerat*, one might guess from their names, are of the sect of *Gokalast'has*, or exclusive worshippers of VISHNU in his *Avatara* of GOKAL, or KRISHNA. GOVINDA and ANANDA, the names of the late and present heads of the *Gaikawar* state, having been borne by KRISHNA and his foster father.—(See *Hindu Pantheon*, Index.—*Gaikawar*, the patronymic, may, I think, be traced to the same pastoral source) *Gài*, *Go*, and *Gao*, meaning *kine*. Of this, perhaps, something in a future page. It may be remarked, that a very redoubted antagonist of KRISHNA was named MUCHU KUNDA (*Hindu Pantheon*, p. 214; *As. Res.* VI. 509); and hence may be derived the name of the district of *Muchoo Kànta*, that hath given rise to this note; but I incline to *Matsya-kanta*. The latter (*Kanta*) is indeed the name by which the district of *Kutch*, or *Kach*, or *Kach'ha*, as it ought to be written, appears to have been locally known; and it has been so called, probably from projecting like a *prong* into the sea. Off *Bombay* light-house there are two dangerous reefs or shoals, projecting a considerable distance from the shore; these, by our navigators and pilots, are always called the *prongs*, and by natives, if I mistake not, *Kanta*. *Matsya-kanta*, will thus mean the promontory of fish; happily designative of the outline, and productiveness of *Guzerat*. E. M.

children; who must, from the nature of the case, be either wives or boys.

111. As a number of *Jarejahs* in that country have disused Infanticide, without any formal renunciation, however, of the practice, the number of deaths may be estimated at 30,000.

112. I shall, lastly, state the lowest estimate that I received of these murders; and although its moderation may appear in favour of its truth, I am disposed to think this account as short of the number destroyed, as the preceding is probably an exaggeration.

113. These accounts, it is to be observed, do not pretend to rest on calculation, but convey the opinions of persons well informed of the state of the country. According to this authority, the number of Infanticides annually in *Hallar* and *Matsyu Kantha*, are between 1000 and 1100, and in *Kutch* about 2000.

114. The disagreements of these estimates would probably defeat any attempt to reconcile them, but they are sufficient to establish the enormity and magnitude of the crime.

115. It has already been remarked, that whenever a *Jarejah* save his daughter, he invariably exerts every means, sometimes to the impoverishment of his family, to obtain a respectable settlement for her in life. It is perhaps this strong desire that prevents the lower orders saving their daughters.

116. The instances that were reported to me of *Jarejahs* who saved their daughters, were of families of rank in the country; but these instances of humanity are few.

117. I shall begin with stating the most remarkable in-

stance, as it was the effect of conscience, although operating by a kind of double faculty.

118. The *Jarejah* MOKAJI, of *Anundgher*, one of the *Byaud*,[m] of the *Goundal* chief, renounced, after a short period, every matrimonial intercourse with his wife, from the apprehension of begetting a daughter.

119. This self-constraint was persevered in for several years; and MOKAJI, during that period, patiently resisted the scoffings and persuasions of his *caste*, and relations, without being in the least diverted from his purpose.

120. The case became serious, and the family assembled to prevent the misfortune, if possible, of MOKAJI dying childless.

121. After every expedient had failed of success, KUMBAJI, the late chief of *Gondal*, in his capacity of *Tilaat*, or head of the family, was obliged to lay a solemn and public injunction an MOKAJI to preserve his daughters. On receiving the order of his superior, MOKAJI returned to his wife, and had born to him in succession four daughters; a circumstance which exposed him again to the taunts of the *Jarejahs*, but which MOKAJI appears to have supported with philosophical indifference.

122. These daughters are still alive, and are married to the present chiefs of *Drangadra*, *Wadwan*, *Limri*, and *Wankanier*.

123. The motives that led MOKAJI to pursue this conduct deserve to be explained; but it is first necessary to mention that he had become a [n]*Kabir Pant*.

[m] Brotherhood, fraternity.

[n] *Kubeer Punt* in the MS. As this sect seem to blend *Mahomedan* and *Hindu* tenets,

124. The *Kabir Pants* form a sect of *Beragis*, who follow the tenets of KABIR, a holy man, who lived about 300 years ago. They deny, in general, the authenticity of the *Sastras* and *Vedas*—and assert that God is one and indivisible; possessing in himself every attribute ascribed by the *Hindus* to different deities. They deny the *avataras*, or incarnations; and they place no confidence in the efficacy of the ceremonies of worship, and purification by washing in rivers; they put their whole trust on the sincerity of devotion, and in good works.

125. KABIR himself was a *Mahomedan* by *caste*, and a weaver by profession. His disciples may be either *Mahome-*

so they have also the languages in naming their founder. *Kabir* is an Arabic word, signifying *great, mighty,* and is not unfrequently given or assumed as a proper name. *Pant*, or *Punt*, is a corrupt abbreviation of *Pandit*, the *Sanskrit* term for a philosopher, and strictly applicable only to a learned *Brahman*; but it is now commonly given to almost every *Brahman*, and often apparently as a proper name. The miracle related in paragraph 125 above, or a miracle something like it, is said to have happened on several occasions, where *Hindus* and *Mahomedans* have come into religious contentions. In my account of an "Hereditary living deity near Poonah," given in Vol. VII. of the Asiatic Researches, it is related, how trays of cows flesh, sent by the *Mahomedans*, covered to the *Deva*, in mockery, as if it were a present, were found, when uncovered, to have been miraculously changed into sacred flowers, dear to *Hindu* superstition.

In the *Ayin Akbery*, II. 19, the following paragraph is of the same stamp; appearing indeed to be only a variety of the same story, as is above related by Colonel WALKER, and told too of a person of the same name, KABIR.

"Many pretend that at this place" (the author is describing the temple of *Jaganat'h)* "is the tomb of KABIR MOWEHHED, and to this day they relate many stories of his sayings and actions. He was revered both by *Mahomedans* and *Hindus*, on account of his wisdom and exemplary virtue. When he died, the *Brahmans* wanted to carry his body to be burned, and the *Mahomedans* insisted on burying it; but when they lifted up the sheet from the bier, the corpse could not be found." The name of this favored person is in the *Ayin Akbery* written KEBEER. MOWEHHED is a derivative from *wahed*, a word signifying *unique, peerless*, and is an epithet of MAHOMED. E. M.

dans or *Hindus*. On his death, the *Mahomedans* claimed a right to bury him—the *Hindus* to burn him—a quarrel ensued, which seems to have been appeased by a miraculous intervention, thus related. The corpse was covered with a cloth; on withdrawing it, the body was found metamorphosed, the upper part into a [o]*Tulsi* plant, the favorite *nymphæ* of KRISHNA; the lower into the *Rehan*, an odoriferous green herb, the sacred colour of the prophet *Mahomed*.

126. As a zealous *Jarejah*, the honour and custom of his sect required that MOKAJI should kill his daughters. As a *Kabir Pant*, the principles of this sect rendered Infanticide unlawful and criminal.

127. In this situation MOKAJI could only avoid disgrace or sin, by that course of celibacy which he prescribed for himself, and from which he was so happily relieved by the commands of his chief.

128. The chief of *Kersura* is the next instance of a *Jarejah* who has brought up his daughter, and who is now married to WAJI SING, the eldest son of the [p]*Thakore* of *Bhownagher*.

It was neither natural affection, nor any conscientious sentiment, that made the chief of *Kersura* save his daughter.

129. The whole merit of this act of humanity is due to an *Arab Jemadar*, who gave up to this sordid and mercenary chief, all the arrears of pay which he had earned in his service,

[o] More classically written *Tulasi*; see a fable hereon in *Hindu Pantheon*, p. 202. The *Rehan* is the sweet *basil*. E. M.

[p] *Thakore*, or *Thakur*, is a title of distinction, equivalent to chief, head, or lord: it is sometimes applied to a deity, and is also given as a proper name. E. M.

and which amounted to a considerable sum, on condition that he would preserve his daughter.

130. It is more pleasing to relate the third instance, as it appears to have proceeded from the natural affection of a parent. DADAJI, the brother of the present chief of *Rajkote*, has preserved his daughter, and from his conversation and manners, I was fully convinced, that it was the effect of principle and duty.

131. A similar instance occurs in the example of HUTAJI, the chieftain of *Kotara Sangani*, who has preserved all his female offspring.

132. It is to be observed, that the families of *Rajkote* and *Kotara* are both in impoverished circumstances; and the principle that has led them to save their daughters, is the more unquestionable and meritorious, as they have voluntarily burthened themselves with the great expense of providing for them.

133. HUTAJI is a professed [9]robber, with whom sentiment and feeling might be supposed to be strangers. The profession which he followed did not prevent me conversing with HUTAJI, nor to avoid a pretty frequent intercourse with him.

134. This man, with the aspect and manners of a barbarian, possessed all the feelings of natural affection, which led him to cherish his daughters, in opposition to the usage and prejudices of his tribe.

The daughters of HUTAJI are between six and eight years of age; and he brought them both to my camp, where they were vaccinated.

[9] See note B in Chap. V.

135. I observed their father caressing them with pleasure, and exulting in them with true parental satisfaction; and their persons and manners were very interesting.

136. It deserves remark, as exhibiting a strong feature in the character of the *Jarejahs*, and of their feelings with respect to their daughters, that these girls wore turbans, and were dressed and habited like boys.

137. As if ashamed or afraid of acknowledging their sex, they assured me that they were not girls, and with infantile simplicity, appealed to their father to corroborate their assertion.

138. The last instance which I shall mention of a *Jarejah* saving his daughter is the chief of *Mallia*; and I believe this comprises the whole number of existing cases that have come to my knowledge.

139. The wife of this *Thakore* prevailed on him to rear his daughters; but notwithstanding this, he was one of the last who subscribed to the instrument for abolishing the practice of Infanticide.

140. My reports for the settlement of the revenue of this country, have occasionally exhibited a solitary instance wherein the *Jarejahs* have saved as well as destroyed their daughters; but my intercourse with the *Jarejahs* brought me acquainted with several who had caused three or four of their female offspring to be put to death; and they spoke of the circumstance with the indifference incident to the most ordinary transaction.

141. The *Jarejahs* carefully select their wives from the most respectable *Rajput* families; and although they generally give a preference to the *Jhallas*, they may marry apparently into any of the numerous *Rajput* tribes.

142. The *Jarejahs* marry the daughters of the *Jhalla, Wagela, Goil, Churassamma, Purmar, Surweys*, [1]*Soda, Jaitwa, Wala*, and *Wadal*, tribes.

They give in marriage such legitimate daughters as they preserve to any of the *castes*, but invariably endeavour to affiance them to the highest rank or tribe, in their power.

143. Illegitimate daughters are not given in marriage to *Raj-puts*, but are bestowed on *Mussulmans*, or on *Hindus* of an inferior *caste*, under the best circumstances they can obtain.

144. I was told, that the *Jarejahs*, from the difficulty of procuring wives, were in the habits of procuring bastards and slaves, but I was satisfied, that this was an untruth.

145. On asking JUSSAJI if this was ever the case, he appeared to feel great indignation, and to think that it was intended to insult him; but on explaining the motive of the inquiry, he acknowledged that the *Thakore* of *Banwar*, under the hope of supporting himself through the great influence which MERU KHAWASS possessed at *Nowanagher*, was affianced to his daughter; but the contract was not completed, and the *Thakore* never admitted the woman into his house: even the poorest and lowest *Jarejah* feels the utmost solicitude not to taint his blood by an improper alliance.

146. It does not appear that the number of their wives is limited by any rule.

147. The practice of concubinage is common among the *Jarejahs*, and in forming these connections they are under little or no restraint with respect to *caste*.

148. It will be observed, that the settlement of their

[1] See note C of Chap. V.

daughters born of a *Rackila*, or mistress, is attended with little expense, or publicity; and the motives therefore which lead the *Jarejahs* to destroy their legitimate daughters do not in the former case exist with equal force.

149. Rao Lakpat, the grandfather of the present sovereign of *Kutch*, had a daughter by a *Rackely*, whom he preserved, and afterwards married to Damaji Gaikawar.

The name of this lady, who has since returned to *Booj*, where she resides, is Mota Bhye Maharaj.

150. It may be observed, however, that this marriage among the *Mahrattas*, is reckoned of an inferior kind, called *Khanda laggan*,[r] or a marriage celebrated by the proxy of a sword; and the children would be considered illegitimate, or incapable of inheriting the *Gaikawar Gadi*.[t]

151. Political reasons induced Rao Lakpat to form this connection with Damaji. The country of *Kutch* was at that period threatened with an invasion from *Sind*, and Rao was desirous of protecting himself by the powerful alliance of Damaji.

152. The marriage was celebrated at *Patten* with great pomp and expense. Damaji survived this transaction but two years, and at his death his [u]widow returned to her relations.

153. This lady derives her support from her own family, and lives on the produce of a *Jaghir*, from the *Rajah* of *Kutch*.

154. The uncle of Rao Lakpat had a daughter by a *Rackeli* of the *Khomarin* tribe, who was famous for her beauty.

[r] *Khanda*, a *scimitar*; *laggan*, a *connection*.

[t] *Gadi*, a throne, or seat of state.

[u] See pages 17. 19. 30. preceding.

The daughter was affianced to the king of *Sind*, a *Mahomedan*.

155. The present chief of *Kutch* has likewise a daughter by a *Rackeli*, who was betrothed to a son of the *Junagher Nawáb*; but FATTEH MAHOMED prevented the celebration of the marriage, and it is now considered to be dissolved.

156. These instances may be sufficient to shew the treatment by the *Jarejahs* of their illegitimate offspring; and they appear to spare them, rather from a contemptuous opinion of their inferiority than from humanity. These children are not considered to belong to the *caste*, and their future situation in life is of little consequence; but the pride and prejudices of a *Jarejah*, make him occasionally also destroy his spurious offspring.

157. It is remarkable, that it is the practice of these *Rackelis*, or mistresses, to perform [a]*Sati* with deceased *Jarejahs*, which is but rarely done by their wives.

158. When RAO LACKA, the grandfather of RAO RAYDUN, the present chief of *Kutch*, died, fifteen *Rackelis* burnt at his funeral pile; two of these women were *Mahomedans* of the country, and another a [x]*Seeden*—the rest were *Hindus* of different *castes*; but not one of RAO LACKA's wives sacrificed herself on this occasion.

159. This deviation from the general *Hindu* practice is merely the effect of another habit, or custom; as there is no

[a] That is, to burn with the corpse of their lord. The word means *pure, holy,* and is that usually given to this species of suicide. See Index to *Hindu Pantheon,* under *Sati.* E. M.

[x] This, I believe, means a female *Sidi*, or *African*, with a woolly head; but the word is not familiar to me. E. M.

law against a *Jarejah* wife burning with her husband, and they sometimes voluntarily devote themselves to the flames.

160. This ceremony, however, is less expected from the wife than the *Rackeli;* and these unfortunate females conceive it a point of honour to consume themselves with their lords; often being inspired by a dreadful emulation to become the first victim.

161. It may be necessary to correct an opinion which many *Europeans* have entertained, that these sacrifices are compulsory.

162. The *Jarejah* wives and *Rackelis* are at liberty to follow this custom, or to abstain from it; and neither disgrace nor opprobrium is attached to those who may chuse to survive.

163. It may be mentioned as another extraordinary deviation from the general custom of *Hindus*, that in the district of *Halvad*, the wives of the lowest *castes* only burn with their husbands; and this may be the reason that the *Jarejah* women excuse themselves; as it is only people of rank who keep *Rackelis*, instances of this nature are not frequent.

164. The influence of example and communication is capable of procuring converts to the most criminal and flagitious courses.

165. The *Jaitwa Rajputs* who rule over the division of *Burrudda*, known at present under the name of *Poor*[7] *Bunder*,

[7] I retain this spelling, rather than alter the name of a place so well known about *Bombay*; otherwise I should write it *Pùr bandır*. The division of *Burudda*, mentioned in this paragraph, is very distant from *Baroda*, or *Beroda*, the residence of the *Gaikawar* court. Until within these few years this latter city and district was usually called by us *Brodera*. E. M.

have been accused of adopting the barbarous practice of the *Jarejahs*, in destroying their daughters.

166. The *Jaitwas* may have thought it no disgrace to follow a custom cherished by their conquerors; and having lost the greater part of their possessions, they may have been desirous, like the *Jarejahs*, of relieving themselves from the burden of portioning their daughters.

167. The *Jaitwas*, however, do not pretend to deny the sin of Infanticide, and avoid an open avowal of the practice.

168. They observe a silence on the subject, and the deed is performed in secrecy; but the singular fact that the *Ranas* of *Poor Bunder* have had no grown up daughters for more than a hundred years, would be evidence against them.

169. The ministers of the *Rana* did not deny the circumstance to me, when I communicated the information I had received respecting this practice of the *Jaitwas*; and their Chief executed the same instrument as the *Jarejahs* did, for renouncing the custom; an unequivocal proof that it existed.

170. The doctrines of the *Hindu* religion have been singularly careful to protect the female sex and infants from violence; and it is unlawful to put a woman to death for any offence whatever.

171. In support of this opinion they quote the following *sloka* or verse:

(As Colonel WALKER has again given this verse, and an amended translation in a note, I shall retain the note only—omitting here both the translation, and the text in the original. —See, therefore, note D of Chap. V. E. M.)

172. As the *Jarejahs*, and many other tribes now calling themselves *Hindus*, are but very imperfectly instructed in the

doctrines of their faith, and entertain many opinions in opposition to its tenets, I imagined at first that the *Jarejahs* might possess precepts favouring Infanticide.

173. Although my enquiries into the religion of the *Jarejahs*, did not support this conjecture, it may not be superfluous to notice some of their religious opinions and practices.

174. The *Jarejahs* are comprehended within the *Hindu* name and pale; but we are ignorant of the origin of the term *Hindu*,[z] which is not of an ancient date; and it is in many instances so loosely, irregularly and indiscriminately applied, as to embrace religions professing tenets in direct opposition to the *Brahmanical* system.[a]

175 The *Sravaka*[b] *Banias*, for instance, deny the existence of the *Trimurti*, the divinity of the *Avataras*, and the authority of the *Vedas*. They have no *Brahmans*, and worship different Gods; but they are, nevertheless, comprized under the general denomination of *Hindus*.

176. The *Jarejahs*, and the *Katties* especially, have also a very doubtful claim to this title. It is to be observed that both these people came from beyond the *Indus*, and derive their descent from a country where it has always been supposed a genuine *Hindu* could not exist. The [c]Sun is the

[z] See note E of Chap. V.

[a] There are among the *Hindus*, as among *Christians*, sects almost innumerable—varying from trifling to the most important points—some worship many deities, some only one or two, some none. See hereon page 2. note, and *Hindu Pantheon*, under *Sects*, in the Index. To the Index and plates of that work the reader is also referred for the history and representations of the *Avataras*, or incarnations of VISHNU and other deities—of the *Trimurti*, or Trinity of the *Hindus*, and some account of their sacred books, the *Veda*: subjects adverted to in this and the following paragraph. E. M.

[b] See note F of Chap. V.

[c] The *Hindu* sect of *Saura* worship SURYA, or the Sun exclusively—many other sects

real object of their worship, and it is not perhaps too extravagant to conclude, that they originally followed the religion of the ancient *Persians*, nor that these religions might have had a common origin.

177. The religion of the *Jarejahs* is far from being strict either in its precepts or practice. The Sun and the [d] *Matta* ASSAPURI are the objects of their worship.

178. Her tenets are reported to hold forth that it is not improper to eat with people of a different faith. In *Hallar* the *Jarejahs* observe some scruples on this point; but in *Kutch* and *Wagar* scarce any distinction is observed.

179. The *Jarejahs* worship DEVI, or the Goddess of nature, under the appellation of HINGLAS, who according to their legendary accounts saved and nourished their common ancestor, one of the four [e] *Jadoons*, who were saved from the universal destruction that befel their race.

combine the adoration of SURYA with that of other deities the Sun is, indeed, generally worshipped among *Hindus*. See *Hindu Pantheon*, under SURYA-*Sun* and *Sauras*, in the Index. E. M.

[d] This name, and that of HINGLAS in a following paragraph, are of PARVATI, or BHAVANI, the *Sacti*, or consort (or the might and glory) of SIVA, of whom so much occurs, with a great many plates under their different names and forms, in the *Hindu Pantheon*. *Matta* I judge to be an epithet of respect equivalent to *Mother*. *Assapuri* is explained by Colonel WALKER in the 180th paragraph. There is a place of pilgrimage called *Hinglaz*, near Cape *Moran*, or *Mudan* more properly, which means a head-land; where there is most likely a temple dedicated to DEVI under this appellation, which, as is usual, gives its name to the place: HINGLAS is not however of classical authority as a name of DEVI, but is probably a provincial appellation.

The *Dasra*, or *Dasera*, noticed in paragraph 181, is in honour of DEVI; and is one of the greatest festivals, among all ranks of *Hindus*, of the year. For some particulars of it, see *Hindu Pantheon*. E. M.

[e] This would perhaps be more correctly written *Yadus*. KRISHNA and his family were descended from a *Yadu*; hence one of his names is YADAVA. E. M.

180. When the Goddess HINGLAS BHAVANI bestowed on the *Jarejahs* the kingdom of *Kutch*, and thereby fulfilled their hopes, they built a temple to her which they called *Assapuri*. By this term the *Jarejahs* expressed their gratitude and their confidence in the favor of the Goddess; *Assa* in the *Sanskrit* signifying *Hope*, and *Puri*, *fulfilled—accomplished*.

181. To their *Devi* ASSAPURI the *Jarejahs* offer up in sacrifice the Buffaloe, at the yearly festival of the *Dasera*, and afterwards feast[f] on the victim.

182. The *Jarejahs* drink wine and spirits in public, and are in general, especially in particular situations, indifferent about the mode of preparing their food; and seem to be excluded[f] only from eating of the flesh of the Cow.

183. The *Jarejahs* hold their *Rajgurs*, or domestic priests, in little estimation, or respect. By the rest of the *Brahmans* the *Rajgurs* are despised; but this seems to arise from their performing the *Kria*, or the ceremonies at the funeral pile, as the *Kartia Brahmans* do in *Guzerat*, and other parts of *India*.

184. Like the *Kartia*, the *Raj-Gurs* receive the alms which are distributed on the twelfth day, or *dowadasa*, which finishes the period of mourning.

185. On the twelfth day the *Raj-Gur* of the family is stretched out like a corpse and placed on the cot of the deceased *Jarejah*; on which is also placed several articles of food and raiment.

186. This is taken up and carried to the spot where the

[f] Perhaps all the warrior tribes of the *Hindus* eat flesh meat. For the generality of this custom, contrary to the common notions on that point, see *Hindu Pantheon*, Index, under *Hindus*. E. M.

Jarejah was burnt, like a funeral procession, provided the crowd allow it to proceed.

The relations of the deceased and the inhabitants follow the procession as if it were a real funeral; but the multitude exert themselves to interrupt its progress, and for this purpose throw dust, stones, and every thing missile within their reach; as all these injuries are aimed at the *Raj-Gur*, he is generally obliged to abandon the cot precipitately and to fly.

187. The intention of this violence and clamour is to frighten away evil spirits, and to prevent their injuring or molesting the survivers; and the food and raiment placed on the cot is to supply the soul of the deceased with such articles in the next world.

188. This ceremony is termed *Seja* from the cot; but it is not peculiar to the *Jarejahs*, as it is practised by some other tribes.

189. The *Jarejahs* will sometimes remark that their *Gurus* are poor, and despised; which they made no scruple of attributing to the sin of Infanticide, and from the wrath of God, for having the weight of that crime on their heads.

190. This singular opinion, which I have expressed nearly in their own words, instead of producing any abhorrence in the *Jarejahs* against the act, has served to confirm their idea, that they have nothing to do with its responsibility and punishment.

191. The *Jarejahs* respect the [1]*Charons* and *Bhats* more than they do *Brahmans*.

[1] The *Charons*, or rather *Chàrànas*, and *Bhàts*, are a curious description of people. There doth not appear to be much distinction between them; *Chàràna* being in *Sanskrit* and among the gods, what *Bhàt* is in the current dialects and concerns of men. The

192. The [h] *Dassendi*, or people who receive their support from the charity of the *Jarejahs*, are called *Kaggar*. They

Chàrànas are the bards of the celestials; the *Bhàts* the bards of mortals: the latter word means *speech, language, oratory*; and is equivalent to our similar word *bard*, and is indeed a corruption of the *Sanskrit Bàrdài*.

As every event, at all remote, is, with the *Hindus*, involved in mystery and mythology, they have a wild legend of the origin of the first *Chàràna*; a being so named, having, they say, sprung from the sweat of MAHADEVA, who entrusted him with the charge of his *vahàn*, or vehicle, the bull NANDI, respecting whom so much occurs in the *Hindu Pantheon*, Index and plates. But Mr. WILFORD (*As. Res.* IX. art. III.) was told that in the *Puranas*, CHARANA is related to have been " born from the churning of the right arm of VENA, father of PRITHU, or NOAH." This story is related in the *Hindu Pantheon*, page 111.

The *Bhàts* of mortals are sometimes dignified by the superior title *Chàràna*. Every great man in *India* had formerly a *Bhàt* in his retinue, as was the custom also in some parts of *Britain*; but the custom is now much disused in both countries. In *Bengal*, where commerce has introduced other incitements, the *Bhàt's* office is seldom filled; and of course still more rarely filled well. In that country the occupation is not reputable. In the *Dekkan*, or southern provinces of *India*, many persons of rank still retain them, and the *Bhàt* forms also a part of the establishment of many villages; and a certain portion of the produce of the lands of such villages is set apart for his maintenance, as other certain portions are similarly for the *Patel*, or head person; to the *Brahman*, or priest; to the barber, &c.; exhibiting in the various local details, a very pleasing picture of the simplicity and innocence that we read of as having existed in ancient times, but which we are now seldom gratified with witnessing. In these situations, the *Bhàt*, if he, as he often is, be a man of talent and virtue, is of course much respected; having opportunities of improving the morals and understanding of his townsmen; who, after the labour of the day be over, will assemble under a tree, or, in default of any other public place in bad weather, in the apartment appropriated to the accommodation of travellers, and listen with great delight to the *Bhàt*, while he instructs them in the history and genealogy of the deities, with interesting episodes from the narratives of their warlike and amorous exploits. These he recites from the *Ramayana* and *Mahabharat*, and other works of a more familiar sort. On the approach of any traveller of exalted rank, the village *Bhàt* goes forth to meet and compliment him, and conduct him to or past his hamlet. In the *Hindu Pantheon*, page 330, a note of some length is given on the subject of the poetical oratory of *India*.

---

[h] The *Dassendi* are literally those who receive the *tenth* or tythe; but this amount has long since been diminished to a mere voluntary donation. A. W.

are a tribe of *Charons* of the *Tombel*, or as pronounced by the inhabitants of *Kutch*, *Toomber*; and emigrated with the *Jarejahs* into this country.

193. Although the *Jarejahs* are not pure *Hindus*, and know little of the ordinances of the *Brahmans*, yet they believe in all their legends: but although the religion of the *Jarejahs* may have but a feeble operation in preventing Infanticide, it certainly presents nothing to authorise the practice; on the contrary, the expedient of making the *Raj-Gurs* answerable for the act, is a plain proof that they view it to be a crime against religion.

With warriors the *Bhâts* take the field, and recite martial songs and tales to animate the troops. The bard CHANDA (or as the *Hindus* call him CHANDRA from the Moon or its regent) noticed in page 13, was *Bhât* to his prince PRIT'HU, so named after the mythological PRIT'HU, or NOAH, mentioned in the early part of this note. Mr. WILFORD (*As. Res.* vol. IX.) calls him CHANDA BARDAI, and says he is so celebrated as to have been surnamed TRI-KALA, knowing the past, the present, and the future. He was an important person at court, and acted a conspicuous part in the wars and amours of his royal patron. *Trikala* means the three periods or times; and we may hence judge that the *Bhât*, like the "Bard" of GRAY, assumes occasionally the character of the seer; and

"With a master's hand and prophet's fire,
"Strikes the deep sorrows of his lyre"——

forcing "Ages unborn to crowd upon the soul."

The title *Bardâi*, or *Bârdâhi*, as it is differently pronounced in *Sanskrit*, is, by ABU'L FAZEL (*Ay. Ak.* II. 120.) translated *musician*; but in *India* the *Bhât* does not play on any instrument; and is not therefore properly so designated. The praise and glory of his employer, and the honors of his family and tribe are the usual topics of the domestic *Bhât*; but with some he is a person of much influence, as may be supposed where such facilities offer, for the application of flattery, by a man of address, to the ear of individuals of high rank and humble talents. Considering the favourableness of such opportunities we may reasonably be somewhat surprized that the influence of the *Bhâts* should have declined so much as it has in some parts of *India*, and in other countries. In *Guzerat*, however, and in some other provinces, they are still very numerous and very respectable. Colonel WALKER, in the text (paragraph 191), seems to make some distinction between the *Châràna* and *Bhât*, using both terms. They are, he says, more respected by the *Jarejahs*, than are even the *Brahmans*. E. M.

194. I have now related such facts and circumstances as have come to my knowledge concerning the practice of female Infanticide among the *Jarejah Raj-puts*.

195. But however singular and extraordinary this practice may appear, it is not confined to the *Jarejahs*.

196. That it prevails among the *Jaitwa Rajputs* I have already noticed; and it also prevails amongst a people still more numerous; and there is not wanting appearances, which would lead us to think, that it is connected with the manners and institutions of some of the ancient nations.

197. The practice of female Infanticide prevailed with the *Raj Khumars*, and other tribes in *Bengal;* where it has been happily abolished. The custom of putting their infant daughters to death, has also been discovered to exist with the *Rhatore Rajputs* of *Jeypore* and *Joudpore;* but this fact when reported to *Europe* was doubted and denied to be possible.

198. It is confirmed however by every intelligent and well informed native of that country; nor does there appear any grounds whatever for questioning its existence.

199. The existence of the custom is traced to other tribes of [i] *Hindustan*, and in particular to the *Jauts* and *Mewâts;* which latter are a sect of *Musselmans*.

200. I am indebted for this information to NIZAM ED DIEN HUSSAIN, and the following is the translation of a memorandum which he gave me on the subject.

" The *Jaut* chiefs of [k] *Bhartpore* are stiled *Sensniwal;* these

[i] The reader will recollect that although *Hindustan* be in *Europe* often applied to *India* in general, it is not so in *India*, where by *Hindustan* is meant the countries north of the river *Narmada*, or *Nerbadda*. E. M.

[k] Or *Bhurtpore*. The scene within these few years of gallant attack, and desperate resistance, by and against the British arms. E. M.

" people, or the *Sensniwal*, are in the habits of putting to death " their daughters at the moment of their birth, by opium, or " by strangling.

" The cause of their doing so proceeds from a supposition " which they entertain, that it is a great disgrace to give their " daughters, even in marriage, to any person. And many " *Mewàts* who are *Mahomedans*, but who are known under the " appellation of *Mewàts*, whose country is near that of the " *Jauts*, kill their daughters from the same cause.

" I suppose the governors of [l] *Hatrus* and *Mursan* follow " the same practice.

" These people are all of the *Jaut caste*."

201. I have learnt from other sources of information on which I rely, that some of the *Rhatore*, the *Harri* of *Bundi Kota*, the *Waish* in the *Poorub*, the *Jauts* in *Hindustan*, and some of the [m] *Katchwas* of *Jeypore*, and other *Rajput* tribes kill their daughters.

202. The *Jarejahs* are aware that the custom of Infanticide is practised by many other tribes besides their own; but although it is probable that they have a common origin, I could not discover the traditionary motive that had led to the introduction of Infanticide amongst so many people of *Hindustan*.

203. The practice however appears to be maintained among them by the same causes which operated with the *Jarejahs*.

l *Hatrus*, E. of *Agra* about 30 miles.

m *Katchwas*—worshippers of VISHNU in his second incarnation in the form of a *Katchwa*, or turtle. See plates and history of this incarnation in *Hindu Pantheon*. See also note in page 17 preceding. E. M.

Pride, avarice, the cares of a family, the disgrace which would attend the misconduct of their women, the difficulty of establishing them in life, and an apprehension of exposing their daughters to ill treatment, were assigned invariably by every person acquainted with this subject, as the causes that induced these tribes to commit Infanticide.

204. I have ventured to suppose that the practice of Infanticide may have some analogy with the customs and institutions of some of the ancient nations. It would be interesting to trace, and develope, the laws and customs of the most distinguished people of antiquity, which sanctioned Infanticide.

205. If we except the fabulous history of the [n] *Amazons*,

[n] The *Hindus* have also their *Amazons*. Their *Stri-Rajah* are women who live and govern themselves independently of men; they are supposed to reside somewhere to the southward, in the direction of *Ramisseram*; between that and *Ceylon*, or on *Ceylon*. The situation of the residence of the *Stri-Rajahs* is not quite certain; but in order to arrive at it, the visitor must wade through an extent of water, breast high, and which will require several days to cross. It is recommended to those who undertake this journey, to carry a cot on their heads which will float on the water, and on which they may sleep at night, or repose themselves when fatigued.

The women of *Malabar*, distinguished at this day by their singular institutions and the peculiar privilege of cohabiting with several husbands, are supposed to be the *Stri-Rajahs* of the *Hindus*. A. W.

I cannot help thinking that the whole fabulous relation of the *Amazons* was borrowed from the *Hindus*—I mean that the idea was thence borrowed, and dressed up in the usual stile, by the embellishing *Greeks*. The armed, one-breasted female, may be often seen in the sculptures and paintings of *India*; and the legends referring to the goddess so depicted are sufficiently consonant with those of western fable, as to give reasonable grounds for imagining them of a common origin. See this one-breasted armed female in plate 24 of the *Hindu Pantheon*, and some notice of it in page 98 of that work.

There is a story extant in several *Hindu* and *Mahomedan* dialects, that may be entitled a history of the travels and adventures of KAMARUPA. This prince is sent by his father to see men and manners, and is accompanied by his tutor—they are shipwrecked on an island

I am not aware that we have any account of a positive law or custom, for the regular and invariable destruction of children of either sex.

206. The *Amazons* are said to have formed a state from which they excluded men. They held a commerce only with strangers, and for the purpose merely of begetting daughters. They killed their male children, and cut off the right breast of their females to render them more fit for war.

207. Among the ancients the exposition of their children was a very general practice, and they do not appear to have considered it as either cruel or barbarous.

208. ROMULUS is said to have laid the citizens under an obligation, to educate all their male children, and the eldest of their daughters.

209. The requiring this obligation from the citizens, must have been suggested by the necessity of restraining the practice of Infanticide; and ROMULUS probably trusted in procuring wives for his males, from the other tribes in his neighbourhood, with as little difficulty as the *Jarejahs* do at present; but the rape of the *Sabines* is an historical proof, that the number of males, exceeded the females in the infancy of the *Roman* state, and might in some measure have originated from the exposure of their daughters.

210. MONTESQUIEU has the following observation on

inhabited by women only—the queen falls violently in love with the accomplished prince, whose name means *Cupid-faced*, or with a face like CUPID. The progress of the story strongly reminds one of that of TELEMACHUS, blended with *Amazonian* fables; nor is it the least of the resemblances that the *Mahomedan* translators render the *Hindu* name of the islanders *Hamazen*, which means *All-women*, and is pronounced very much as we sound *Amazon*. I do not recollect the *Hindu* name of the islanders; perhaps *Stri-Raja*, which means Royal, or governing, women. E. M.

this subject, which makes the resemblance still more complete; and proves that the same motives prevailed with the *Roman* fathers for exposing their children, as with the nations of *India* who commit Infanticide.

" We find not any *Roman* law that permitted the exposing " of children: this was without doubt an abuse introduced " towards the decline of the Republic, when luxury robbed " them of their freedom, when wealth divided was called " property, when the father believed that all was lost which " he gave to his family, and when this family was distinct " from his property."

211. It appears that infants newly born were placed on the ground. Those who were agreeable to the father, he took up, or educated, for these were synonimous terms; but those who were displeasing to him he neglected and exposed.

212. In *Greece*, Infanticide, or the exposure of children, appears to have formed a part of the policy of those states.

Solon gave permission by law to parents to kill their children.

213. Aristotle appears an advocate for the exposing of children, and conceives where this is not the case, that the number of those brought forth ought to be limited.

He proposes expedients for this purpose, more barbarous than any usage of the *Jarejahs*.

214. The *Greeks* appear to have been led to expose their offspring from the sterility of the territory, and the apprehension of want, excited by a redundant population.

215. The same motive arising from a fear of famine has induced the government of *China*, if not to permit, at least to tolerate parents, to sell and expose their children.

216. The [o]*Carthaginians* are reported to have frequently sacrificed their children; but this appears to have originated in motives of religion and patriotism; the first taught them that the sacrifice of children was acceptable to their Gods; and the love of their country inspired the noblest of the *Carthaginians*, to offer up their offspring as victims, to avert or remove any public calamity. A similar custom was also practised by the *Phenicians* and *Tyrians*, the founders of *Carthage*, and which was also extended to the *Greeks*, the *Gauls*, and the *German* nations. Among the *Canaanites* also, previous to the invasion of the *Israelites*, similar sacrifices prevailed, and which are termed in scripture "passing their seed through the fire to MOLOCH."[p]

217. In ROBERTSON's history of *America* we are informed, that the difficulty of training up an infant to maturity amidst the hardships of savage life, often stifles the voice of nature among the *Americans*, and suppresses the strong emotions of parental tenderness. Some of these women are stated in particular, to destroy their female children in their infancy.

"But," the historian remarks, "though necessity compels "the inhabitants of *America* thus to set bounds to the increase "of their families, they are not deficient in affection and "attachment to their offspring: they feel the power of this "instinct in its full force."

At *Otaheite* and other islands of the Pacific Ocean a peculiar society exists, who destroy their children; and other nations

[o] The senate of *Carthage* at the instigation of HANNOO proposed to sacrifice the infant son of HANIBAL after he had gained the battles of *Ticinus* and *Trebia*. A.W.

[p] This subject is farther discussed in note I of Chap. V.

in a rude state have been found who do not suffer those to live, who are born with any natural defect or deformity.

A more attentive and extensive research would multiply these examples, and illustrate this subject.[1]

218. However disgusting it may be to human nature, we find that many nations have tolerated, or permitted, parents to destroy their own offspring; and we are certain that parents have deprived their children of life by availing themselves of this privilege; but the custom of exclusively murdering females, although the regulation of ROMULUS evidently points to their destruction in preference to that of the males, and a systematic Infanticide, seems to be confined to the *Raj-puts* of *India*.

219. It will now be necessary to relate with precision and briefness, the proceedings and expedients, which finally led the *Jarejahs* of the Peninsula to relinquish Infanticide.

220. I entered on this underdaking with sanguine expectations of success, but which were, for a long time, disappointed; and I must own that the natives had formed much more just opinions on the subject, when they foretold the difficulties that would attend the attempt; which few of them thought could be overcome, but by the Company making a conquest of the country.

221. I conceived that reason and feeling would effect the relinquishment of a barbarous custom unconnected with the principles of society; and which all the passions of the human mind, and all the forms and maxims of religion, were combined to destroy.

222. As it was evident also that the most disinterested

[1] It is my intention to offer, in a future page, something farther on this point. E. M.

humanity had led the Honourable Company to interfere for the abolition of female Infanticide, I conceived that this reflection, and the respect due to their mediation, would have disposed the *Jarejahs* to comply with a request, which it was scarcely to be supposed could be at variance with their own sentiments.

223. But sentiments of nature and humanity have no influence with the *Jarejahs*; and I was soon, however reluctantly, obliged to relinquish the favourable expectation I had formed of success.

224. The difficulties were many and formidable.

225. I had been for several years in habits of friendly correspondence with JEHAJI, the chief of *Murvi*, and he had continually expressed a strong desire to cultivate the favour of the English Government.

The artifices of this chief, and his *Vakil*, who resided in my camp, deceived and amused me for some time with promises, which proved fallacious.

226. I availed myself of the agency and influence of SUNDERJI SIVAJI after his arrival in camp, but with no better success.

At last JEHAJI transmitted a [1] paper, in which he offered to accede to my wishes by preserving his daughters, provided I would reduce *Mallia*, and restore the village of *Hurralla*, of which he had been deprived by the *Gaikawar* Government.

227. The possession of this paper I considered of importance, as it discovered the selfish and mercenary motives, that attached the *Jarejahs* to Infanticide.

I preserved it as a testimony which refuted their pretences

[1] See this paper in Chap. IV. No. 5.

of the inviolability of the practice, as a custom of the *caste;* and destroyed every argument which they attempted to found on principle.

228. When JEHAJI perceived the disadvantage which attended the possession of this paper, he made several applications to induce me to restore it, with which I did not comply.

229. As my intercourse and knowledge of the *Jarejahs* increased, every circumstance tended to shew that they followed Infanticide from mean and interested motives only. It was also evident that it would be very difficult to awaken their natural feelings; and that the same motives of conveniency and interest, would have more influence in inducing them to relinquish the practice, than any arguments derived from humanity, morality, or religion.

230. It appeared likewise from the communications of JEHAJI and others, that the reproach and odium of being the first to renounce an ancient practice operated as a considerable motive.

The weight and authority of this example could not be complete, unless it was set by a chief of acknowledged rank and superiority.

231. The *Rao* of *Kutch* seemed to possess these qualifications, from his family, and extent of territory.

232. I was induced therefore to select this chieftain; but addressed myself principally to *FATTEH MAHOMED, whose authority is paramount in that country, and from whom as a zealous *Mahomedan*, I was led to expect the exertion of his influence for suppressing a crime against nature and religion.

* See Nos. 18. and 19. of Chap. IV.

233. The answer however of FATTEH MAHOMED (N° 20 of Chap. IV.) destroyed every hope of success from that quarter.

This *Jemadar*, who rose from the humble station of a goat-herd, and is extremely illiterate, had the sentiments of his letter probably dictated to him; and by the hand of his writer, transmitted, in an inflated and ostentatious style, an elaborate defence of the practice of Infanticide; such as could be expected to proceed only from an infuriated and bigoted *Jarejah*.

234. It may not be unworthy of remark that this defence of Infanticide was written and composed by a *Nagar Brahman*,[1] and promulgated in the name of a *Mahomedan*, whose religion inspires them with horror against these murders.

235. In the mean while every effort and endeavour was continued to prevail on the *Murvi* chief to abandon Infanticide, which the long detention of the detachment in the vicinity of that city afforded.

It was the daily subject of letters, messages and conferences.

236. The humanity and tenderness congenial to the sex induced me to expect the assistance of the women of JEHAJI's family. The preservation of their offspring appeared naturally and peculiarly their business.

237. I conceived that my appeal to wives and mothers, and to women who came from tribes that rejected Infanticide, would be attended with every advantage. I was farther led to entertain great hopes from this plan, on account of the

[1] See *Remarks* after No. 20. of Chap. IV.

high character of the mother of the chief of *Murvi*, for prudence, propriety of conduct, and a benevolent disposition.

238. As this lady possesses considerable influence over her son, I expected that she would exert it in favour of a measure, agreeable to her own feelings.

239. The embarrassed state of JEHAJI's affairs, and the countenance which he stood in need of from me for retrieving them, were circumstances which I conceived would occur to the discretion of his mother; and urge her to obtain from her son a concession which might give the family a claim to my support.

240. My [u]overtures to this lady were at first received with the feelings natural to her sex; and she seemed disposed, with the rest of the women, who held several consultations together on the subject, to unite their influence for the abolition of Infanticide.

241. But these ebullitions were of short duration:—the *Jarejahs* were alarmed, and their women contended for the ancient privilege of the *caste;* they were led away from the path of nature and humanity by the example and influence of their husbands.

242. The mother of the chief of *Murvi* requested that she might be excused soliciting her son on this head, and referred me for any farther [x]information to JEHAJI.

243. At this period my prospect of success was very obscure and distant:—but although these efforts had failed of their desired effect, they were, notwithstanding, useful; and

[u] See No. 10. of Chap. IV.

[x] No. 13. of Chap. IV. contains the answer of JEHAJI and his mother.

paved the way for success, by turning the attention of the country to a subject, which, it would appear, had never before attracted any public notice.

244. By discussing the subject frequently in the public [7] *Katcherry*, and exposing the enormity of the practice, as contrary to the precepts of religion and the dictates of nature, every *caste* came to express an abhorrence of Infanticide; and the obstinate prejudices of the *Jarejahs* began to be shaken.

245. The maxims and passions which favoured Infanticide, were probably for the first time canvassed, and censured with freedom.

246. The progress of this system was slow, but it was insensibly spreading its influence, and became a subject of universal conversation.

The novelty of the attempt, and the extraordinary nature of the subject, also attracted general attention.

247. But whatever influence these circumstances might produce, as JEHAJI was the first chieftain that I had addressed on the subject, it was of the utmost importance to make some impression on him. I bent every exertion therefore, and tried various expedients, to reclaim this chief, who had already destroyed two of his daughters, from the practice of Infanticide.

248. At last I obtained from JEHAJI a conditional writing to the following effect:—

" From motives of friendship the Honourable Company
" have urged me to preserve my daughters; to this I consent,
" if the chiefs of *Nowanaggar* and *Gondal* agree."

249. This was the first considerable step towards the attainment of this great object; and the writing appeared to

[7] Or court of justice.

reduce the question to a kind of point of honour, or respect for antiquity, in setting the example of sanctioning an innovation on a general habit.

250. From the character and behaviour of JAM, I could have no hopes that he would set this example; but as the family of DEWAJI of *Gondal* had already preserved several of their daughters, I was led to entertain the most favourable expectations from the general disposition of this chief, and his reputation for humanity.

251. It may be proper to mention, that JEHAJI first proposed to insert the names of the *Rao* of *Kutch* and JAM of *Nowanaggar* in his writing; but I positively refused to receive the paper unless it comprised DEWAJI of *Gondal*.

252. The compliance of JEHAJI with this request, it may be but fair to consider as a favourable indication of his sentiments; and that he was secretly not extremely averse to agree to the abolition of Infanticide.

It may be presumed he was acquainted with the disposition of DEWAJI, and of the general opinion that this chief, when pressed, would renounce the practice of killing his daughters.

253. From DOSSAJI[1] of *Mallia* I obtained a similar writing to that received from the chief of *Murvi*.

254. I had conceived great expectations from DOSSAJI,

[1] The reader will recollect that the names of persons and places, although strange to us, in this and other letters, are well known to the corresponding parties—occurring often in political and revenue concerns: the writers could at the time have had no idea that their letters would ever be published. This leads me to remark that many very curious and valuable tracts might be taken from the records of the governments of *India*, and at the India House; and without compromising any thing of a secret or political nature, unfit to be imparted to the public. E.M.

who had preserved a daughter, and had by his *Vakil* afforded repeated assurances that he was ready to renounce Infanticide; but it is remarkable that this chief used every evasion and delay to avoid executing a formal deed in renunciation of the practice.

255. It is necessary to notice here, that there were several petty *Jarejah* chiefs in my camp, whose distressed and dependant circumstances rendered them obsequious to any measure proposed by Government; and they were ready to bind themselves by any engagement to renounce Infanticide: but I conceived that their early formal acquiescence would not have the force of example with any of the superior chiefs, and would rather prejudice the cause.

256. Under these ideas, I declined for the present entering into engagements with the petty chiefs who followed the camp.

257. The narrative must now accompany the operations of the Detachment, which traversed the country of JAM and arrived at *Kandorna*.

I employed this time, as often as circumstances and opportunity permitted, in favour of the design for abolishing Infanticide.

258. WASSONJI ESWARJI, the *Vakil* of the *Gondal* chief, residing in camp, enabled me frequently to converse with him on the subject; and this sensible and respectable *Brahman* was easily persuaded to unite his influence with mine, to prevail on his master to enter into a formal obligation for discontinuing Infanticide.

259. During these events, WASSONJI had occasion to proceed to *Gondal* on some revenue affairs; and before his

departure he privately gave me such assurances, as I conceived might be confided in, that he would, on his return, obtain authority from DEWAJI, to enter into any engagements which might be required, for preserving the daughters of the *Jarejahs*, residing in that part of the country.

260. In this, and every endeavour for suppressing Infanticide, it is with great pleasure that I mention the cordial and zealous assistance of WITTOL RAO DEWANJI, the commander of the *Gaikawar* army.

This officer, with the peculiar ardour of his character, embraced every occasion of exposing the enormity of the crime, and of promoting, by his arguments and influence, a detestation of the practice.

261. The mission of WASSONJI ESWARJI was entirely successful; and on his return to camp, after expressing the reluctance of his master to set an example which might bring on him the reproach of his *caste*, a deed of the most solemn, effectual, and binding nature was executed, renouncing for ever the practice of Infanticide.

262. The following is a translation of this instrument:—

" Whereas the HONOURABLE ENGLISH COMPANY and " ANAND[a] RAO GAIKAWAR SENA KHASKIL SHAMSHIR " BAHADER, having set forth to us the dictates of the *Sastras* " and the true faith of the *Hindus;* as well as, that the " *Brahma-vaiverteka Purana* declares the killing of children to " be a heinous sin; it being written that it is as great an " offence to kill an embryo as a *Brahman;* that to kill one " woman is as great a sin as a hundred *Brahmans;* that to

[a] I shall take some notice of these names and titles, and of their probable origin hereafter. E. M.

" put one child to death is as great a transgression against the " divine laws, as to kill a hundred women; and that the " perpetrators of this sin shall be damned to the Hell [b]*Kule-* " *sootheela*, where, he shall be infested with as many maggots " as he may have hairs on his body; be born again a leper, " and debilitated in all his members; We *Jarejah* DEWAJI " and *Koer* NATHU, *Zemendars* of *Gondal*, (the custom of " female Infanticide having long prevailed in our *caste)* do " hereby agree for ourselves, and for our offspring; as also " we bind ourselves in behalf of our relations, and their " offspring, for ever, for the sake of our own prosperity, and " for the credit of the *Hindu* faith; that we shall from this " day renounce this practice; and in default of this, that we " acknowledge ourselves offenders against the [c]*Serkars*. More- " over should any one in future commit this offence, we shall " expel him from our *caste*, and he shall be punished according " to the pleasure of the two governments, and the rule of the " *Sastras*."

" The above writing is duly executed."

263. With the exception of JAM, every *Jarejah* chief, readily, and without offering a single objection, subscribed to a counterpart of this instrument.

264. JAM continued to oppose the measure as long as he was able, and used every subterfuge and artifice, to avoid making the same declaration that his brethren had done.

[b] I have retained the MS. spelling of the name of this place of torment; not knowing exactly how, according to the mode of orthography adopted by me, it would be better written; but should surmise *Kala sut'hla*; a provincial pronunciation perhaps of *Kala Surra*; the sixth of the one and twenty hells enumerated in the *Hindu Pantheon*, page 297. See also note in page 8, preceding. E. M.

[c] *Serkar*, means the *head* of *affairs*, the Government. E. M.

His first attempt to make the plan miscarry, was to persuade DEWAJI of *Gondal* not to sign the engagement. For this purpose JAM used the influence of letters, and messages; but fortunately ineffectually.

265. When JAM JESSAJI found notwithstanding his opposition and remonstrances, that DEWAJI had executed the agreement for renouncing Infanticide, and that the rest of the *Jarejah* chiefs would follow his example; he probably foresaw that he would also be obliged to comply: but even at this moment he was instigated by his pride and arrogance, to offer an exception, by which he expected to save his honour, and to circumscribe the extent of his obligation.

266. JAM proposed, that neither himself, nor his own offspring should be included in the engagement; but that he should bind himself for his relations and their offspring only, to renounce Infanticide.

267. On the grounds however that an unqualified abolition was become the custom of the country and the order of government, JAM was informed that his request could not be complied with; and he finally, like the rest of the *Jarejahs*, concluded and executed a corresponding instrument.

268. It is sufficient to expose the unworthy motives of this chief, to mention, that after he had agreed to the engagement for renouncing Infanticide, he had the effrontery, and meanness, to solicit an abatement of his revenue; in order to reimburse the expence which, as he alledged, he would in future be liable to, in consequence of bringing up his daughters.

269. The character of this chief exhibits an extraordinary contrast of great arrogance and extreme submission; of in-

solence and timidity; and the treachery and cruelty of JAM are only restrained by the cowardice of his disposition.

270. The originals of these instruments are in my possession, and will be deposited in the Honourable Company's treasury at *Baroda*, where they may perhaps be better preserved than in the *Gaikawar* [d]*Dafter;* and can readily be produced on any occasion of appeal, or reference.

271. Copies of the original instruments remain with the commander of the *Gaikawar* army in *Kattawar*, and among the enclosures of this Report, [e]N° 24, is a list of the names of every chief who has subscribed to the deeds for renouncing Infanticide.

272. This list contains not only every chieftain of note, but every inferior *Jarejah* chief who enjoys the least share of independence, and comprises within its obligations every *Jarejah* family inhabiting the Peninsula of *Guzerat*.

273. Having accomplished the renunciation of Infanticide in this part of the country, I was willing to think that the example might produce a favourable effect on the *Jarejahs* of *Kutch;* and in this expectation I addressed myself again to [f]FATTEH MAHOMED.

274. The *Jemadar's*[f] answer contained a second defence of Infanticide, but in more moderate terms; and it disclosed a circumstance, which is probably true, that his situation rendered it improper for him to say any thing on the subject to the *Jarejahs*.

275. It appears that the *Jarejah Byaud* of *Kutch* could

[d] *Dafter*, or *defter khanah*, the office for records

[e] See No. 24. of Chap. IV.

[f] See Nos. 21. and 22. of Chap. IV.

easily overturn the usurped authority of FATTEH MAHOMED; and that they only sanction or submit to it, in consideration that they have acquired thereby an extension of their own authority, and many illegal possessions; but it is generally understood that if this *Jemadar* should attempt to deprive them of any of their privileges, or to circumscribe their unjust acquisitions, they could, without much difficulty, deprive him of his own power.

276. Under these circumstances we cannot probably indulge any strong hope that the suppression of Infanticide will soon be attained in *Kutch;* and in the actual state of affairs in that country, they may afford some apology for FATTEH MAHOMED appearing as a constrained [g] advocate, perhaps, for the unnatural crime of Infanticide.

277. I have the honour to enclose [h] translated extracts from my correspondence with the native chiefs concerning Infanticide, and several other documents connected with the subject; which I have occasionally referred to in this address.

278. I shall now proceed to offer some remarks on the nature and efficacy of the engagements for the renunciation of Infanticide.

279. The apparent ease and readiness, after the example of the chief of *Gondal,* with which the *Jarejahs* were induced to relinquish the practice of killing their daughters, is difficult to account for, on any common principle of human conduct.

280. This sudden change in the sentiments, and dere-

[g] See Note G of Chap. V.

[h] Chap. IV. Nos. 1. to 24; and perhaps some of the papers or notes of Chap. V. but on this point I am not exactly informed. E. M.

liction of their manners and prejudices, were not probably entirely the effect of example.

The *Jarejahs* were prepared for the event from the perseverance with which the measure had been pressed on their attention; and they were probably apprehensive that they might expose themselves to some inconvenience and punishment, if they continued an opposition which they had been accustomed in every case to see ending to their disadvantage.

281. However this may be, the difficulty with which these people were first led to discontinue the absurd and wicked custom of destroying their daughters, may be viewed as no unequivocal proof of the stability of the arrangement; and that it was at length entered into with more sincerity, than if it had been the result of an instant compliance with an arbitrary mandate.

282. But to estimate correctly the determination of the *Jarejahs* to respect their engagements, it is necessary to refer to the terms, and the extent of their obligations; and the unquestionable power of the Honourable Company, and of the *Gaikawar*, to maintain these contracts in force.

283. The instruments ascertain with precision what the parties have stipulated to perform; and besides inflicting the penalties derived from *caste* and religion, those deeds confer on the Company and the *Gaikawar*, a clear and legal right of punishing the offenders.

284. It seems to be incontrovertible, that, whatever may have been its origin, the *Jarejahs* continued Infanticide from motives of interest or convenience; and the same motives are now brought into operation to counterbalance their former prejudice;—for if they were to relapse, and again kill their

daughters, they would be liable to the disgrace of expulsion from their families, and to arbitrary punishment; exposing themselves evidently to much greater disadvantages and vexations, than can possibly arise from preserving their children.

285. The illiterate condition of the *Jarejahs*, the confined state of their information, and the acquiescence of successive generations, had shut their eyes to the atrocity of Infanticide; but it is not too much to expect, that the instruction and lights they have lately received, may produce a beneficial change in their sentiments.

286. The crime of Infanticide has been exposed to the community; and many men who never reflected upon it before, will now, under the impression of its enormity, insensibly impart their sentiments to the *Jarejahs* who live amongst them.

287. The intercourse of life, and the equal state in some points of the members of this society, afford abundance of opportunity for this communication; and it will produce that influence, which is generally the consequence of a free exchange of correct opinions.

288. Among the causes also which are likely to maintain the observance of these engagements, superstition may be mentioned, which was before acting in favour of Infanticide.

289. The *Jarejahs* now understand the punishment denounced by the *Sastras* for the crime; and the same spirit of religion which transferred the sin to the *Raj-Gur* will be equally disposed, by a kind of retributive justice, in consequence of their own voluntary deed, to make them in future answerable for every violation of their contract.

290. Even a temporary disuse of Infanticide would assist towards its entire abolition, by allowing reason and natural

feelings to recover their ascendancy. The great satisfaction of the country, and the general contentment of the *Jarejahs* themselves, after they had signed the instruments for abolishing Infanticide, whatever repugnance they had before expressed to the measure, appeared to me to afford strong grounds for believing that the engagements would be permanent.

291. The efficacy, however, of these engagements, and the entire suppression of this vice, must be maintained by the vigilance and vigour of the Company's and the *Gaikawar* governments.

Their power or influence must be exerted to punish the first instance of transgression.

292. It may appear to have been desirable, but it was not easily practicable, to have defined the nature of the punishment to be inflicted on future offenders.

293. The great inequality in the power and rank of the *Jarejahs*, rendered it difficult to fix with any advantageous precision, on a common standard of punishment.

There may also be some advantage in leaving this matter uncertain and unlimited.

294. I have now, Honourable Sir, brought to a conclusion, the several observations which have from time to time occurred to me on the very extraordinary subject of female Infanticide, as lately existing among the tribe of *Jarejah Raj-puts;* and which I have committed to paper as they arose with little attention to order.

295. The extent to which this horrid practice has been carried, affords a melancholy picture of human manners and depravity. The fact which would scarcely obtain credit among the more civilized nations of *Europe*, is now established

to demonstration; and the Honourable Company's government have the merit of having directed their philanthropic attention, to the abolishment of a custom as singular, as barbarous; and as contrary to the general feelings of parents and of humanity, as ever disgraced the history of man.

296. It is remarkable that none of the Governments who have acquired an ascendancy in *India*; have ever been induced to attempt the abolition of Infanticide; and that a custom, so repugnant to every principle of reason and natural affection, should have been permitted to exist and be tolerated, even at the very walls of the capitals of the *Mahomedan* sovereigns of *Delhi*, and *Guzerat*, without an attempt to abolish it; while the harmless [1] rites of the *Hindu* religion should have excited the most bigotted and intolerant persecution.

297. It is satisfactory however to reflect, that this honour has been reserved for our Nation. I trust the engagements which have been executed will be perpetual, and I see at present no reason to doubt but they will be observed. The abolition of Infanticide is one of the most popular acts of the Honourable Company's government in *Kattawar;* and even the *Jarejahs* themselves seem to conceive it to be a benefit to be relieved from the performance of an act, which, for the honour of human nature, it must be hoped could not always be practised without some pity and compunction.

[1] "Major WALKER," Mr. DUNCAN observes in a note on this passage, "here adverts to those rites of the *Hindu* religion that are really innocent, or at least unhurtful to the public; under which may be comprehended generally all the customs ordained by the modern ritual. But there are likewise some strange and pernicious doctrines appertaining to the *Hindu* system, as appears in its having, in ancient times at least, admitted of human sacrifices:—a practice that is still imputed to the tribe of *Karara Brahmans* in the *Konkan*."

In Note H of Chap. V. Colonel WALKER has detailed some curious particulars of this tribe of *Brahmans*; on which point I may perhaps offer some remarks. E. M.

298. The same motives which directed the Honourable Company to obtain engagements for the abolition of Infanticide, will also induce them to superintend, with anxious care, the advantage thus gained to the cause of humanity, until natural feeling shall have gained an ascendancy sufficient to prevent any infraction of the present agreement.

I have the honour to be with the greatest respect,

Honourable Sir, &c. &c. &c.

(Signed) ALEXANDER WALKER,
Resident.

Baroda, 15*th March*, 1808.

Postscript *to the foregoing Letter.*

1. Since the conclusion of my letter of this date, a dissertation has fallen into my hands on the horrid sacrifices, which were formerly performed by almost every nation on the Globe; which derives credit and authenticity from being the production of the celebrated Jacob Bryant.

2. The numerous facts which the investigating genius of that learned man has concentrated, give a most melancholy picture of the enormities which were at different times so universally practised, under the impressions of a bigotted and gloomy fanaticism.

3. Even the ancestors of our own nation are implicated in those horrid impieties; proving in a most forcible manner the great and manifold advantages, which attend the progress of modern civilization.

4. But if these sacrifices were so horrid and numerous, as to induce the *Grecian* Biographer to doubt "whether it would not have been better for the nation of *Scythia* to be ignorant of the existence of a Deity, than to propitiate him by such cruel offerings," what would have been his sentiments had he been acquainted, that a numerous nation, without compunction, doomed to irrevocable death, the whole of their female offspring!

5. Horrid and detestable as the sacrifices related by Mr. BRYANT were, they were yet the result of the most noble sentiment that can animate the human mind; although under melancholy and mistaken impressions.

6. To avert calamity from the nation, to gain some common blessing, was the general motive; but among the *Jarejahs* it originated in the prostration of every manly and humane principle; and was nourished by pride, avarice and other selfish feelings of convenience.

7. Mr. BRYANT does not appear to have been aware of the existence of human sacrifices among the *Hindus;* and it is melancholy to add to the list of human infirmity, by citing the translation of the sanguinary chapter *Rudhiradhyaya* from the [k]*Kalica Purana* by Mr. BLAQUIERE, as an evidence of this barbarous rite being sanctioned by the *Hindu* ordinances.

8. It was not only enjoined, but in the ancient rites of

[k] See *Hindu Pantheon*, p. 145, where this subject is discussed; and under *Naramedha*, in the Index. E.M.

the *Hindus* was frequently practised, under the denomination of *Nermedha*—the sacrifice of a Man.

9. There is at this day a numerous class of *Brahmans* who are accused of this practice.

They are called *Karáda*, and are inhabitants chiefly of the *Kokan*, or *Konkan*.

10. The object of their worship is [1]MAHA LAKSHMI, to whom human sacrifices are acceptable; and the more so, if the victim be a *Brahman* learned in the *Sastras*.

11. The public performance of this sacrifice, has long since fallen into disuse; but a sect of the *Karada Brahmans* are accused of effecting, by the secret operation of poison, that object which they dare not publickly avow.

12. I know several *Karada Brahmans* in respectable situations, intelligent, charitable, and humane, who would abhor the commission of this detestable crime; and who, though they admit the former existence, most strongly deny its present practice: but the power of prejudice is sometimes stronger than the completest evidence of moral conduct; and many people, under the influence of this feeling, would decline to eat of food prepared by a *Brahman* of this tribe, of which he himself should not at the same time partake.

13. Since my return to *Baroda*, I have met with an account of Infanticide, which ascribes its origin to a circumstance more probable than the disappointment felt by the *Rajah* at not finding a suitable match for his daughter, as related in my preceding letter.

14. It is said that some of the early *Musselman* invaders of the *Jarejahs'* country, experiencing the determination with

[1] See Note H of Chap. V.

which they defended their liberties, united policy to their arms; and sought to consolidate their interests in the country by demanding the daughters of the *Rajahs* in marriage.

15. The high spirited *Jarejaks* would not brook the disgrace, and pretended they did not preserve their daughters; but fearful of the consequences, and that force would be resorted to in order to obtain what was refused to entreaty, they in this extremity, listened to the advice of their *Rajgurs;* and deluded by the fictitious responsibility which they accepted, the practice of Infanticide originated, and has since been confirmed.

16. In consistency with this relation is an account which I have heard of one of the *Rajahs* of *Noanagger;* whose daughter was demanded in marriage by the Emperor of *Delhi*, and which also throws some light upon the doubtful point, whether a grown up daughter is ever put to death.

It appears that although much discredit would attach to a *Jarejah* who killed his daughter after having preserved her for any time; yet that such occurrences, however unfrequent, are not without precedent. It is probable that the *caste*, or family, would resent such a deed, and refuse to eat with the perpetrator.

17. In some period of the history of the *Jarejahs*, it is said that one of the JAMS was despoiled of his country by the King of *Delhi*, who promised to restore it, provided JAM gave him a daughter, whom he had preserved, in marriage. This must have been a legitimate daughter, as JAM disdainfully rejected the alliance, and transmitted his refusal through the Governor of *Ahmedabad;* who was the medium of the proposal on the part of his Sovereign.

18. After some time, however, given to reflection, JAM was counselled by his friends to comply apparently, and to depart for *Delhi* accompanied by his daughter:—when he might evade the disgrace, save his honour, and recover his country, by putting his daughter to death; and give out that she died of sickness or fatigue, during the journey. The plan was accordingly put into execution, and this conduct does not appear to have received the disapprobation of the *caste;*—probably it was applauded.

19. As Mr. BRYANT's production is interesting and generally relates to the subject of my Reports, I beg to annex it to this [m] Postscript.

[m] See Note I of Chap. V.

CHAP. IV.

Extracts, translated from the Correspondence between Major ALEXANDER WALKER, SUNDERJI SIVAJI, *Jarejah* JEHAJI, FATTEH MAHOMED, *and others, on the Subject of* INFANTICIDE—*referred to in the foregoing* Report.

No. 1.

From Major WALKER *to* SUNDERJI SIVAJI, *dated Camp at Gootoo, 13th*[a] *September*, 1807.

(After[a] *compliments)* .... Another indispensable article is the relinquishment of Infanticide. This is a concession to the Company:—it is necessary to ensure their regard, and will render the character of JEHAJI illustrious for abolishing a practice which all civilized people so strongly condemn.

No. 2.

From SUNDERJI SIVAJI *to Major* WALKER, *dated 20th September*, 1807.

The state of affairs are—that having had an interview

[a] The dates of this correspondence are reduced from the native, to our era; and the compliments usually *prefixed* to letters written in a country language, are omitted. In this

with JEHAJI [b]THAKUR, some time elapsed in making him acquainted with my message—by his answer it appeared that the relinquishment of Infanticide will not compose an article of the [c]*Fil Zaminy*:—but he will give a separate writing to that effect into my hand; provided you will cause the village which BABAJI has taken, to be restored—then his consent to the relinquishment of Infanticide is given.

No. 8.

From Major WALKER *to* SUNDERJI SIVAJI, *dated 20th September*, 1807.

In respect to the *Thakur* JEHAJI, I am very sorry to observe that the full assurances which I gave you and BHANJI MEHTA have been lost—I did not expect the objections which have been made—and all the trouble which I have taken may now prove fruitless.

The relinquishment of the custom of Infanticide must be unconditional; it must be clear, and from the heart, and

point the usage of *Hindustan* and of *Europe* are at variance:—in another, that of the unmeaning nonsense of 'Your most obedient humble servant,' &c. &c. they perfectly agree, differing only in position. The adulatory strain in which natives commence their letters, is, however, if possible, more contemptible, while it affords greater scope for poetical flourish, than the circumscribed monotony of our epistolary termination. E. M.

[b] *Thakur*, or *Takur*, is an honorary title, of indistinct and indefinite application—sometimes given to a mere man, at others to a *Brahman*, and even to a deity, and is sometimes a proper name. In this work it generally is equivalent to *The Chief*. E. M.

[c] The *Hindus* have borrowed and adopted from the *Mahomedans* many revenue terms—this is one, and usually means being bail for the conduct of another; but it appears to be here used as an item in an obligatory instrument. E. M.

without any reservation. The advantages to the *Rajah* would be many, besides those arising from humanity, from religion, and from the natural affection of parents to children.—It will ensure him the friendship and favour of the Company's government.

' The *Thakur* must not expect the friendship of the Company if he continue this practice; and nothing will be ceded on this point to induce him. It must be relinquished as the only terms on which the Honourable Company's favour and friendship can be retained—but there is no objection to the engagement to relinquish it being expressed in a separate paper.

Since writing the above I have received your second note, but its contents cause no alteration in the sentiments I have above written, further than you may tell the *Raja*, that I do not know how the Honourable Company can become [d] *Banderry* for any civil obligation of men who disregard the most sacred of all obligations—that of protection to offspring.

No. 4.

From SUNDERJI SIVAJI *to Major* WALKER, *dated 20th September*, 1807.

...........I related this morning the conversation I had yesterday with the *Thakur* JEHAJI, with which you will have become acquainted. At present the Mother of the *Thakur* with the Brethren of the *Raja* having assembled, they repre-

[d] *Banderry—bondsmen—*from *band*; a word equivalent to our *bond*. E. M.

sented that 'the relinquishment of female Infanticide will be agreed to by us according to the conditions to which RAO *Saheb of *Kutch* and JAM *Saheb* may agree—prior to them nothing will be concluded by us.

If Major WALKER should cause the village taken by BABAJI to be restored, it is well—otherwise he is a free agent —but according to the adjustment which RAO and JAM may make, not to commit Infanticide, we will agree.'

No. 5.

From Jarejah JEHAJI *to Major* WALKER, *dated 21st September*, 1807.

You have often urged me to adopt some course to preserve my daughters; and I am convinced you look upon me as your own when you desire me to do this; but the *Jarejahs* have from ancient times killed their daughters, and I cannot first set a new example.

I am much annoyed by *Mallia*—if therefore you reduce *Mallia*, and keep it subject to the Company or give it to me, as well as restore *Hurralla*—if you should favour me so much, my present distress will be removed, and I will meet your wishes in preserving my daughters.

This is my petition.

* *Saheb*, is an affixture of respect equivalent to *Sir, Master, Lord,* and extensively applied, from a private person to any one short of a prince—perhaps, indeed, to that length. The East India Company are sometimes called *Kampny Saheb* كنبني صاحب Mr. *Company*; oftener however كمپني بهادر *Kampny Behader*, the *Valiant Company*, or *Kampny Saheb Behader*, the *Mighty Lord Company*. E. M.

No. 6.

From SUNDERJI SIVAJI *to Major* WALKER, *dated 22d September*, 1807.

............Having arrived at *Murvi* and had an interview with the *Rajah*, I saw that no clear answer could be obtained, without threats; notwithstanding that, according to the best of my ability, I used both soothing and warm language; yet I grasped the wind, and nothing but dregs remained in the cup. The arrangement respecting the children in particular appeared helpless.

No. 7.

From SUNDERJI SIVAJI *to Major* WALKER, *dated 23d September*, 1807.

I yesterday wrote the particulars of my interview with the *Thakur*, and his refusal to relinquish Infanticide.

Affairs are thus—that what I yesterday wrote is still the language of to day—therefore favour me with an answer to yesterday's and the present communication; for to wait longer without effect would be discreditable; but I am subject to orders.

No. 8.

From Major Walker *to* Sunderji Sivaji, *dated 23d September*, 1807.

Your notes of yesterday and to day are both received, and understood; I delayed to answer the first in expectation of the second. I have now the pleasure to send you two letters, one to the *Rajah* and one to his Mother—that to the *Rajah* being delivered first, observe what effect it has; and then if you think it will prove of any use, deliver the other to his Mother.

If this should induce any alteration in the *Rajah's* mind, you will of course make the most of it—but if it do not, we can only regret that our efforts should be unattended with the effect we wished.

It will however be still proper to keep open the gate, so that this business may be hereafter resumed; and you may therefore, with this view, suggest to the *Rajah* the propriety of answering my letter in terms of friendship.

No. 9.

From Major Walker *to the* Rajah *of* Murvi, *dated 23d September*, 1807.

I have learnt with much dissatisfaction from the respectable Sunderji Sivaji that, notwithstanding the assurances which I have given him and Bhanji Mehta, you still continue to persist in refusing to contract an engagement to relinquish female Infanticide.

If the custom be a bad one, it cannot require any person's example to leave it off—if it be a good one, no person's example ought to be sufficient to cause its abolishment.

But it is universally allowed to be unnatural, and against your religion; and the objections you urge against it are unbecoming your rank and situation. The friendship and favour of the Company can only be procured by leaving off a practice so contrary to the usage of mankind.

I am well disposed to serve you; but my support to you must depend on yours to the cause of humanity.

On this subject, and on the adjustment of your future [f]*Jamma*, hear the advice of SUNDERJI, to whom I have communicated my sentiments.

No. 10.

From Major WALKER *to the Mother of* Jarejah JEHAJI *of* Murvi, *dated 23d September*, 1807.

The army being in the neighbourhood of *Murvi*, I have unavoidably learnt a number of circumstances, and I have heard of your wisdom and prudence with great pleasure.

The [g]*Serkar* is very anxious that the cruel custom of female Infanticide should, by your advice and assistance, be

[f] *Jamma*, or *Jamma-bandy*, is the gross fixed rental of a district, or occupation of smaller extent, payable by the landholder to Government. With natives it is common for a *Zemindar* to hire a district, and to be answerable to Government for the whole amount of the *Jamma-bandy*; he recovering it from the cultivators. E. M.

[g] The Government—the head of affairs. E. M.

abolished. Do you therefore, by every means in your power, endeavour to persuade your Son to desist from this practice. I hope you will labour in this affair; for it is very unnatural for a mother to allow her own offspring to be put to death.

Your father and your mother have nursed and brought you up—wherefore then should it hurt you to rear up your daughters?—Should you not do as I request, what answer can you return to your God?

Should you fully consider it you will perfectly observe the impropriety of this sad custom.

Should other *castes* do as the *Jarejahs*, how could the *Jarejah* race exist?

What more can I write?

No. 11.

From SUNDERJI SIVAJI *to Major* WALKER, *dated 24th September*, 1807.

Your kind letter and its two enclosures, with which you favoured me, arrived in proper time—They were both delivered—After four hours had elapsed, the *Thakur* came to my quarters and appeared very submissive—but although I pushed the point as far as possible, he never consented to abandon the practice of Infanticide; but he said thus much, "That whatever JAM may conclude in this business—it has also my consent.—Before that I cannot engage for any thing—therefore let this subject be dropped—but the Company are powerful."

No. 12.

From Major WALKER *to* SUNDERJI SIVAJI, *dated 24th September*, 1807.

I have received your letter, and I understand its contents, but to day being [h]*Wittepad*, which is an unlucky day, I therefore am unable to write a particular answer—until tomorrow I beg you to wait—still I request you will not slacken in your endeavours, until you have accomplished the point of obtaining a renunciation of Infanticide.

This object is for the good of the *Thakur* JEHAJI; and your reputation will be increased in the opinion of Mr. DUNCAN by gaining it.

No. 13.

From Jarejah JEHAJI *of* Murvi, *and his Mother, to Major* WALKER, *dated 24th September*, 1807.

Your letter, Sir, I have received; in which it is written to rear up and protect our daughters—but the circumstances of this case are, that from time immemorial the *Jarejahs* have never reared their daughters, nor can it now be the case.

This is my petition:—

My situation and circumstances are all known to you,

[h] *Wittepad*—an unlucky day in the *Hindu* Calendar; in consequence of which the officer commanding the *Gaikawar* troops did not come to my camp. A.W.

Sir; and I now, Sir, with folded arms, make my petition—that if, Sir, you will continue to observe the same course of favour towards me as you have hitherto done, I may then hope to secure my ends, and to meet the demands upon me—I have agreed to a sum of *Jammabandy*, even beyond my actual means; and let your protection so extend, that I may be able still to walk with rectitude, and be able to pay my dues.

From the Mother of JEHAJI *to Major* WALKER, *dated Camp at* Gootoo, *24th September*, 1807.

Your letter has been received and its contents understood. You have called upon [1]*Koer* JEHAJI to rear up his daughters; but it is so that for many years past none of the *Jarejah* tribes have ever reared their female offspring. Further particulars of this concern you will learn from *Koer* JEHAJI's writing—and you must excuse him on this score. As *Koer* JEHAJI has attached himself to you, let his *Jammabandy* be so settled that his credit will be preserved.

No. 14.

From Major WALKER *to* SUNDERJI SIVAJI, *dated 25th September*, 1807.

Should any thing wear a favourable appearance I request

[1] *Koer*, appears to be a family, or familiar, appellation, equivalent to *brother*, *son*, &c. without meaning precisely either—it is here applied by a mother to her son; but it is hereafter used in apparently a different degree. E. M.

you will let me know—the former and strong aversion to renounce Infanticide appears now to be less.

Do you on this account keep *Thakur* JEHAJI assured of my friendship.

No. 15.

From Major WALKER *to* SUNDERJI SIVAJI, *dated 25th September*, 1807.

I have received your note, and understood its contents; but I request you will again take the trouble to explain to the *Rajah* JEHAJI my concern, at the difficulty which appears to exist to persuade him, and the obduracy with which he resists every argument, to relinquish the practice of female Infanticide.

What can induce the Honourable Company to make such efforts? and what can induce me to request from you the utmost exertion of your abilities in this respect, except the cause of humanity? and the desire of the Honourable Company to put a stop to a practice, which will redound to the advantage and credit of the *Rajah* JEHAJI?

No. 16.

From SUNDERJI SIVAJI *to Major* WALKER, *dated 26th September*, 1807.

Your letters of the third and second days past have been received; the second at about eight o'clock at night, when the

Thakur was with me, who saw the [k]*Peon*. Before I received this letter I had been engaged in strong conversation with the *Thakur*, but without effect—the difficulty still remains—and this practice will not be relinquished by the *Thakur* JEHAJI.—" Whatever JAM agrees to I will,"—as I before reported, and the same is still dwelt upon.

You say that, should the *Thakur* agree to relinquish the practice of Infanticide, it would be a source of advantage to him, and the cause of increase of reputation to me in the opinion of Mr. DUNCAN:' but, Sir, your servant has come to *Murvi* solely on the Honourable Company's account; and in whatever he may attempt, he is not that person who will not exert his best ability. Other business has arrived at a point of conclusion;—but to the Infanticide relinquishment consent is not procurable;—and my further detention here is unnecessary;—but as you say that owing to the rain, the [l]*Dewanji* had not arrived; but that I should receive an answer to day, I accordingly await its arrival:—pray favour me with it before the close of the day.

If the relinquishment of Infanticide be a question assuredly to be effected by the Company, its accomplishment must be effected by force, which would be but advisable and proper; but in future whatever is your pleasure I am your servant, and your orders, whatever they may be, will be conformed to.

[k] A *peon* is a man who goes on errands, and attends at hand to all calls of his master. In other parts of *India*, *herkàra* has nearly the same meaning. E. M.

[l] A *dewan*, is a deputy or agent, or minister. *Dewanji* is a respectful way of speaking of him; equivalent to Mr. *Dewan*, as we say Mr. *Alderman*, &c. E. M.

No. 17.

From Jarejah JEHAJI, *dated 21st October*, 1807.

From motives of friendship, the Honourable Company are urging me to preserve my daughters—to this I agree, if the *Nowanaggur* and *Gondal Wallas*[m] agree—if they do not preserve them, I will not do it.

No. 18.

From Major WALKER *to* FATTEH MAHOMED, *dated 28th September*, 1807.

It is now a long time since I had the pleasure of hearing from you; it is proper that in contradiction to the past you should favour me with friendly letters.

The object of my present writing to you is to disclose a plan which the Honourable Company are very desirous of seeing adopted, and which would, if effected through your influence, redound to your credit and honour.

It is known to you that the tribe of *Jarejah Rajputs*, who are very numerous in the country of *Kutch*, do not rear their

[m] *Walla* is a term rather familiar, equivalent to *men, people*; sometimes to *fellow*, but without disrespect. *Europeans* are frequently called by natives *Topy-walla, hat-men*; or folks who wear hats. A groom is vulgarly called *Gora-walla*, the *horse man*. The word may be used both in the singular and plural; but never elegantly: see page 31. E. M.

female offspring; but under the blind influence of prejudice suffer their female infants to be destroyed.

This practice is no less contrary to the laws of the *Gospel*, than it is to the precepts of the *Korân*; and it is also equally and fully prohibited in the *Sastras* and ordinances of the *Hindus*; which the *Jarejahs* ought to respect.

Then you will observe that no motive of ambition, interest or advantage can prompt the Honourable Company to wish to see a practice, so contrary to every law, abolished.

Their desire in this respect can arise solely from humanity, and a wish to inspire the tribe of *Jarejahs* with that affection for their female offspring which parents ought to possess.

But what argument can be necessary to prove to you the advantage and credit which will attend your co-operating in this useful and humane attempt? to which you are invited by every consideration of humanity and religion.

Your effectual aid and assistance in this respect, will secure the respect and consideration of all persons; and I feel a confidence that you will exert your best endeavours.

Accordingly, as his Highness RAO SAHEB is the Senior of all the tribes of *Jarejahs*, it is highly probable that none of this tribe will hesitate to follow an example that is set them by the head of the family; especially, as they do not appear averse to it in other respects, and some of them have, of their own will, laudably broke through the custom.

To make this universal, it requires that it should be formally renounced; and that the separate independent heads of the *Jarejah* families should give some public document testifying its abolition.

I have therefore written upon this occasion a letter to his

Highness RAO SAHEB, and trust that his answer may be in conformity to the above; and be productive of the very desirable result of terminating the practice of Infanticide.

No. 19.

From Major WALKER *to* RAO SAHEB, Rajah *of* Kutch, *dated 3d October*, 1807.

In these parts it is represented that all is well—gratify me by writing me accounts of your welfare—and in the terms of friendship that subsist between you and the Honourable Company.

Just now, whatever is most profitable to your interest, and to the welfare of your family and race in the opinion of the Honourable Company, has been written to FATTEH MAHOMED; and that respectable and worthy person will disclose the whole to you for your consideration.

I am satisfied that you will reply conformably to the wishes of the Honourable Company's Government:—and friendship, from this cause, will be much increased.

No. 20.

From FATTEH MAHOMED Jemadar *to Major* WALKER, *without date, received 21st October*, 1807.

(After compliments, and, as is usual, recapitulating the contents of Major WALKER's letter to him, which he states having received at a fortunate moment, and that it afforded him much pleasure, he proceeds:)—

..........It is notorious that since the *Avatara* of *Sri* KRISHNA, the people, (the *Jarejahs,*) who are descended from the [a]*Jadus*, have, during a period of 4900 years, been in the habits of killing their daughters;—and it has no doubt reached your knowledge, that all of God's creation, even the mighty Emperors of *Hindustan*, SHAH JEHAN, AURUNGZEBE, and AKBER, who have successively reigned in *Hindustan;* those of *Khorasan*, and *Iran;* and the *Rajahs* of the four quarters of *Hindustan;* besides all others the conductors of the affairs of this world, who have existed from time to time, have always preserved friendship with this Court; and never acted in this respect (female Infanticide) unreasonably.

Even the King of the world, who is protected by God, the King of [o]*Rum*, descended from a long line of illustrious ancestors who have reigned over that country from the earliest time, and in whose dominions is situated the inestimable and glorious *Mecca*, never once thought of putting a stop to the custom which prevails among the *Jarejahs* of killing their daughters; but on the contrary has preserved friendship at all times with this [p]*Durbar*:—and merchants possessing *lakhs* of wealth belonging to his country reside here, and people of equal wealth of this country reside there—but he never once uttered any thing on this subject.

But you, who follow the paths of the King, and who are

[a] *Jadu*, or rather *Yadu*, is the tribe to which KRISHNA belonged; hence he is called YADAVA. A copious account of the *Avatara* of KRISHNA, with many plates, is given in the *Hindu Pantheon*. E. M.

[o] The *Grand Segnior*, as we curiously call him, is here meant. By *Rum*, or *Room* روم the *Persians* and *Indians* mean *Rome*, or *Greece*, or the whole *Roman* empire; their notions of which are not very exact. *Iran*, and *Turan*, mean *Persia* and *Turkey*. E. M.

[p] *Durbar*—Court; or royal residence. E. M.

an [q] *Amir* of the great *Sirkar*, the Honourable Company, having written me on this subject, I have derived much uneasiness; for it does not accord with your good character.

You should reflect, that though the authority of many Kings and *Rajahs*, the King of *Rum* excepted, has decayed, or passed into the hands of others, still the Government of this Country contains so many brothers of one heart, descended from a common parent, as is not to be found in any other quarter; but they have not to this day departed from the habit of female Infanticide: they have however approved of two good customs:—First, In this country neither birds or animals are killed, goats excepted; and but few eat them—and secondly, Charitable places for [r] *Fakirs* going and coming from *Mecca*, and *Hindus* performing pilgrimages, are so strongly planted that the pilgrims suffer no annoyance.

This *Durbar* has always maintained friendship beyond bounds with the *Sirkar* of the Honourable Company; and notwithstanding this, you have acted so unreasonably in this respect, that I am much distressed.

God is the giver, and God is the taker away—if any one's affairs go to ruin he must attribute his fortune to God. No one has until this day wantonly [s] quarrelled with this *Durbar*, who has not in the end suffered loss.

[q] A prince, or lord. E. M.

[r] *Fakiri*,—poverty, meekness, humility. *Fakir*,—a poor person, a pilgrim, a beggar. E. M.

[s] It will be recollected that the writer, or rather sender, of this flourishing letter, is a *Jemadar*, or military officer, under the *Rajah* of *Kutch*, although, as said in the 232d paragraph of the Report forming Chap. III. his authority was paramount in that country. The *Rajahs* of *Kutch* are known to adopt a similar style, and to have long had very haughty notions of their prowess. Mr. WILFORD in Vol. IX. of the *Asiatic Researches*,

This *Durbar* wishes no one ill, nor has ever wantonly quarrelled with any one. Every thing that may happen is from God. —I bow obedient.—Do not again address me on this subject.

REMARKS.

In the 234th paragraph of his Report, whence reference is made to the preceding No. of this chapter, Colonel[1] WALKER remarks that the above defence of Infanticide was composed and written by a *Brahman*, in the name of a *Mahomedan*, whose several religions equally inculcate an abhorrence against such murders.

A *Brahman* writer, employed by a *Mahomedan* is not usual, as is the converse, in political correspondences; on which subject I find, among my memoranda, and beg to offer, the following remarks—not, indeed, confined precisely to that point, but extended to rather a miscellaneous range.

It is a curious fact, that a great portion of the political

has the following passage applicable to this topic:—'The *Rajas* of *Cach'ha*' (as this learned gentleman classically writes the name that in this work is generally spelled *Kutch)* 'boast of their independence; and pretend that, since the beginning of the world, they have never been conquered, and that they once ruled all over *Gujja-rasht (Guzerat)*. They have forgot the conquest of their country by MENANDER, which is well attested; for unquestionable vestiges of it remained in the second century, such as temples, altars, fortified camps, and very large wells of masonry, with many coins of MENANDER, and APOLLODOTUS; and these monuments were found as far south as *Baroach*.' *Periplus*, pp. 24. 27. E.M.

[1] This officer having been promoted subsequent to the correspondence comprised in this chapter, is, with some apparent incongruity perhaps, designated by different prefixtures of rank. E.M.

correspondence in *India* is carried on in a language foreign to both parties, and of which both are ignorant. The introduction of the *Persian* language so generally into the political correspondence of *India*, is of course to be ascribed to the conquests of the *Mahomedans;* and its retention, to the convenience found to arise in employing them on matters of business; and farther perhaps in having a sort of common language, if it can be so called, in a country where dialects, and independent states, unwilling to adopt each other's tongue, are so numerous.

Between the *Mahomedan* governments of *Delhi, Oude, Arcot, Hyderabad,* &c. and the *English*, all correspondence is, of course, carried on in *Persian*, as it is likewise between us and the *Poona durbar;* although no member of that government, and very few of its ministers (I know not of one) or its subjects, understand a word of the language: treaties of peace, alliance, or commerce, are also exchanged in *Persian* and other languages. In this point the *English* possess a great advantage in having servants of their own nation competent to transact every description of business, with any power or person of *India*, without the intervention of a native.

Individuals of high rank or station of all three descriptions, *English, Mahomedan*, and *Hindu*, are in the habit of impressing their dispatches and official letters (impressing rather a waxen appendage similar to the great seal of *England)* with enormous signets; containing in *Persian* characters the name, rank and titles, of the addressing party: the titles bestowed by the King, (or *Great Moghul.)* Impressions of many of these seals of state have fallen into my possession.

Among other subjects of like value, I am fortunate enough

to possess an *unopened letter*, written by the late *Great Moghul* شاه عالم *Shah Allum*, to a personage of high consideration, with his signet unbroken. Any *virtuoso*, desirous (as all such must surely be) of enriching his cabinet with so great a curiosity, may be accommodated with it on reasonable terms.

To return, however, for a while to the subjects of *Indian* correspondence, and the influence of *Mahomedan* example on the natives of that country, I have to remark, on the former, that many refinements and niceties are introduced into it, unknown in other countries. Between princes and grandees the letter itself is finely written on paper exactly suited to the relative rank of the parties, more especially of the one addressed. To the King, and to persons of the first rank, the paper is of a gold ground, spangled with flowers, and of a very beautiful texture; to those of inferior rank there are different descriptions of paper and style, minutely attended to by those entrusted with this branch of etiquette: it is no offence to exceed, unless in an unreasonable and evident degree, in the article of paper, &c.; but care must be taken not to fall short of what is due on that point. The letter is folded up in a long narrow form—one inch by six perhaps—the ends tucked in, in a peculiar manner, so as not to admit of being developed; the exterior end of the paper is pasted down, through its whole breadth (or what is the same thing along the whole length of the letter, the paper being seldom wider than six or seven inches) instead of being sealed, like our letters, in the middle only. The titles of the addressed person, preceded by a complimentary flourish, are superscribed; and sometimes also the name of the writer, and the date. The writer's signet, usually a seal ring, containing his name, and a brief or principal title, is placed over the pasting in the middle, where our seals generally are; this is not done in wax, but in ink; the inscription cut in the seal receiving no ink, leaves no impression, but appears in white letters.

The letter is now placed in a loose bag of that elegant manufacture called *Kamkhàb* (vulgarly *kincob)* which is tied up by a small silk and gold cord, run through, and having appended to it, the state, or great seal of the addressing party. Some of these, such as the King's, DOWLAT RAO SINDEA'S, Lord CORNWALLIS'S, Lord WELLESLEY'S, the *Gaikawar's* (all of which I think I have) and others, are four or five inches in diameter. Others of less exalted rank, of which I have some, have them of more modest dimensions.

This *Kamkhàb* bag containing the letter is put into another of the finest muslin; into which is also put a small slip of paper with the name, titles, &c. of the addressed person, similar to the superscription of the letter. This latter bag is loosely tied, having the seal dangling outside, being too large to go into the bag.

The *Kamkhàb* is of various qualities, according to the rank, more especially, of the addressed party—some is entirely of gold thread, other of gold embroidered flowers, on a blue, red, or green silk ground—and the paper, I might have said, is also ornamented with gold or silver flowers, stars, or merely dusted or spangled. The entire packet or dispatch is called *Kharìtah;* and I have I think specimens of each sort, quite complete, with bags, seals, &c. and some with letters even, as originally dispatched by and to the greatest potentates of *India;* nay, some of them unopened;—change of circumstances having, in the interim, rendered it politically inexpedient to deliver them.

In developing the dispatch, a hole is usually ripped in the *Kamkhàb* bag, and the letter is extracted. The bag may, among those " with saving knowledge blest," do again—a species of economy that the magnificent establishments under *Bengal* may perhaps smile at; but which I have known attended to, where thrift is more necessary. In some of the offices for country correspondence, a monthly allowance is made for furnishing stationary, including wax, *karìtahs*, &c.

The English Government's embassadors, or residents as they are denominated, at the different courts of *India*, general officers commanding armies at stations or in the field, and some others of high rank, adopt the above style. The letters from his Majesty or the Court of Directors, addressed to the Princes of *India* are usually written in *English;* sometimes very finely on vellum, and illuminated. One from his present Majesty, written in 1798 to his Highness BAJY RAO, the *Peishwa*, or head of the *Mahratta* empire, was in this style, handsomely ornamented on the outside. It was enclosed in a plain mahogany box, out of which it was taken before presentation. It was not addressed conformably to Eastern etiquette; but that was of little moment, as it was not understood. No translation into any country language accompanied the letter; nor, by some omission, was any copy sent to the *Bombay* Government; in consequence of which the *Peshwa* and his ministers were, I know, some time before they could gain a knowledge of its contents; and in the end perhaps, for they did not choose to apply to any of our legation, but imperfectly.

This letter was in reply to one that my much respected friend Sir CHARLES MALET, many years our Ambassador at the *Poona durbar*, brought from the present *Peshwa;* and I had the honour of proceeding to his Highness's court, and delivering his Majesty's answer. Presents, as is usual, had been sent with the letter from *Poona*, and some were looked for in return. None, however, were sent; and a deal of negociation and arrangement was found necessary, not perhaps wholly in consequence of this omission, to induce the *Peshwa* to receive the honour done him by his Majesty in a proper manner:—and after all he deviated in several particulars that the silly etiquette of Eastern courts deem important, from the promised arrangement.

At the time I am speaking of, we had no subsidiary force in the *Mahratta* country, and no English gentlemen went to *Poona* but on an occasional visit to their friends at the Residency; and for these it was necessary to obtain passports from the *Poona durbar*. It was so likewise with the persons proceeding on this occasion with his Majesty's letter. The reader may perhaps be not displeased at seeing the nature of the passport, of which here follows a translation from the *Mahratta* original.

Translation of a *Pass* from BAJI RAO RAGHUNATH MUKH PARDHAN.

"To all [t]*Komavisdars*, [u]*Chokydars*, Travellers, [x]*Mokadams*, &c.

[t] I do not know this word.

[u] A *Chokydar* is the commander of a *Choky*, or watch, or guardhouse.

[x] A *Mokadam* is the head man of a village, or town, or retinue, or persons of various sorts. E. M.

of all towns and villages. Dated 16th of *Rejeb*, of the *Deftary* year, 1200, or the 14th December, 1799.

A [1]*Serdar* from the Honourable Mr. DUNCAN, Governor of *Bombay*, is coming with a letter from his Majesty the King of *England* to *Poona*. He has with him one company consisting of about seventy-five Sepoys, a *Palky* and baggage. You are accordingly ordered not to offer him any hinderance on any account, but to station guards and sentries wherever he shall take up his abode."

On this pleasant journey I was honoured with the company of my gallant and valued friends Marshal Sir WILLIAM BERESFORD, and his brother Lord GEORGE BERESFORD; who not expecting a long residence in *India* took this opportunity of visiting a native court; and were gratified at being presented to his Highness the *Peshwa* in full *durbar*, and also at the court of DOWLAT RAO SINDEA, who was then with his army in the neighbourhood of *Poona*. Not only to the presence of mere Sovereigns and semi-divine *Brahmans* had we the good fortune to be admitted; we visited an hereditary living Deity! and could not fail of being amused and interested, how much soever we may be forced to regret its existence, by such an instance of priestcraft and superstition. Of this visit I furnished a particular detail to the *Asiatic Society*, and it is published in the seventh volume of their Transactions. I will not finally quit the subject without expressing the great increase of enjoyment we derived in our journey from the unremitting attentions and valued society of

[1] A military officer. E. M.

my much respected friend General WILLIAM PALMER, then our ambassador at the *Mahratta durbar*. To see him, was indeed, my chief object in proceeding to *Poona;* that court and city offering but little novelty to me.

Concluding the subject of *Indian* correspondence, it may be remarked that illuminating letters from our Kings to Eastern Monarchs is of old date. JAMES I. sent one to the King of *Persia* early in the seventeenth century, as appears in WALPOLE'S Anecdotes of Painters in *England*, Vol. III. p. 160. 4to Ed. whence the following article is extracted:—

"Among the accounts of the Lord HARRINGTON is this entry:

'Paid to EDWARD NORGATE' (a miniature painter) 'by warrant from the council, April 24, 1613, for his paynes taken to write and lymne in gold and colours certain letters written from his Majesty to the king of *Persia*, the sum of ten pounds.'

"These letters," Lord ORFORD remarks, "were undoubtedly in answer to those brought by that singular adventurer Sir ANTONY SHIRLEY, embassador *from* the *Sophy to* his own Sovereign."

Thus much I have taken the liberty of offering on the subject of *Indian* correspondence; and shall touch for a moment on the other alluded to some pages earlier in this note, on the influence of *Mahomedan* example on the natives of that country. On this latter point I shall in this place confine my notice to one trifling example, which is the different style of dress that of late years has been thought decorous at the *Poona durbar*. A very few years ago, not twenty, you might have seen courtiers, chiefly however, soldiers, come into the presence of the *Peshwa* and his ministers, without any clothing save a *turban* and a pair of short breeches reaching only half way to the knee; and these, officers of such rank and respectability as rendered it proper for the *Peshwa* and all the Court to rise at the annunciation by the [1]gold stick in waiting, of the visitor's name and titles. About the year 1797, the *Moghul* army of *Hyderabad*, among other immense armies, was encamped in the neighbourhood of *Poona*; its commander, AZIM *al* OMRA, the prime minister of the *Hyderabad* government, chusing to be present to fish in the troubled element of *Poona* politics: and as the *Mahomedans* are scrupulously attentive to all the decorums and niceties and elegancies of dress, the contrast, when these trim perfumed coxcombs came to the *Poona durbar* to seat themselves

[1] It is probable that the refinement of gold stick, adopted in the English court, was borrowed from the East. Most men of exalted rank in *India*, *Hindu*, *Mahomedan*, or *English*, retain this description of attendant; mostly however bearing a silver stick, but having the common name of *Choabdàr*, or staff-bearer. The *choab*, or *baton*, is about five feet long, and as thick at the upper end, where is a sort of head, as one's wrist, or as one of our constable's staves. The duty of the *Choabdàr* is to attend the person of his lord, to receive and carry messages, which they do with unequalled grace and elegance; and to receive and announce visitors. In doing this they proclaim his name and titles with a degree of pomposity, truly *Asiatic*; dwelling with open mouth very audibly on some of the most sounding and emphatic syllables, in a way that appears to strangers almost ludicrous. In public, princes and persons of very high rank have several *choabdars* in attendance, who bawl out the title of the grandee, very ostentatiously; adding sometimes an epithet expressive of his virtues, qualifications, or achievements. The *Choabdàrs* dress very elegantly, in large flowing robes, and are certainly a refined appendage to a royal or noble establishment. Persons of inferior rank, who do not choose to go to the expense or show of a *Choabdar*, have a second rate sort of staff-bearer, called a *Sontabardàr*, who bears a silver baton, like our constable's shorter staves, about two feet long, sometimes crooked at one end. E. M.

beside their shirtless, unshorn neighbours, was very ridiculous. And when these *semi-nudes* first attended the levee of AZIM *al* OMRA, the officers in waiting would scarcely admit them, in *buff*, if we may apply that term; and this was at length found to be uncomfortable, and the *Mahrattas* by degrees became less distinguished by this paucity of clothing, and the *Poona durbar* is now attended by well dressed persons only.

The *Peshwa*, however, and the very great men among the *Mahrattas*, such as DOWLAT RAO SINDEA, &c. are always in public magnificently dressed, with a profusion of diamonds, emeralds, pearls, &c. of immense value. NANNA FURNAVEESE was remarkable for a peculiarly elegant neatness in dress, without ornaments; save, perhaps, one splendid diamond ring.

In DANIEL's fine painting of the *Poona durbar*, done for Sir CHARLES MALET, not only is the portrait and character of each leading personage preserved, but the dress and ornaments are also accurate. I have often seen the *Peshwa* and NANNA in the very ornaments and apartment there portrayed; and the utensils for *atr*, *&c.* on the carpet are old acquaintances. This painting has been finely engraved, and is published by CRIBB in *Holborn*.

I was once amused at the method in which a very soldierly, stately looking personage received the *atr* (or *otter* as it is called in *England*) on a ceremonious visit in camp. He attended PARASU RAMA BAO (usually called PURSERAM BHOW) the famous *Brahman Mahratta* General, with whose army I served in the campaigns of 1791-92, against TIPPOO, on a visit to our lamented commander Colonel FREDERICK.

The person in question was habited as before described—his head and loins merely covered; and as

> "He had ne'er a hand idle,
> "For one held his sword, and the other"—no "bridle,"

but his shield, I was curious to see how he would, in this lack of garment, or shawl, or hands, receive the *atr*—he held forth his shield, and receiving it thereon, carried it to his nose with great solemnity. I have noticed this, among other points relating to the *Mahrattas*, in my Narrative of the Operations of those Campaigns, p. 376, to which the reader may, if he think fit, refer.

Having noticed the *Peshwa's* dress, jewels, &c. I will conclude this miscellaneous, but I hope not tiresome item of *Remarks*, with an anecdote touching his family jewels, that were so long in the hands of the *English*.

When *RAGHUVA, commonly called RAGOBA, or RAGABOY, father of the present *Peshwa*, was forced by the just indignation of his countrymen about 1773, to flee from *Poonah*, he brought away what valuables he could, and among them his family jewels. Seeking refuge in *Bombay*, that government unwisely espoused his cause; which however they were unable to uphold; but I shall not touch on the political, military, or moral errors incident to their injudicious interference. Straitened for cash, RAGHUVA deposited some of his jewels with the *Bombay* government, as security on a certain occasion, for about, if I recollect right, six *lak'hs* of rupees, or 70,000 *l.* and never having been able to redeem them, they

* The probable origin of this name, which is very common among *Hindus* of different tribes, is noticed in page 5. E. M.

remained many years in the *Bombay* treasury; and were, by orders from home, at length sent to *England.* Not being of much use in this country, they were, after some years, sent to *Calcutta,* where they remained for some more years unappropriated.

When the vicissitudes of *Mahratta* politics had brought RAGHUVA's family from their lengthened imprisonment in *Junìr*, and placed BAAJY RAO in the post illegally sought by his father, of *Peshwa,* the first officer of the state, (which is the meaning of the word, and we must not call a *Brahman* by the title of King) the family jewels were well remembered; and after waiting a reasonable time in view to ascertain the stability of the reigning family, it was determined, by that consummate and most fortunate statesman, Marquis WELLESLEY, to return the jewels in the shape of a present, on some occasion when such an act of munificence might afford an eligible degree of *eclat.*

After having been put up, and put down, and put up in various modes, BAAJI RAO seemed fixed in his seat; to which, although his father was not, he undoubtedly was the rightful claimant; and the occasion alluded to was thought to offer, when my good friend General PALMER, with a suite from *Bengal,* succeeded the diplomatic establishment, that till then had been filled by *Bombay* servants.

The jewels were accordingly sent under the charge of my old, eccentric, but worthy friend, Captain DONALD MICHIE, who to the great regret of a large circle of friends was killed in *Egypt.* His party joined General PALMER's on the march from *Bengal,* and they came to *Poonah* together.

On the day when his highness the *Peshwa* should return

the General's visit of presentation, it was determined to display and return to him the splendid regalia of his fathers.

Previously to which, however, it was thought proper to brush them up a little, and arrange them, and so forth; and in doing this, the well-secured *teak* wood case was found all right—clamps fast, seals unbroken, &c. &c. but on opening it, instead of being dazzled by the blaze of diamonds, and emeralds, and rubies, and carbuncles, and what not, how were the party astonished at seeing nothing but clods, dirt, and disgusting filth!

This would formerly have passed for a miracle; but as in these sceptical times, the Government of *India* might have demurred at such a mode of accounting for the disappearance of the jewels, the parties concerned were induced to seek a little farther for an explanation of what had excited their just amazement.

They had not far to seek; for one of them poking with his sword among the dirty mass in the case, thought he saw something heterogeneous; which on being drawn forth, and rubbed and cleaned, proved to be a diamond—searching farther, others were discovered; and so on, until by rubbing, and washing, and sifting, every gem was recovered.

The cause of this was easily seen. The chest into which the jewels had been packed in *England* was of deal—this had, at *Calcutta*, been put into one of *teak;* and although the latter appeared well and closely put together, those destructive insects, the white ants, had insinuated themselves through the joinings, and got at the deal box, which, with such of its contents as were edible, they had devoured; leaving on the exterior *teak* case no appearance of their presence. White ants are especially attracted by fir wood, and abhor *teak*. In many parts of *India*, a deal box placed on the ground at night, would be devoured by the morning. They abound most in a dry argillaceous soil, impregnated with iron. They commence their operations, by incrusting their destined object with a thin covering of earth, which they moisten by their own secretions: this is laid over, but not exactly *on*, the surface, for between that and the crust there is room for the ants to move to and fro, to extend the cover under which they intend to act. This covering is very thin; thrice the thickness of a wafer perhaps, and is held to its object by connecting lines of earth, which form roads, and between which the ants pass under cover of the crust to work and eat. The crust when put on is moist, but quickly dries, and falls off by a very slight touch, discovering hosts of these destructive workmen; who eat through and through whatever they attack, honey-combing it in such a manner as to leave barely sufficient to support their incrustation: so that a kick, or stroke with a stick, would pass through an apparent post half a foot thick, and tumble the whole to the ground. In *Calcutta* they have been known to work their concealed way to the cieling of a room, which when sufficiently eaten, has given the first indication of the enemy, by falling altogether on the floor.

To conclude my story, I have only to add, that among the contents of the *teak* case were found all the jewels, although mingled together in a curious manner. Jewellers were sent for from the city to re-string and furbish them up; and as some who knew the arrangement of the strings, and form of the combined ornaments, were still in *Poona*, every thing was soon restored, little or nothing the worse for the intrusion above described.

Those who recollect the impetuosity of our deceased friend DONALD MICHIE, may guess his astonishment at seeing his charge metamorphosed from gems to filth—so unaccountable, at the first blush, to him, who had always chained the case to his tent post, and scarcely ever ventured it out of his sight. E. M.

No. 21.

From Major WALKER *to* FATTEH MAHOMED, *dated 9th January* 1808.

The Honourable Company's government impressed with horror at the inhuman practice of female Infanticide in existence among the *Jarejah* tribe, was induced to take measures to put a stop to it.

The designs of great men are always in concordance with the secret will of the Divinity; and that secret assistance of the Omnipotent, which (praise to his name!) always attends the victorious standards of the army of the Honourable Company, has, in this instance, in a short period crowned the wishes of their government with success; and extended and confirmed their reputation for humanity.

The fame of the great character which you bear in the country of *Kutch* for humanity, and your love of justice, has not remained a secret to me. Do you, my friend, put a stop to the custom of Infanticide in *Kutch*, and you will perpetuate that name by an act which will ever be remembered with delight; and be assured, that the reward of so good an action will await you in the other world. I am fully satisfied, that you will exert your utmost influence to do away this horrid practice, and thereby entitle yourself to the gratitude of your fellow mortals, and the most perfect bliss in the next world:—for this the Almighty has bestowed on you the power to do.

I have heard that all the *Jarejahs* who have become converts to *Islamism* have renounced this practice:—true it is, that it is contrary to the dictates of MAHOMED, and to the religion of JESUS CHRIST, as well as to the tenets of the *Puranas* and *Sastras* of the *Hindus*:—indeed it is, according to all these, the most heinous crime and sin.

I feel a strong desire to write you much at length on this subject; but to the wise, a hint is enough.

My friendship requires me to desire you always to write me accounts of your welfare, and of the advancement you may make in the attainment of the object of my present letter.

No. 22.

From FATTEH MAHOMED *to Major* WALKER, *without date. Translated 13th February*, 1808.

.... Your other letter is expressive of the grief of the Honourable Company on account of the horrid practice of female Infanticide among the *Jarejahs;* and stating that you would derive much pleasure from the abolition of this custom, which you have urged on account of the friendship that subsists between this *Sirkar* and the Company; and supported by several arguments well composed; from the perusal of all which, I have derived much pleasure.

The reputation of your government and of mine are now long established; and this is known to the whole world; and, God be praised! it will daily increase.—Previous to this, I wrote you on the subject of female Infanticide; and from that you must have learned every thing:—what can I now say on this subject?—for this custom has prevailed for 5000 years, since the incarnation of KRISHNA—and thus it has been, and is now, practised.

This is not a practice confined to a few, that it can be dispensed with. Every one also who wishes to nourish his daughter, is at full liberty—and he who wishes to kill them at their birth, has full powers so to do.—In this world, none of the Kings of the seven [b]countries occupying its four quarters, have ever written on this subject—but on the contrary, have always preserved the connections of friendship—and this government has, with these Kings and rulers, always maintained amity; which I also preserve: and it is not fit with true friends, such as we are, constantly on this subject, to create any ground of uneasiness.

[b] The term here translated the *seven countries*, is I imagine هفت اقليم, meaning rather the *seven climates*, into which the *Mahomedan* geographers have divided the earth. The term is meant to include the whole world, and kings sometimes hyperbolically assume the title of king of the seven climates. *Heft Kishwer* هفت كشور has the same meaning and allusion as *heft aklim*; and the sovereignty of the world is sometimes assumed under that title. The sea, as well as the planets and the earth, is also subjected to a septenary arrangement. E. M.

It is the decree of Heaven—God, the Merciful, the King of the two worlds, be praised! every one is pleased with his own faith.—On this account—and as the *Jarejahs* are the relations and brothers of MAHA RAO SAHEB, and I am an adherent of his *Durbar*, it is not proper for me to say any thing on the subject to the *Jarejahs*: and it would not have effect—nor ever will.

Therefore, this business excepted, I beg you will write me on any other; that I may from performing it, shew to you my regard; from which we will derive mutual advantages; and to say more than this to a person of your wisdom, would be as foolish as to teach knowledge to LUKMAN.*

No. 23.

Communication from Jarejah DADAJI, *Chief of Raj-kut: who states,*

That many of the *Jarejahs* of *Kutch* preserve their daughters; and that previous to the birth of a child, the father if he wishes to preserve his daughter signifies such a wish, and his will is invariably obeyed. If the mother wishes, and the father is averse to preserve his daughter, it is killed. Exceptions to this take place now and then; when the mother has great influence over the father.

When the daughters are killed, they are almost invariably

* لقمان A person very famous, among *Mahomedans*, for wisdom—he is by some supposed to be ESOP the fabulist. E. M.

put to death immediately after their birth. On the birth of a daughter, the mothers seldom apprise the father, but put it to death at once.

Daughters when put to death, are always buried in the state in which they were born; without undergoing any purification, or being wrapped in clothes.

DADAJI has a daughter alive. He states, however, that he expressed a wish to preserve it eventually, previous to its birth.

Some *Jarejahs* preserve their daughters that may be born within the space of six months after the death of a chief—though this is little observed, it is still reckoned proper—but he says the avarice, or other passions, of the parents, make them disregard this practice.

DADAJI says there is no uniform mode of killing the infants.—Sometimes they terminate their short life by opium, sometimes by placing the navel string on their mouth and suffocating them. DADAJI, on being interrogated as to any other mode, expressively said, " what difficulty is there in blasting a flower?"

DADAJI observes, that there is no impropriety in *Jarejahs* preserving their daughters.—Sometimes the mothers, if there be no female attendants, kill their infants themselves; but in general, women of station never perform this unnatural office.

DADAJI, in allusion to this subject, and as descriptive of the motives for Infanticide, states, that in *Kattawar* and *Hallàr*, the *Rubaries*, or goat herds, allow their male kids to die when there are many of them brought forth;—and the *Charons* follow the same practice with their male buffaloes: both being reckoned unproductive in a country where little flesh is consumed:—the only profit arising from these classes of animals being from their milk.

In regard to the origin of the custom of Infanticide, *Jarejah* Dadaji related the story of the *Rajah* and his beautiful daughter, as before given—but although he did not appear to put much confidence in the truth of this history, Dadaji could give me no other account of the origin of that practice. He says, that his race at one time occupied a country on the other side of *Sind*; and that being suddenly surrounded with *Mahomedans*, they were necessitated to kill their daughters, not being able to provide them with husbands; and that the custom, which had its origin in a desire to preserve their *caste*, has been maintained in consequence of its favouring the avaricious feelings of some; but in general without any motive at all, farther than that of following a custom of the tribe.

Dadaji farther states *Persia* to be the country which tradition assigns the *Jarejahs* as their original residence; and that the word *Jam* is derived from [d]Jamshid—the name of a famous *Persian* monarch.

[d] The idea that the *Jarejahs* are descended from *Persians*, seems to have gained some ground. The military pride of this class would naturally lead them to claim their descent from the most illustrious personage, and we accordingly find them tracing their line to Jamshid. This ancient king of *Persia*, called indifferently Jam or Jamshid, جمشيد is often confounded with Bacchus, Solomon, and Alexander; so vague is the historical knowledge of *Mahomedans*. He is the subject of much fable, and of very frequent allusion by poets and other writers. Almost the whole circle of the arts and sciences are attributed to him, or to Pythagoras, who they make his prime minister. The cup of Jamshid, called *Jam i Jam*, discovered, filled with the elixir of immortality, when digging for the foundations of *Persepolis*, is more famous in the East, than even the cup of Nestor, among the *Greeks*; furnishing the poets with numberless allegories, and allusions to

SUNDERJI SIVAJI, referring to the above, states that all the *Jarejahs* in *Kutch* kill their daughters; but he is not acquainted with the particular mode in which they do it. Others have reported that they place the navel string on their mouth, or give them opium.

He thinks that it is not customary to report the birth and death of a daughter to the father.

The *Jarejahs* of *Kutch* marry into all the *Rajput* families of *Guzerat*, of *Thur*,[e] and *Pankur*. He states that they never marry their slaves; and that when they keep them as *Rackelas*, or mistresses, they allow them a separate house, even though the *Jarejahs* be not married.

SUNDERJI's *Munshi*,[f] who is a native of *Sind*, states that in that country the custom of female Infanticide has been relinquished by all except a tribe of *Mahomedans*, named *Kalora*. This is not a very numerous tribe. The Sovereigns of *Kutch* formerly belonged to it. A. W.

wine, the philosopher's stone, divination, enchantment, &c. See WILKINS's edition of RICHARDSON's Persian Dictionary, art. جمشید E. M.

[e] I am not quite sure how the names of these places, or tribes, ought to be written; the MS. not being very clear. Perhaps *Thir* and *Pankir:* the former name occurs in a note in page 25. E. M.

[f] A writer, or secretary; especially a *Persian* one. E. M.

No. 24.

List of JAREJAHS, including BYAUD, (or *brethren,*) not specifically mentioned, who have renounced INFANTICIDE.

Names.	*Taluks*, or villages.
Jarejah HOTIJI, ...	*Kotara Sangni.*
.... DOSAJI, ...	*Mallia.*
Koer SATAJI, ...	*Ditto.*
Jarejah JIAJI, ...	*Murvi.*
.... RANMALJI, ...	*Rajkut.*
Koer LAKMAJI, ...	*Ditto.*
JAM JESSAJI, ...	*Noanagar*, or *Nowanagher.*
Jarejah RAMALJI, by the agency of *Koer* VERAJI,	*Sirdhar.*
.... DEVAJI, ...	*Gondal.*
Koer NATHUJI, ...	*Ditto.*
Jarejah BOPAT SING, ...	*Dherole.*
.... HOTIJI, ...	*Kersura.*
.... SALAJI, ...	*Jallia.*
.... KHENGARJI, ...	*Harmatia.*
.... JIAJI, ...	*Kotori.*
.... RAMSINGJI, ...	*Amba.*
.... KIMAJI, ...	*Lodeka.*
.... DEWAJI, ...	*Pall.*
.... MORJI, ...	*Gauridher.*
.... DOSAJI, ...	*Kotaria.*
.... KHANJI, ...	*Wadali.*

Names.	*Taluks*, or villages.
Jarejah Tezmalji, ...	*Virwa.*
.... Khanji, ...	*Gadka.*
.... Bhanji, ...	*Ditto.*
.... Raising, ...	*Shapur.*
.... Raoji, ...	*Kang-siali.*
.... Hadoji, ...	*Ditto.*
.... Fulji, ...	*Drapa.*
.... Saliyalji, ...	*Ditto.*
.... Raibji, ...	*Ditto.*
.... Ramsingji, ...	*Ditto.*
.... Jiji Rasonji, ..	*Ditto.*
.... Mairuji, ...	*Rajpura.*
Koer Usaji, ...	*Ditto.*
Jarejah Banaji, ...	*Barwa.*
.... Samatji, ...	*Mengni.*
.... Fullaji, ...	*Sisang.*
.... Sujaji, ...	*Ditto.*
.... Dadaji, ...	*Ditto.*
.... Makanji, ...	*Ditto.*
.... Pemji, ...	*Dedi moli.*
.... Wagji, ...	*Ditto.*
.... Suraji, ...	*Keruri.*
.... [s]Kana Mulu, ..	*Saludher wawri.*
.... Hakaji, ...	*Ditto.*
.... Kana Rokaji, ..	*Ditto.*

[s] *Kana* seems here rather a family distinction, than a name;—something similar perhaps to *Koer*, noticed in a former page, and which again occurs above. They appear to be provincial terms, and denote some relationship, perhaps, to a *Rajah*, or chief. E. M.

Names.	*Taluks*, or villages.
Jarejah KANA PUCHANJI,	*Saludher wawri.*
. . . . KANA NATHUJI,	*Ditto.*
Koer SATAJI, the brother of JAM.	
Rana SERTANJI, ...	*Purbander*, or *Poorbunder*.
Koer HALAJI JAITEAS, . .	*Ditto.*

CHAP. V.

NOTES—*chiefly by Colonel* WALKER, *illustrative of his General Report of* 15*th March,* 1808—*and notices of some singular customs and opinions of the* HINDU *inhabitants of* GUZERAT, *and others.*

NOTE A.

THE instance here[*] alluded to was a *Jarejah* who was reported to have murdered his daughter after she had been preserved for some days. This circumstance illustrates also another superstitious ceremony of the *Hindus.*

A *Jarejah* of *Raj-kut* was accused of causing, according to the custom of his *caste,* his infant daughter to be destroyed:—this was just at the period when most of the chiefs had subscribed to an engagement renouncing the practice.

Although this deed was supposed to have been committed before the penalties of the engagement could in strictness be enforced, I conceived it advisable to notice the circumstance, and to embrace every occasion of marking with disapprobation and horror, the commission of this unnatural crime. In this instance too, the fact was reported to have been attended with unusual barbarity; for, some time previous to the delivery of the woman, the chief of *Raj-kut* had caused it to be intimated to her that should she have a daughter, it must

[*] See paragraph 89. of Chap. III. page 57.

be preserved. The husband was absent; and a daughter being born, the mother followed the injunctions of his chief, and doubtless her own inclinations, and nurtured her child. After two or three days the husband returned; and in the most brutal rage threatened to kill his wife, and ordered the immediate destruction of his daughter.

Thus were the circumstances related to me; and DADAJI, the chief of *Raj-kut*, who resided in my camp, confirmed the facts of the delivery, and the injunctions which he had issued for preserving the offspring.

The attendance of the *Jarejah* was obtained; but as he affirmed, and with some appearances in his favour, that the child had died a natural death, we were contented, in a case where complete evidence could not be procured, to have recourse to the expedient of deciding the question by lot.

This extraordinary mode of appeal to justice may be found to have existed formerly among most nations, and is still practised by the [b] *Hindus*.

[b] A curious article, the twenty-third in the first volume of the *Asiatic Researches*, is on the Trial by Ordeal as in use among the *Hindus*. Several modes are there detailed. The trial by jury, called *Panchayet*, was likewise formerly in extensive usage, and is not now entirely discontinued, in some districts of *India*. See WILK'S *Mysoor*, Vol. I. p. 501. Trial by ordeal is also in use on the coast of *Africa*: "All criminal charges are tried by the *Pynins*, or judges, who hear and weigh the evidence produced. But if there be no evidence the cause is decided by a species of ordeal called *doom*, which consists in administering to the person accused a certain quantity of the bark of a tree deemed poisonous. If he retain it on his stomach, he is pronounced guilty; if otherwise, innocent. The refusal to submit to this ordeal is considered as a decisive proof of guilt, and the judges proceed accordingly." Fourth Report of the *African* Institution. Letter from Mr. MEREDITH on the gold coast, December, 1809. This reminds one of a similar ordeal with the *Hindus*, among whom in both Peninsulas the usage is very general: extending to *Siam* and *Pegu*; the inhabitants of which vast countries, being *Baudhas*, I have considered, in the *Hindu Pantheon*, as heretical *Hindus*. E. M.

The appeal being supposed to be made in the presence of the Divinity, it is attended by religious rites and ceremonies; and in cases of importance nothing is spared that may add solemnity to this mode of trial.

The parties, accompanied by their friends and by *Brahmans*, assemble and proceed to a place of worship; where, after the requisite *puja*, or religious ceremonies, have been performed, two *chits*, or notes, are made out in the tremendous name of the Deity unto whose justice the appeal is made—one implores that if the accused be innocent, the *chit* of innocence may be drawn—this is called the *dherma* note; the word meaning, as well as justice, charity, religion, innocence, &c.—the other is called the *pap* note; *pap* meaning sin; and if the accused be guilty, this note of iniquity is invited to come forth.

These notes are thrown into a cloth, or into a vessel; and the parties, or those whom they may appoint, draw the tickets which are to decide the contest.

The following are translates of the notes used on this occasion.

No. 1. *Prosperity!*[c] SRI RANCHURJI is Infallible!

If RAJAJI KARCHERAWALLA killed his daughter, let the *pap chit* come forth.

No. 2. *Prosperity!* SRI RANCHURJI is Infallible!

If the daughter of RAJAJI KARCHERAS died a natural death, let the *dherma chit* come forth.

The accused was acquitted.

Another instance of reference to trial by lot occurred in a civil case; but it was not decided thereby, as the result left it still dubious.

[c] See *Remarks*, at the end of this Note.

The object was to ascertain whether certain words in a will were genuine or forged. The case had been referred to arbitrators, but they were unable to decide; and they agreed to put six tickets before the god—three for the complainant, and three for the defendant, to determine whether the words in question were the hand writing of the deceased or not. The first time the ticket was in favour of the defendant, and two subsequent times for the complainant. If the three tickets had been in favour of either party, the case would have been decided in his favour. A. W.

Remarks.

SRI is a name of the goddess LAKSHMI, importing prosperity, increase, abundance, &c. in one case it is SRIS, reminding us of the CERES of the west, with whom in many points, as well as in name, LAKSHMI corresponds. SRI is also, as in the above instance, a prefixture of reverence to names of other deities, both male and female; as well sometimes, as to the names of men. See *Hindu Pantheon*, under those words, in the Index. RANCHUR is a name of VISHNU, the husband of LAKSHMI. *Ib.* p. 405. The termination *ji* is, to names both of gods and men, as is seen above, an appendage of distinction; not indeed of much, for it is now assumed as a thing of course by whole tribes. It may be observed that the name of the accused terminates differently in the two notes—the second name is however of locality, or of office—*Karcherawalla* and *Karcheras*, may mean one of a town or place of the name of *Karchera.*—*Walla* being equivalent to *man*, or *fellow*, but without any light or debasing allusion (see page 120.) It is common for both *Hindus* and *Mussulmans* to be distinguished by the names of their town or country, by the addition to their name of *Surty*, (of *Surat*,) *Bombayker*, *Madrassy*, *Bengally*, *Poonaker*, *Hyderabady*, &c. These terminations, that is their genitive case, are arbitrary, and appear to be assumed in reference to their concord with the name; or it may be regulated by some grammatical rule. *Karcherawalla* and *Karcheras*, both mean of a place of that name; as *Kutcheraz* in page 27 denotes the person so surnamed to be of *Kutch*. Perhaps, indeed, both *Karcheras* and *Karcherawalla*, may be only other pronunciations denoting *Kutch* to be the country of the accused. *Raj-kut*, a town and district in *Guzerat* is named in the text as his residence; but he may nevertheless have been originally from *Kutch;* for it is more common to surname a man from his native place, than from that of his immediate residence. E. M.

NOTE B.

The profession of Robbery (Chap. III. paragraph 133) is not in *India* so disreputable as may at first sight appear. It is, like begging, an hereditary craft; and an individual, in answer to a direct interrogation, would have little scruple in avowing himself either of the robber, or of the beggar, tribe. The dexterity thus acquired by the former tribe, handed down from generation to generation, improved occasionally by a man of genius, is surprising; and many curious anecdotes have been related of their adroitness and enterprize. A thief has been known to undermine the foundation of a house, and ascend through the floor, which, seldom being boarded, may be done with less noise and difficulty than in *Europe*. I have known a lady and gentleman awake in the morning, and find their tent completely stripped; even to the bed curtains that surrounded, and the bed clothes that covered them. No great degree of moral turpitude attaches in the estimation of others, to the followers of this profession:—none, if the individual be fortunate in escaping detection, and hath the reputation of being wealthy. In the *Mahratta* countries, this tribe of robbers abounds the most—and, indeed, it may be safely said that the *Mahratta* nation are an associated band of robbers. There is no nation or state that they would not, and do not, rob and plunder, when they can do it with reasonable impunity; and in default of rich and weak neighbours they will rob each other. This I could exemplify by several instances in point. Not by land only; the *Mahrattas* have, to use a western term, organized, as well as authorized, robbery also by sea; and whole families, it may, indeed, be said, whole nations, claim and exercise the trade of Piracy, as a hereditary right. Authors who wrote more than two thousand years ago describe these people pretty much as they now exist;—or rather as they were thirty or forty years back; for the *English* have of late sadly circumscribed this once flourishing occupation.

The western coast of the *Indian* promontory from the *Indus* to *Goa*, and perhaps farther, has been heretofore distinguished by geographers as the "Pirate coast." ANGRIA the famous Pirate is well known even in *Europe;* but he is not, nor, I believe, ever was, the head, or of the head family, of the Pirate sect. The chief of the Southern Pirates, both in reference to family respectability, and power, is SIVAJI BHUNSLA, the *Raja* of *Kolapore;* so named from his principal place north of *Goa*—inland he is more usually styled the *Raja* of *Panella,* from his strong hill fort of that name, called also [d]*Pavangher.* He is a lineal descendant of the daring founder of the *Mahratta* empire, his namesake, SIVAJI; and inherits a portion of his independent spirit; for his obedience to the usurped power of the *Peshwa* has ever been, and is, at best, precarious; and in troublesome times, altogether nominal.—Sometimes not even that. During the distractions at *Poona* in 1796-7, he, as usual on such occasions, took the field, with 7000 men, and levied contributions in the neighbourhood of *Tajgom* and *Meritch.* *Hubly* being a place of great wealth, and with no fortifications, he took possession of it. At sea his people are called *Malwàns; Malwàn,* or *Malundy,* being the port whence most of his vessels take their departure. It is less than a degree to the north of *Goa.* This privilege of Piracy in *Malwàn* is a royal one; none but the *Raja* can fit out Pirate vessels—he sends out yearly about a dozen, of the descriptions called *Galivat, Shebàr,* and *Grab:* the first have generally two masts, and are decked fore and aft—and have square top sails and top gallant sails, and are rigged mostly after the *European* fashion. The *Shebàr* is also of two masts—the hinder mast and bowsprit very short—they have no

[d] Being very elevated it is poetically styled *Pavangher,* the residence of *Pavan,* the *Hindu* regent of the winds. See him and his history in the *Hindu Pantheon. Panella,* may perhaps have the same origin—*Pàn,* an abbreviation of *Pavan.* E. M.

top-masts, and very little rigging—haulyards, braces, and bowlines being the chief; they are not decked—their largest sail is extended on a yard of very great length, running up to a point, many feet higher than the mast—they sail well and are fine vessels in fair weather and smooth water—many of them are of more than 150 tons burthen. The *Grab* is distinguished from other vessels by having, instead of bows, a projecting prow—they are decked, and have either two or three masts, and are rigged in the *European* manner with topmasts, yards, shrouds, backstays, &c.—Each of the *Raja's* vessels of all these descriptions carries eight or ten small carriage guns, and about a hundred men. Their general rendezvous is *Pigeon Island.* On leaving port each pirate *lascar*, as we are accustomed to call native seamen, receives two rupees—the commander, or *serang*, eight—and on their return they get corn, according to their success, and three or four rupees, and more, corresponding to their rank and good fortune. Their cruize seldom exceeds fifteen days. All prize is the property of the *Raja*, who is at the whole expense of the outfit.—The vessels taken are seldom retained, unless indeed peculiarly adapted to the service.—The cargo becomes the *Raja's* property, and the vessel is released to bring another.

They sail without any written commission; and with instructions, it is understood, to take all vessels that they can master, except those having *English* colours and passes.—Sometimes, however, they are regardless of the *English* protection, which they thus contrive to evade—one Pirate boat boards the intended prey, and demands her pass; and while some persons pretend to read it, others pick a quarrel with some of the crew, and commence a scuffle, in which the pass is removed or destroyed—however, they take but little, perhaps nothing, and depart. Soon after another Pirate boards the destined vessel, and finding no pass, pretends that the reasons offered for its absence, are lies, and takes all.

In these cases complaint is of course made by the plundered owner to the *Bombay* government; and restitution is demanded, and generally made without much demur; one can hence scarcely see the utility of the robbery—but it is the impulse of habit, enforced by the hope, however remote, of being able to parry or evade the necessity of restitution. Sometimes, indeed, the *Raja* is not so prompt in his obedience to our demands, as is judged proper; and I have known his ports occasionally blockaded by a detachment from the *Bombay* marine, of a cruizer and an armed boat or two, and no intercourse admitted, until satisfaction and indemnity were obtained, for the insult and loss and expense incident to the measure. The *Raja* perhaps will offer some extenuation by alleging that it is his indefeasible and immemorial right to levy contributions on vessels sailing in his seas, either in the shape of payment for protection, or of plunder—His protection may I believe be purchased, and his vessels would respect the pass. That he doth not exact this from the *English* arises, he says, from his respect and esteem for that nation, whose property is never touched without some suspicion of an abuse of his confidence—for he will allege that our passes are sometimes given to vessels and property not *bona fide British*—This may or may not be true—for I do not imagine, but may be mistaken, that the *Bombay* Government are very particular as to whom their passes may be granted:—

they are renewed every year. I think I have a recollection, but find no record, of a complaint having been forwarded to the *Poona durbar* against the *Raja* of *Kolapore,* for a piratical trespass on *British* property, with an application for an order to their supposed vassal, for restitution and satisfaction—and that the answer of the *durbar* was that the *Raja* was a contumacious subject, who deserved chastisement; and that no objection existed to its being inflicted by the *Bombay* Government. I do not imagine that the *Poona* government would, at any time, seek satisfaction for any of its subjects plundered by the piratical *Raja;* or indeed that any *Mahratta* would think of applying to the *durbar* for it.

Besides SIVAJI BHUNSLA and RAGHUJI ANGRIA, there are other piratical potentates to the southward of *Bombay.* One is a female named SAKUBI, but I know nothing of her. She and ANGRIA have not above three or four vessels each.

As well as to the southward, the traffic of the *Malabar* side of *India,* is infested by Pirates to the northward of *Bombay;* and these do not often go much farther south—they then perhaps infringe on the privileges of some brother or sister Pirate. The northern folk are a more desperate and enterprizing set than those to the south:—they have generally no other avocation but that of robbery; whereas the *Mahratta* Pirate states have also trade, agriculture, and other civilizing pursuits: although perhaps the individuals engaged in Piracy, do nothing else.

The northern Pirates inhabit chiefly the coast about the mouths of the *Indus,* and thence to the gulph of *Kutch,* where they have strong forts, and large towns; and in all, perhaps, some hundreds of vessels. They are comparatively a barbarous race; and are not only regardless of the *English* flag, but frequently ill use their captives. Of this I have known instances, even of *English* officers,—and of their attacking our armed vessels with desperate ferocity.—Their boats sail and row very well; and being well manned, we can seldom catch them. When we do, the crew are kept as prisoners, and put to work on the docks or roads. In 1797 the Company's ship Sir Edward Hughes took a *Malwan* Pirate, after chasing her fifty miles.

It is confidently said that the northern pirate boats, which we generally distinguish by the name of *Kuli* or *Cooley* boats, come, not unfrequently, as traders, into *Bombay* harbour, and there wait until they see a promising vessel sail unprotected, when they will slip out, in the night, and carry her off. They are so daring that our coasters between *Bombay* and *Surat* almost always sail in large fleets and with convoy: in the cotton season two or three hundred perhaps in a fleet; and even then several are captured every year.

The preceding portion of this Note is taken chiefly from memoranda made at *Poona* in 1797. I may now add that the *Bombay* Government, unable any longer to put up with the audacity of the northern sea robbers, have recently sent a force to deprive them of the means of farther annoyance. They had, as they thought, secured their vessels under the guns of their forts, and it became necessary to take the latter also; which was effected, after a desperate resistance, in a most gallant manner, and all their vessels were destroyed.

The historians of Alexander make frequent mention of the Pirates who resorted to the convenient harbours formed by the many mouths of the *Indus*. In the following extract from Mr. WILFORD's essay (art. III.) in Vol. IX. of the *Asiatic Researches*, it appears that strong measures, something similar perhaps to those noticed in the preceding paragraph, have of old been resorted to with these people. Some portions of the extract do not bear on the subject now under discussion, but have reference to other parts of our work. " . . . . . It is also my opinion that the *Sardonyx* mountains are misplaced by PTOLEMEY: and indeed such is the construction of his map in that part, that there is no room for them in their natural place; and I take them to be those situated to the east of *Baroche*, between the *Narmada* and the river *Mahí*, where to this day they dig for precious stones. In consequence of this erroneous construction, the rivers *Paddar*, *Sabhra-matí*, and *Mahí* are confounded, and the whole peninsula of *Gujarát* disappears. The reason I conceive to be that the shores were not frequented on account of the vicious and untractable disposition of the natives. In the fourth century mention is made of *Diu*, under the denomination of *Dibu*, or *Divu:* its inhabitants were called *Divæi*, *Dibeni*, and *Diveni;* and it appears that this denomination extended to the whole peninsula. In the same manner, the *Mussulmans* gave formerly the name of *Soma-natha*, to *Gujarát*, from a famous place of worship of that name.

" It seems that the inhabitants of that country had, by their piracies, greatly offended the *Romans;* for we read, that they were forced to send an embassy to *Constantinople*, and give hostages for their future good behaviour, and the famous THEOPHILUS was one of them."

The history of Piracy in *India* and elsewhere would make a curious article. In these latter times we can with difficulty reconcile the forcible transfer of property with our notions of morality. But formerly it would appear that no such delicacy existed. In TURNER's history of the *Anglo-Saxons*, is the following passage:—

"In the ninth century, it was the established custom in the north, that all the sons of kings, except the eldest, should be furnished with ships properly equipped in order to carry on the dangerous but not dishonourable profession of Piracy. So reputable was this pursuit, that parents were even anxious to compel their children into the hazardous and malevolent occupation. By an extraordinary enthusiasm for it, they would not suffer their children to inherit the wealth which they had gained by it; and it was their practice to command their gold, silver, and other property to be buried with them. Inherited property was despised; that affluence only was esteemed which danger had endeared." Vol. II. ch. 11.

BRYANT has a passage in his *Analysis* bearing on this subject, and referring to the very people perhaps of whom we are more particularly speaking, viz. the people about the mouths of the *Indus*, and between that river and the gulf of *Cambay*. The *Sacæ*, here spoken of, have been thought the *Sacyas* of *India*, that is, the adherents of SACYA, or BUDHA, with which sect the territories of *Sind* and *Kutch* abound. BRYANT thus translates a passage from CHÆRILUS, who gives a curious history of the *Sacæan Cuthites*, of whose ancestry he speaks with great honour in describing the expedition of ALEXANDER the Great:—

"Next march'd the *Sacæ*, fond of past'ral life,
Sprung from the *Cuthite Nomades*, who liv'd
Amid the plains of *Asia*, rich in grain.

> They from the Shepherd race deriv'd their source;
> Those Shepherds, who, in antient times, were deem'd
> The justest of mankind."

" Yet we find," says BRYANT, " that these *Sacæ* have been by some represented as cannibals; whence we may perceive, that people of the same family often differed from one another.

" There was another custom, by which they rendered themselves infamous, though in early times it was looked upon in a different light. They contracted an uniform habit of robbery and plunder; so that they lived in a state of Piracy, making continual depredations. This was so common in the first ages, that it was looked upon with an eye of indifference, as if it were attended with no immorality or disgrace. Hence nothing was more common in those days, when a stranger claimed the rights of hospitality, than to ask him, with great indifference, whether he were a Pirate or a merchant. This is the question, which NESTOR puts to TELEMACHUS and MENTOR, after he had afforded them a noble repast at *Pylos*. ' It is now,' says the aged prince, ' time to ask our guests who they be; as they have finished their meal—Pray, Sirs, whence come you, and what business has brought you over the seas? --Are you merchants destined to any port? Or are you mere adventurers, and Pirates, who roam the seas without any place of destination; and live by rapine and ruin.'—*Odyssey*, v. 69. The same question is asked by other persons in different places, and the word which means robbers and Pirates, is said by the *Scholiast* not to be opprobrious, nor the profession culpable. On the contrary, Piracy and plunder were of old esteemed very honourable. THUCYDIDES speaks of *Greece* as devoted to this practice in its early state. But he refers to hostilities by land; but the depredation of which I principally speak, were rovers at sea, who continually landed, and laid people under contribution upon the coast: and in making these levies one of their principal demands was women; and of these the most noble and fair." *Anal.* vol. V. p. 220. 8vo Ed.

By other ancient maritime people Piracy seems to have been equally honourable; but not equally disinterested. E. M.

NOTE C.

The following memorandum from an agent of the *Jemadar* of *Kutch*[e] *Bhooj*, who holds the present power of that principality, will illustrate this paragraph[f].

"It is a vulgar error that the tribe called *Sodi*, or *Soda*, or *Sogdi*, or *Swddah*, encourage the practice of Infanticide among the *Jarejahs*, from the consideration that as the riches of their tribe consists in their daughters, the preservation of the daughters of the *Jarejahs*, would, by lessening the demand for, lessen the value of their own."[g]

[e] This town, or city, is the capital of *Kutch*. See pp. 19. 31. There written *Booje*. It is also called *Pooj-Booj*. It would be spelled, in conformity with the geographical orthography adopted in this tract, *Buj*. More classically *Buja*—it having been called after a prince of that name, surnamed BUJA KACH'HA because he reigned in *Kach'ha*, or *Kutch*. See *Asiatic Researches*, vol. IX. p. 231. E. M.

[f] See paragraph 142. of Chap. III.

[g] This is, however, a common error, if it be one. It is noticed by Captain SETON, in page 25, where, and in pages 22 and 23, some particulars of this *Soda* tribe are given. It appears that this tribe is also called *Swadah*. In the *Hindu Pantheon*, some speculation on this word is pointed to under it, or *Swadha*, in the Index, but it is not easy to trace any

The evidence of KUBIRJI is sufficient to prove, that these women only follow the practice in common with others when united to a *Jarejah;* but it may also be observed that the above reason could not operate, as neither the *Jarejahs* or any *Rajputs* ever marry a woman bearing the same family name.

KUBIRJI MEHTAH, agent of FATTEH MAHOMED, describes RAO[h] RAIDHUN the *Rajah* of *Kutch* to have had six wives—three are dead—the three that remain are

1. A *Jhulla*, or *Jalla*;
1. A *Sodi;*
1. A *Wagila.*

There is no distinction whatever in the customs of these *castes* —the ladies, from whatever *caste*, destroy their children when married to *Jarejahs;* and not when married to any other classes who have not that habit.

The *Sodi*, mentioned above, may appear to be the same people described by ARRIAN, as quoted by Major RENNEL—

connexion between its application to a tribe, and the "food offered in sacrifice to the *Dii manes*," or as a grace after partaking of such food. "In all ceremonies relating to deceased ancestors, the word *Swadha* is the highest benison." Institutes of MENU, Chap. III. v. 252. The word has other meanings and allusions. The *Edinburgh Review* for January 1807 states "SWADHA to be a goddess whose adventures are very poetically narrated in the *Brahma Vaivartika Purana*, originally a nymph of *Golaka*, the paradise of VISHNU. Her celestial charms excited the jealousy of BADHA, who perfectly represents the *Grecian* JUNO in her caprices, her jealousy, and her fury. Hurled by the goddess from the *Empyrean*, VISHNU, to console her under her banishment, gave her in marriage to the *Dii Manes*. She is the goddess of funeral obsequies; conveying to the *Manes* the offerings of men, and rewarding the latter for their piety to ancestors." It may not, as I have said, be easy to trace any connexion between this word as applied to a tribe, and to a goddess, and a sacrifice; but it might still perhaps be done, although I shall not here attempt it. E. M.

[h] In page 19, this name is spelled RAEE RAEE DHUN, by Captain SETON; and RAHI RAHI DHUN by me. E. M.

they are also noticed in the *Ayin Acberry* under the *Sirkar* of *Tatah*, by the name of *Sowrah* :—

"The country from *Behkur* to *Nassubpoor* and *Amerkote*, is peopled by the *Sowrah*, *Jareetcheh*[1] and other tribes." *Ay. Ak.* II. 145.

Whether the *Sodi* be the *Sogdi*, mentioned by the historians of ALEXANDER, must be ascertained where the sources of information are more abundant; but there are many reasons for believing that the tribes who opposed that conqueror are still existing; and that their manners and institutions are little altered from those of their ancestors. A comparison in this respect would be curious; and might be easily made by referring to the original writers, who have related, although with exaggeration, the exploits of this Hero.

The tribes, however, who opposed ALEXANDER, will not be found exactly in the same situations that they occupied at that period. They have progressively advanced into *India*; while their former places have been supplied by nations equalling them in rudeness and barbarity, but surpassing them in courage and ferocity. The *Kati*, the *Jhallas*, the *Jarejahs*, the *Sodi*, and other tribes, have successively crossed the *Indus* and obtained more southern establishments; but it appears probable that they were obliged to seek for their new settlements from necessity, and not choice; the more warlike tribes of *Arabia*, *Persia*, *Parthia*, and *Scythia*, expelled them from their own country, and forced them into *India*. A. W.

[1] *Mahomedan* writers seem to terminate this word, which evidently is *Jarejah*, uniformly in this manner; using the چ for the ج – جاریچا I suppose for جاریجا or جاریجه. *Jarejah* is, however, the usual pronunciation of the people themselves. See page 25, note. E. M.

NOTE D.

In the 171st paragraph of Colonel WALKER's Report, forming Chap. III. reference is made to this Note, for an amended translation of a *Sloka*, or verse, quoted with the view of showing how the doctrines of the *Hindus* protect women and children from violence. The *Sloka* was quoted from the *Dherma Sastra;* but is not accurately written, nor conformably to the rules of *Sanskrit* grammar. I shall therefore here also omit the verse in the original. The following is the translation given by Colonel WALKER:—

" To kill a hundred *Cows* is equal to killing a *Brahman;*
To kill a hundred *Brahmans* is equal to killing a *Woman;*
To kill a hundred *Women* is equal to killing a *Child;*
To kill a hundred *Children* is equal to telling an *Untruth.*"

This poetical aggravation of the sin of lying, is not to be received as the measure of its relative importance; for on this score the *Hindu* moral code has been found rather lax: not only tolerating falsehood in cases where there appears no necessity for it (when, indeed, it may be asked, did, or can such necessity exist?) but admitting of the contradictory combination of [k]*virtuous perjury.*

The *Sloka* translated above errs on the other side; but it is evidently not to be taken literally. In the measured language of the *Hindu* sacred books several instances occur of this *centenial* accumulation of guilt: and taken too literally they have been quoted disadvantageously, or rather unfairly; for in the above instance, how obviously improper it would

[k] This subject is discussed in p. 129 of *Hindu Pantheon.* E. M.

be to calculate, and say that the *Hindu* sacred books estimate the guilt of murdering a *Brahman*, at only the ten-millionth part of that of telling an untruth? The object of this verse and law, is evidently to enhance the turpitude of falsehood, by an exaggerated comparison with other monstrous crimes.

If the object were to interdict any other species of crime, a similar phraseology would be adopted. An instance occurs in *Remarks* (3) after Note H of Chap. V.; where we find that in stating the unlawfulness of any individual not of the warrior tribe assuming the royal prerogatives, it is said that such offender is degraded to the disgusting level "of a slaughterer who employs ten thousand slaughter houses." The passage affording a striking exemplification of that in discussion, substituting a decimal, for a centenial aggregation of guilt, I will quote it from the Institutes of MENU.

Ch. IV. v. 84. From a king, not born in the military class, let him (a *Brahman)* accept no gift, nor from such as keep a slaughter house, or an oil press, or put out a vintner's flag, or subsist by the gain of prostitutes:

85. One oil press is as bad as ten slaughter houses; one vintner's flag, as ten oil presses; one prostitute as ten vintner's flags; one such king as ten prostitutes;

86. With a slaughterer, therefore, who employs ten thousand slaughter houses, a king, not a soldier by birth, is declared to be on a level; and a gift from him is tremendous.

The object here is to prevent civil commotion in general struggles for a throne. It can be aspired to only by the *Khetri*, or military class: a *Brahman* being thus forbidden to reign. It may be imagined that these extravagant denunciations, like heavy penalties for light offences, have a contrary effect to what was intended; and that no man of whatever class was ever deterred, by the above law alone, from ascending a throne within his reach. This conclusion would not however be wholly correct. *Brahmans* are never kings. Perhaps no instance can be given of it. The existing political fiction in the Government or *Peshwaship* of *Poona*, shews the cogency of the above law.

We do not readily discern the justice of stigmatizing the useful occupation of the *oil-presser*, in the manner seen above by MENU. It is still, as it evidently has long been with the *Hindus*, a degraded business. In *Bombay* the pressers and dealers in oil are *Jews;* to the exclusion nearly, if not wholly, of every other description of men. In *Bombay* they are often called *Taly*, or *oil-men*. Their common appellation is *Yahodi*. *Jews* abound all over *India*. In the native regiments on the *Bombay* establishment they are of all ranks, from the drummer to the commissioned officer, and are very clean, good soldiers. They usually have scripture names—DAOD, for DAVID—YAKUB, or JACOB—ISRAEL—IBRAHIM—SOLIMAN, &c. Their women are named REBEKA, SARAH, &c. There are at least 5000 resident *Jews* on the island of *Bombay*. They have a synagogue; and the *Pentateuch*, and perhaps other portions of the scriptures in *Hebrew;* and are a peaceable and tolerably moral race of people. The *Borahs*, a tribe of *Mahomedans*, follow in *India* the habits of the lower classes of *Jews* in *England*. In *Bombay*, where they are very numerous, and rarely respectable, they go about the town, as the dirty *Jews* do in *London*, early and late, carrying a bag, and inviting, by the same nasal tone, dishonest servants and oth rs, to fill it with pilfered clothes, empty bottles, old iron, &c. &c.

The tribe of *Borah* have many peculiar, and very curious customs and opinions. A good account of them is wanted. E. M.

NOTE E.

Several opinions have been advanced respecting the etymology of the word *Hind*, or *Hindu*. Those *English* gentlemen who possess the greatest knowledge of the *Sanskrit* have yet discovered no authority for it in that original language.[1]

Neither is it, I have been assured by an intelligent *Yati*, known among the *Jainas;* and no *Brahman* with whom I have conversed, hath been able to trace it in his native dialect.

It is not known in the *Malabar*, or *Tamul* languages, either as the name of a country or people; and the languages of that portion of the peninsula have less admixture of foreign words than most others.

The word *Hind* would therefore seem to have a foreign origin; and the following surmise was offered to me by BAPU MET'HA, a very intelligent *Nagar Brahman*, well acquainted with *Persian:*—it seems tolerably well grounded.

In the *Sekander Nameh* of NIZAMI, the following verse occurs:—

بهندوستان پیری ازخر فتاد پدرمرده را بچین گاو زاد

B' HINDUSTAN *pìrì az khur 'ftàd*—
Pedr merdeï rà b' CHIN *gào zàd.*—

In *Hindustan* an old man fell from an ass.
In *China* a cow was born to one whose father was dead.

[1] I shall notice this point, and others that occur in this Note, in some *Remarks* at the end of it. E. M.

The *Sekander Nameh* abounds with verses of like recondite meaning. One of its commentators, *Syed* SIEF *ad* DIN, says on the above passage, that *Hind* is *dark* or *black*, the colour appropriated to the planet SATURN, under whose influences *Hind*, or *Hindustan*, is reckoned. BAPU MEHTA related this from memory.

In support of *Hind* being synonimous with SATURN and *black*, he produced the two following extracts from books of authority:—

1st. from the *Mudar al Fazel*:—

"*Hind*—The climate is known—one boundary is *China*, the other *Sind*. According to the *Ibrahimi*, *Kabul* does not belong to *Hind*, but I have heard that it does; this they say is a city on the boundaries of *Khorasan*, which is beyond *Kabul*, and one of the cities of *Badakshad*. *Hind* is in that climate which is subject to the planet SATURN."

2d. from the *Kashf al Lughát*:—

"*Zohul*—a planet well known; possessing two places in the *Zodiac*, *Capricornus* and *Aquarius*. Its place is in the seventh heaven—its colour is *black*, and its temperament cold and dry. The climate of *Hind* is subordinate to this planet." In both these works also, in explanation of the phrase پیری هند *pìrì Hind*, the commentator interprets *pìrì*, a *star*, and *Hind*, SATURN; but which, were it not for the aid of those works, might more obviously be translated, *an old Hindu*, or *an old man of Hindustan*.

Hence it would seem that *Hind* was originally applied by the *Mahomedans* to the country that we call *India*, as the climate or division subject to the planet of that name. *Hindu*, would derivatively be expressive of its inhabitants, and

Hindustan of their abode. The influx of *Mahomedans*, has, by the prevalence of their dialects, given currency to the terms, even to the extent of their general adoption by the people themselves.

Again, *Khoristàn*, now called *Khorasàn*, is the country of the Sun: *Turkistàn*, the country subject to the influence of MARS—*Turk* and *Merikh* being names of that Planet. A. W.

Remarks.

The following note from page 223 of the *Hindu Pantheon*, will show the ancient name for *India*, and illustrate this portion of the foregoing note.

" *Bharàta*, or *Bharàta versha*, is the only name formerly used by the natives for the countries that we include in the term *India*. *Hindu*, for the people, and *Hindustàn*, for their country, now generally applied by natives and foreigners, are probably of *Persian* origin. BHARATA was an ancient king of *India*, and hence Mr. WILKINS (*Hetopadesa*, p. 333.) derives its name; rejecting, of course, the supposition that the river *Indus*, (properly *Sindhu*, vulgarly pronounced *Sindh*) either gave a name to the country or received one from it: also of INDU, a name of the moon, being the origin of *Hindu*, or *Hindustan*; the *Sanskrit* having no such words."

It is, however, occasionally seen in *Sanskrit* writing; but this is no proof of its being a *Sanskrit* word. In the translation of a royal grant of land in *Carnata*, given in Volume III. of the *Asiatic Researches*, art. iii. " *Hindu Princes*" occurs, and the translator, the lamented Sir WILLIAM JONES, gives thereon the following note:—

"The word *Hindu* is applied likewise in a verse of CALIDAS to the original inhabitants of this country *(India)*; but the *Pandits* insist that it is not *Sanskrit*. Since the first letter of it appears to be radical, it cannot be derived from INDU, or the Moon; but since a sibilant is often changed into an aspirate, it has been thought a variation of *Sindhu*, or *Indus*. To that etymology, however, we may object, that the last consonant also must be changed; and that *Sindhu* is the name of a river, and not of a people."

The Royal grant where the word "*Hindu*" appears, is dated 1526 A.D. The age of CALIDAS, was determined by Sir WILLIAM JONES to have been the century anterior to our era, but this has been of late controverted.

The *Sekander Nameh*, is the History of ALEXANDER, in *Persian*. Its author, NIZAMI, died in 1180 A.D. The verse thence quoted is probably enigmatical, or contains a date. The works entitled *Mudar al Fazel* (meaning, among other things, the *Circle*, or *Seat of Excellence*) and *Kashf al Lughàt*, are *Persian* dictionaries. In the *Sharaf Nama*, another dictionary, *Hind* is similarly described as a people; and a large country, having one side bordered by *China*, and the other by *Sind*.

In a former page notice is taken of the division of the earth and seas into *climates*, by the *Arabian* geographers; and of the fanciful influences of a *Planet* over each portion. Astrologers have similarly arranged the heavens under planetary regencies. See page 141.

The name of *Syed* SIEF *ad* DIN occurs in the foregoing

Note as a commentator on the *Sekander Nama*. The prefixture of *Syed*, denotes this person to be a lineal descendant from Mahomed. Such persons distinguish themselves by wearing a green turband, and sometimes a green gown, or outer garment. If otherwise respectable characters, and this consciousness of sanctity certainly tends to make them more circumspect in their conduct, the *Syeds* are looked upon with considerable reverence. They are usually addressed by their title rather than by their names—*Syed Saheb*, or, as noticed in page 111, Mr. *Syed*. In like manner, those persons who have performed, as all true believers are required once in their lives, in person or by proxy, to perform, the *haj*, or *pilgrimage* to *Mekka*, are thereafter styled *Haji*, that is, *Pilgrim*, or *Haji Saheb*, Mr. *Pilgrim*. This also is a very respectable appellation; and such distinctions are assuredly of a tendency to render men more deserving of them.

Although not particularly in place, I will here notice some of the various methods of writing the name of the prophet Mahomed. Between this mode of writing it, and Mohamed, or Mahommed, &c. there is, perhaps, no particular preference; but Mahomet, or any way ending with a *t*, is decidedly incorrect, notwithstanding it be sanctioned by the authority of Gibbon and other imposing names. In reference to its orthography in the *Arabic*, the best spelling would perhaps be Mahammad, giving the *a*, especially in the middle syllable, rather a hollow sound, and dwelling on the medial *m*. In the *Arabic* it is written with four letters Mhmd; the sound of the medial *m* to be prolonged or doubled, as indicated by the mark ّ over it: thus, محمّد Whether this be written Mahommed, or Mohommed, or Mahammad, or

MOHUMMUD, &c. is of little moment. The *t* final, is chiefly to be protested against.

The sound of *ma*, in our word *ma-chine;* of *hum*, as our *hum;* and of *mud*, like our *mud*, will give the usual and uniform pronunciation of this important name, as nearly, perhaps, as can be. E.M.

NOTE F.

People of the *Jain*, or *Sravaka*, persuasion are very numerous in *Guzerat.*

The *Jatis*, or *Yatis*, are priests, or more properly Ascetics, for they perform no religious rite; but it is their duty to expound and read to the *Sravakas*, the scriptures, or *Sastras*, of the *Jaina* system.

The *Yatis* are people devoted to religion from their infancy. They are either the children of people (principally *Banias*, or *Kalmbies)* who devote them to this duty—or they are children of *Brahmans*, *Banias*, or *Kalmbies*, purchased while young by the *Yatis*, and educated by them.

It is frequent for *Banias* (or [m] *Wanias)* who have no children

[m] The *b* and *v* are frequently substituted for each other, in many dialects of *India;* this sect, for instance, being indiscriminately called *Bania*, or *Wania*—by the former appellation most frequently. It is usual with the *English* to call these people *Banians*, or *Banyans;* and, indeed, they call themselves so in our settlements, or where they find that term best understood. Of all sects of *Hindus*, this of *Bania* abstains the most rigidly from eating flesh: it is indeed I believe the only one that universally foregoes eating animals.—Hence probably is derived our distinction of *Banyan* day on board ship; the ration of that day, which when in full allowance occurs once a week, including no meat. See on the subjects of this note *Hindu Pantheon*, pages 347, 348. E. M.

to promise their first born to their *Sri puja*, to obtain the blessing of fecundity in their family.

They serve their noviciate with their *Guru*, or preceptor; and perform for him many domestic offices; and after a proper period, when they have arrived at a sufficient age, and made progress in their studies, they are then admitted as *Yatis*.

The ceremony on this occasion is simple—The noviciate is carried out of the town with music and rejoicing in procession, followed by a crowd of *Sravakas*, who assemble on the occasion. He is taken beneath any tree, the juice of which is milky; but generally the *Indian*[n] fig (or *Banian* tree, as we call it)—a circle is formed by the *Yatis*, and all others are excluded. The [o]hair, or lock of the noviciate is pulled out by the root, at five pulls—camphor, musk, sandal, saffron, and sugar, are applied to the scalp—he is then placed before his *Guru*, stripped of his clothes, and his hands joined.—A [p]*mantra* is pronounced in his ear by his *Guru*—he is invested then with the clothes peculiar to *Yatis*—a cloth of three cubits for his loins; one of five cubits for his head; a [q]*Kamly*, or country

[n] *Ficus Indica* of LINN. *Kabir burr* by *Mahomedans*, and *Pipala* by *Hindus*. E. M.

[o] The idols of the *Jainas*, (whom I consider as sectarists of the *Baudhas*, or worshippers of BUDDHA, itself a schism of *Vaishnava*, or worship of VISHNU) have always woolly heads. See many of these idols, some colossal to a degree perhaps unequalled, others very diminutive, among the plates of the *Hindu Pantheon*: see also some speculation on their woolly heads referred to under BUDDHA in the Index. E. M.

[p] *Mantra* is a term of considerable compass—it means a *charm*, an *incantation*, an *imprecation*, &c.—there are also *tantras*, and *yantras*, for the meaning of which I must refer to the *Hindu Pantheon*, under those words in the Index. E. M.

[q] The cloth called *Kamly* (frequently written and pronounced *Camaline* by the *English*) is in very common and extensive use in *India*. It is usually made in pieces of two or three feet broad, and five or six or more long—and generally very coarse, of a dark or black colour. Sometimes, however, they are manufactured larger, and finer, and striped, on

blanket to cover him; a [1]*Tripuni*, or water pot; a plate for his victuals, and a cloth to tie them up in; a long stick to guard himself from injury, but not to injure others; and, lastly, the indispensible instrument, a [1]*Raj-haran*, or broom, made of cotton threads to sweep the ground, to prevent him from destroying any insect.

That night is passed at a strange place; and the next day he returns to his preceptors, the initiation being completed.

A *Yati* is with the *Jainas* equivalent to a *Sanyasi* among the *Hindus*, but they deny the term.—The *Yatis* recite a verse which expresses their state: "That person who keeps his five senses under restraint is a *Yati.*"

The duty of a *Yati* is to read and expound their books to the *Sravakas;* some of whom daily attend:—at morning and evening twilight the [2]*Sandhya* is performed, with the face turned towards the East, during which no light is admitted.

A true *Yati* should live by charity; his daily consumption of victuals is procured ready dressed from the houses of *Sravakas*, *Brahmans*, or *Kalmbies;* a *Yati* may purchase victuals ready dressed from the *bazàr*, but must not dress them himself:—the fragments are thrown to animals.

spotted, black and white. Natives use the *Kamly*, as a wrapper, in one piece. I have seen great coats made of the finer sorts, and look very well; much resembling in appearance, as well as in name, our *camlet*. The stuff is, I conjecture, made of sheep and goat hair—in warm climates the covering of sheep can scarcely be called wool. E. M.

[1] These names for the water pot, and broom, used by the *Jainas*, are provincial, and do not occur generally, or in sacred writings. E. M.

[2] *Sandhya* literally means *junction*; and the ceremonies performed at the junction of the night with the morning; the day with the night; the forenoon with the afternoon, or at the meridian; are thus called by the *Brahmans*. The prayers pronounced by the *Jainas* are, from the same reason, called by the same name; but do not mean the same ceremony. A.W.

A *Yati* never eats or drinks when the Sun is below the horizon.

The food of a *Yati* consists of all kinds of grain, vegetables and fruit, produced above the earth; but no roots; such as yams, onions, &c.—Milk and [1]*ghee* are permitted; but butter and honey are prohibited.—Nothing that contains animal life ever composes part of the food of a *Jaina*.

[1] *Ghee*, or *Ghì*, is butter boiled with salt, and clarified from its impurities. When fresh and well made it is a very nice and delicate article, for culinary purposes, or wherever melted butter is required. It is eaten daily by every *Indian* who can afford it—no good meal, indeed, can be made without it. The quantity that some individuals will eat, or drink, of it, even when rancid from keeping, exceeds credibility. Large quantities are annually exported from *Guzerat*; a province yielding a great superabundance of all necessaries of life. *Ghì* is always exported and kept in vessels made of hides; perhaps of oxen or buffaloes hides; and although sometimes so large as evidently to require several hides, yet no joining is visible. These vessels are called *dapper*, or *dubber*—are of nearly a globular form, roundish at the bottom, so as not to stand well—the aperture is round like that of our bottles—large in proportion to their size—the neck is short—*dappers* are made of all sizes—some to hold not a wine glass—I once saw one in *Bijapùr* that was estimated at two hundred gallons. The method of stopping the mouth of the *dupper*, is also curious—strips of common cotton cloth three or four inches wide, and perhaps three feet long, are doubled and put four or five inches down the neck, each end hanging out nearly half the length of the strip—several strips are used; three or four, or more, and they cross each other at their doublings, forming a bag, or lining to the neck of the vessel—the ends that hang over are tied externally round the neck, with a strong cord, and then turned up and thrust down on the inside, adding to the bag before made, into which is now rammed wetted tenacious clay, which forms a secure and lasting stopper to the *dapper*.

The cloth used for this, and for every ordinary business in *India*, is of the sort called *Kàdì* when white, *Kàrava* when red, and *Hàrava* when green—when blue, I have forgotten its name. Tents, and all rough works, are made of this useful cloth, which on the *Bombay* side of *India* we, I know not why, call *Dangheri*—commonly written *Dungaree*. It may, possibly, have been so named from a manufactory of it in a very extensive village in *Bombay* of that name; a name given it from its vicinity to a hill, or *dundga*—*dund* meaning a hill in some *Indian* as well as in some ancient *European* dialects. The finest *Ghì* used on the *Bombay* side of *India*, comes from *Kranchì*, a port far north, near the mouths of the *Indus*. E. M.

Some strict *Yatis* drink no water but what hath been first boiled, lest they should inadvertently destroy any insect; it being less criminal to kill them than to destroy them in their own stomachs; and others will only drink that which is received from the house of a *Sravaka.*

A *Yati* having renounced the world, and all civil duties, he consequently can have no family; nor does he perform any office of mourning or rejoicing:—he renounces all gratifications of sense.

The object of the worship of the *Jainas* is the Supreme Being, incomprehensible, omniscient and omnipresent, whom they call ARHANG [a]PARAMATMA.

They have twenty-four *Aryhuntas*, or *Gurus*, who have appeared on earth—these were prophets or holy men, who by study and abstraction reached *mukht*, or reunited themselves with the Divinity. The names of these *Aryhuntas*, as written from the pronunciation of a *Yati*, are as follow:—

1. RISHABA DEVA. 2. AJITA DEVA, (each having the epithet of *dev*, or *deva*, meaning *divine*, or *godlike*, appended to his name, this common termination will be omitted in the rest.) 3. SAMBHAVA. 4. ABHINANDHANA. 5. SUMATI. 6. PADMAPRABHA. 7. SUPARSU. 8. CHANDRAPRABHA. 9. SUVADHI. 10. SITALA. 11. SRIANGSU. 12. VASUPUJA. 13. VERMALLA. 14. ANANTA. 15. DHERMA. 16. SAOTHI. 17. KUNTHU. 18. ARHA. 19. MALLI. 20. MUNISAVRATA. 21. NAMI. 22. NEMI. 23. PARSA. 24. VARDAMANA. With the exception of the ninth, these are the

[a] From *Parama,* Supreme, and *Atma,* soul; one of two vowels being dropped in composition. E.M.

same names as those given by Major MACKENZIE in the *Asiatic Researches*, Vol. IX. art. iv.[1]

These are the twenty-four Images which are represented in the *Jaina* Temples:—these are also called *Tirthunkar*.

The founder of the *Jaina* faith was RISHABA DEO—or REKUB DEO, as he is sometimes called. The *Yati* who gave me the principal outline of this memorandum, referred to a book, from which he said that when the Sun, MERCURY, and JUPITER were in conjunction in *Libra*, VENUS in *Scorpio*, MARS and SATURN in *Aquarius*, and the Moon in *Cancer*, RISHABA DEVA was born.

[1] The names there given, are corrected to the classical orthography by Mr. COLEBROOKE, the most learned and respectable president of the *Asiatic Society*. The first *Arhyunta*, as he is called in *Guzerat*, is in Major MACKENZIE's list, styled VRISHABHANAT'HA, being the same as the first of Colonel WALKER's, RISHABADEVA, as he is called in *Guzerat*. Several of the names have obvious mythological significations.—Among others, No. 6. PADMAPRABHA, means the glory of the lotos.—No. 8. CHANDRAPRABHA, the splendour of the moon, or of its regent CHANDRA.—No. 12. VASUPUJA, is the worship of the minor deities called *Vasus*, respecting whom I must refer to the Index of the *Hindu Pantheon*, where the reader will find them copiously discussed. No. 5. SUMATI, is a mythological female, who, on an emergency, was delivered of a *gourd*, containing 60,000 sons! This could be no common event, and the reader will find it detailed in the work just named. No. 14. ANANTA is eternity; otherwise the name of a vast mythological serpent, of whom various plates and particulars are given as above. No. 9. named SUVADHI by Colonel WALKER, is called PUSHPADANTA by Mr. COLEBROOKE—this means with flowery teeth—this writer says he is surnamed SUVID'HI, corresponding very nearly with his *Guzeratty* appellation. The armorial bearings of this pontiff was the marine monster *Makara* (COLEBROOKE)—so it is of KAMA, the god of love; another of whose names PUSHPADANVA (see *Hindu Pantheon*) or with a flowery bow, comes very near in sound to that of the ninth *Arhyunta*, or *Tirthunkar*, as they are also called in *Guzerat*, as well as in *Bengal* and *Kanara*, varied to *Titt'hayar* in the *Prakrit* dialect, and in *Kanara* to *Tirt'hùrù*, and *Tirt'hakar*. The fourth and fifth articles of Volume IX. of the *Asiatic Researches*, are on the *Jainas*, by Major MACKENZIE, Dr. BUCHANAN, and Mr. COLEBROOKE, and contain many very interesting particulars of that curious race of people, corresponding in several instances with Colonel WALKER's account of them in *Guzerat*. E. M.

Rishaba Deva was the author also of the books of the *Jaina* faith, which he verbally promulgated in eighty-four divisions. He was followed by the other *Arhyuntas;* but when men degenerated, and became exposed to death and mortality, they were reduced to writing—about 1000 years since they were abridged to forty-five, to accommodate them to the degenerate comprehension of the human mind.

A catalogue of these forty-five books will be given presently; besides these they have many other works on a variety of subjects; and some of very ancient date.

There were formerly eighty-four tribes, or sects of *Jainas* (a sect is called *Gatcha)* both among the *Sravakas* and the *Yatis*; but of these many have become extinct—the *Lounka Gatcha*, both *Yati* and *Sravaka* differ considerably from the other sects.

They are more careful of animal life—they worship the Supreme Being alone; and wholly reject the agency of *Dewtas*, and the *Arhyuntas:* they despise the worship of the *Arhyuntas* in the *Jaina* temples, and ask how an image can grant a petition?

The high priest of the *Sravakas* and *Yatis* is called [7] *Sri-puja*.

The *Sri-puja* of the *Lounka Gatcha*, or tribe, is at *Baroda*; this is his principal station; but their duty is to take a circuit among their dependents every year; the high priests of the other sects are elsewhere.

The *Lounka Gatcha* had four stations (of which one no longer exists) at which their *Thiveras* were stationed; viz. *Delhi*, *Ajimere*, and *Jalour*. These *Thiveras* are deputies, or

[7] *Sri*, holy; *puja*, worship. E. M.

legates, who are entrusted with a general superintendance over the morals of the *Yatis*.

The *Sri-puja* is chosen by adoption; generally from among the *Wannias* of the *Veesavosavar*[1] sect, which is deemed the most respectable; when the *Sri-puja* is at the point of death, the *chila* is placed on the [2]*gàdi*—his lock of hair plucked out, and the *mantra* particularly appropriated for this station, is whispered in his ear; and the assembly of *Yatis* are desired to obey their future chief.

About a hundred years ago, this sect gave birth to a new description of *Yatis*, who carry mortification to a great extreme.

It happened that a *Yati* of the *Lounka Gatcha*, disputed the mandate of the *Sri-puja*, and was expelled from his *caste*; he threatened vengeance; and that he would transfer the veneration heretofore paid to the *Sri-puja*, to himself.

He accordingly withdrew; and by extreme mortification and penance, gained many disciples, and founded the sect of *Dhundia*, which is exclusive of the eighty-four *castes*. The *Dhundia* wears only such clothes as are given to him, and only eats such victuals as are voluntarily offered by the *Sravakas*;—he can have no property—he never stirs out in the rain, for fear of killing some animal; and never sits down without first brushing the ground.—Some sweep the ground as they walk, and cover their mouth as they speak; they never wash their clothes, perform any ablutions, or cleanse any part

[1] This is perhaps the same word that is more classically written *Visuvavaswa*, meaning literally *universal good*, but applicable in a less strict sense, to temporal concerns. E. M.

[2] *Chila*, is a disciple, but here means the high priest, or *Sri puja*, elect. *Gadi*, a throne, or seat, or cushion of state. E. M.

of their person.—The *Dhundias* reject all but ten of the *Jaina* books.

A *Sravaka* is a layman of the *Jain* religion; and of course he has every necessary intercourse with the world, and conforms to its customs—marriage is considered as a civil act; and on that account it is performed by *Brahmans* hired for the occasion.—These *Brahmans* are of the *Sravaka* tribe.

The *Sravakas* also perform [b] *Sradha* and other ceremonies; their domestic worship, or *Puja*, is performed at home, either by themselves, or by *Kalmbies* engaged to perform that duty; or personally at their temples.—This should be performed daily.—The *Sravaka* should first bathe himself; then bathe the idol of the particular *Arhyunta* to which he may offer his devotions—he mixes camphor, sandal and saffron, with which he marks the idol in nine places; the mixture is left for the subsequent votaries.—These ceremonies are not performed by the *Yatis*; and they are wholly rejected both by *Sravakas* and *Yatis* of the *Lounka Gatcha*.

The *Jainas* class the religions of the world in six divisions; viz.

1. SIVA *Mutti*.
2. BUDHA *Mutti*.
3. *Veda Mutti*.
4. *Nyack Mutti*.
5. *Memangsika Mutti*.
6. *Jaina Mutti*.

Any of these *castes* except the fifth may become *Yatis*. The *Memangsika* includes *Christians*, *Mahomedans*, and every other religion, except that above denominated.

Although any of the above *castes* may become converts, yet they do not choose their disciples, or *chilas*, from the

[b] This is a ceremony in honour of deceased ancestors, and is deemed a most important one. Its rites are amply detailed in the *Hindu Pantheon*. E. M.

military class.—This, at least, is the case with the *Lounka Gatcha*.

The *Jain* temples are numerous in *Guzerat*. In their external structure they differ little from the usual architecture of the country religious buildings: the images of the twenty-four *Arhyuntas* are placed in the inside; the images are of different sizes in regular gradation to the exterior idol. The *Yatis* and *Sravakas* have no objection to any person entering these temples and handling the idols; and they are far from being averse to free communication on every article of their faith.[c]

The most remarkable circumstance of the *Jain* temples is a subterranean apartment: this is called a *Bhoiri* (a cavern) corresponding with the room above, and furnished with similar idols situated directly underneath.—The cause of this I could not ascertain. The freedom with which they permit strangers to descend, is a proof, that this apartment could not have been intended as a sanctuary, to enable the *Sravakas* to practise their religious worship during a period of persecution.

Another establishment peculiar to the *Sravakas* is the [d]*pinjripul*, or hospitals for animals and reptiles however vile.

[c] This is different from what has been observed in other parts of *India*, where the *Baudhas*, or worshippers of BUDHA, have been found very reserved on matters touching their religion. I may be wrong, but I consider the sects of *Jaina*, *Mahiman*, or *Memangsika*, *Sravaka*, and *Dhundia*, to be specific varieties, or schisms as they will call each other, of the generic faith of BUDHA—itself, as I have detailed at length in another place, a sect of the theological, or mythological grand division of *Vaishnava*. See *Hindu Pantheon*, Index, under BUDHA, and *Sects*. E. M.

[d] These curious receptacles are found in many towns of *India*, and have attracted the attention of many travellers. That in *Surat* is usually called, by the *English*, the monkey-hospital; these animals, which almost every sect of *Hindu* venerates in a greater or less degree, being the most conspicuous of its inhabitants. There is one in *Poona*. I was not

There are many of these in *Guzerat*; the name signifies an enclosure of protection.—There is also another extraordinary establishment called a *jevuti*.—This is a dome, with a door large enough at the top for a man to creep in.—In these repositories, weevils, and other insects that the *Sravakas* may find in their grain, are provided with food, by their charity, and extraordinary protection to every thing possessing life.

Among the *Jainas*, of *Guzerat* at least, there is not the least appearance of any distinction of classes, similar to those among the *Hindus*. The idea of carrying arms is contrary to their principles and faith, the great object of which is the preservation of life.

It would appear that an individual of any of the *Hindu* sects may become a proselyte to the *Jaina* faith; but by this he forfeits every claim to the character of [e] *Hindu*.

I have been assured by a learned *Brahman*, that were any *Brahman* to go to a *Jaina* temple to worship, he would be thereby degraded from his holy character, and others would not eat or drink in his [f] company. I understand that in

aware until now that these charitable institutions were founded chiefly, by the *Jainas*:—it is, however, in strict consonance with the leading tenet of their religion, 'to deprive no animal of life.' I recollect that the *pinjripùl*, or as it would be more correctly written *pinjrìpàla*, in *Surat*, is sometimes called the *Banian* hospital; indicating that the sect, or tribe of *Bania*, have the reputed merit of this ill directed instance of charity, the funds of which are suspected of frequent misapplication. E. M.

[e] This is at variance with an opinion offered by me in the *Hindu Pantheon*; it was however offered under an avowed ignorance of the subject, and I may easily be mistaken; a portion of the next paragraph accords with my opinion. E. M.

[f] Or what is understood by the term "losing *caste*:" this being however an *European* idiom, and there not being, that I know of, any corresponding expression current in *India*, I do not adopt it. I say *current*; meaning in common use among well informed natives out of the reach of our colloquial influence. The writers and *dubashes* and native *Christians*, about the persons of *Europeans*, use the term frequently; and may perhaps translate it into

Bengal, from the prevalence of the *Jaina* faith, many *Brahmans* observe the exterior rites of their own sect, yet conform to the *Jaina* tenets; but these must be considered as interested temporizers, the abuse being connived at from the prevalence of the practice, and the expediency perhaps of thus seeking the patronage of *Jainas*. Such *Brahmans* would, however, be considered by their brethren of *Poona* and the *Dekkan*, as outcasts, and to them they would not return the salute of the *nanazkàr*.

These sentiments do not prevent the *Sri-mala*[s] *Brahmans* from performing the marriage rites and the ceremonies of *Sradha* for the *Sravakas* who may employ them; nor is this deemed by the *Brahmans* as unlawful; it having, they say, no connexion with the *Jaina* religion. The *Yatis* and *Sravakas* consider marriage and *Sradha* as civil rites, unconnected with the tenets of their faith. These remarks are to be considered as applicable only to *Guzerat*:—the conformity between the principles of the *Jainas* and the *Brahmans*, may be more marked in other parts of *India*.

The forty-five works, mentioned in a former paragraph, which the *Jainas* profess to have derived from the founder of their religion RISHABA DEVA, bear the following titles—they

country dialects; but I deem it unauthorized, like many other words in common use among the *English*—*Pagoda*, for instance, as used either for a temple or a coin; *Gentoo*, &c. See hereon *Hindu Pantheon*, page 346. E. M.

[s] So named, I imagine, from their peculiar selection for the performance of the marriage ceremonies. *Mala* is a chaplet; and one of flowers (hence called *pushpa mala)* is thrown by the priest over the neck of the bride. *Sri* means *holy*—as a name of LAKSHMI, the CERES of *Hindustan*, it farther adverts to *increase*, *prosperity*, &c. See *Hindu Pantheon*, under SRI in the Index. E. M.

are written in the *basha*, or dialect, called *Maghada*, and in the *bàlbat* character.

1. *Acharyanga*—on the conduct and actions of a *Yati* in points of religion, &c. This work is comprised in 2000 books or chapters, called *granta*.
2. *Sugaranga*—on the human body, and its appearances; in 2100 *ditto*.
3. *Tahnanga*—on physiology; in 3700 *ditto*.
4. *Sumavayanga*—on theogony; a history of the *devatà*, or gods; their dimensions, &c. 16,067 *ditto*.
5. *Bhagavati*—on theology; in praise of God; forms of prayer, worship, &c. 157,502 *ditto*.
6. *Gynata-dherma-kattanga*—history of celebrated *Rajas*; 6000 *ditto*.
7. *Upa-saga-dasanga*—the history of ten celebrated *Sravakas*; 812 *ditto*.
8. *Antagher-dasangha*—shewing how the above ten saints reached the kingdom of heaven; 890 *ditto*.
9. *Anutaro-vayi*—history of the inferior deities of the heavens; 11,200 *ditto*.
10. *Purushna-vyakerna*—a commentary on religious duty; 1250 *ditto*.
11. *Vipàk sutra*—the doctrine of crimes and punishments; 1290 *ditto*.
12. *Vahi sutra*—on the generation and birth of mankind and animals; 1160 *ditto*.
13. *Rahipasani*—history of Pradasi *Raja*, illustrative of the *Jaina* doctrine of the preservation of animal life; 2078 *ditto*.

14. *Jiva bagam*—on things animated and inanimate; on charity, humility, &c.; 4700 *grantas.*
15. *Pomòna*—a dictionary of arts and sciences; 7787 *ditto.*
16. *Jambudwipa panati*—comprises a history of the earth in 4146 *ditto.*
17. *Chandra panati*—a history of the moon; 22,000 *ditto.*
18. *Nehreawali*—of the sun; 1179 *ditto.*
19. *Pushpeka*—on botany.
20. *Kalpa vatanga saka*—description of the heavenly mansions of the gods.
21. *Pushpa vatanga saka*—on the same subject.
22. *Vanedasa*—a dissertation on fire; what and how far it pervades.
23. *Utara adahain*—a religious treatise on the difference in the sects of *Yati;* 2000 *ditto.*
24. *Ahvesyuka nirjakty*—comprising the several religious avocations of the *Jainas;* 3200 *ditto.*
25. *Pinda nirjakty*—a dissertation on the soul; 700 *ditto.*
26. *Dasweh-kalak*—a ritual of penance—read and expounded during the last illness of persons of note. It seems to have in view an intercession for his transgressions; it contains 700 *ditto.*
27. *Nandi sutra*—on [h] *Nandiswara dwipa*; 700 *ditto.*
28. *Anuyugadvara*—on mind, speech, and existence; 1199 *ditto.*

[h] Nandiswara, the lord of the bull Nandi, is a compound name of Siva, who is called Isa and Iswara, and his vehicle, the bull, Nandi. See *Hindu Pantheon,* Index, under those words. Nandeswara *dwipa,* means therefore, the *dwipa,* or country, of that deity, or of Siva. E. M.

29. *Chowsaran*—an intercession, read at the decease of individuals; 63 *grantas*.
30. *Aur patcha kan*—on fastings and prayer; 84 *ditto*.
31. *Maha patcha kan*—on excessive fastings, of one, two, or three months; 134 *ditto*.
32. *Bakty perignya*—duty to tutors; 171 *ditto*.
33. *Tandula vyàli*—on fishes, and the inhabitants of the waters; 400 *ditto*.
34. *Chandra viji*—history of the moon; 176 *ditto*.
35. *Guna viji*—on the lucky marks on the human body; palmistry; 100 *ditto*.
36. *Marran saymuhi*—on death; 656 *ditto*.
37. *Devindra stuve*—a dissertation on the gods, and [1]INDRA, their chief; 300 *ditto*.
38. *Santàrak*—on sleep, rest, &c; 121 *ditto*.
39. *Kalpa sutra*—a religious treatise, read with peculiar efficacy in the months of *Shravana* and *Bhadrasped*, on the twenty-four *Arhyuntas*;[k] 1216 *ditto*.
40. *Nisit sutra*—on crimes, penance, and punishment; 815 *ditto*.
41. *Maha nisit sutra*—on more heinous crimes and their consequences; 3500 *ditto*.
42. *Vavahar sruti*—on ethics and moral obligations; 500 *ditto*.

[1] The diversified history of this important king of the firmament is given in the *Hindu Pantheon*. E. M.

[k] This work is more especially the life and institutions of VARDHAMANA, the last of the twenty-four *Arhyuntas*, or *Tirthukars*, or saints, enumerated in a former page of this Note. It is a work of great authority. See *As. Res.* IX. 310. where Mr. COLEBROOKE gives an abstract of the history of this pontiff. He deems the work to have been composed about 1500 years back—a copy in his possession is nearly 250 years old. E. M.

43. *Dasah sruti*—on life and its preservation; 500 *grantas.*
44. *Yatikalpa*—Institutions of the eighty-four sects of *Yatis*; 105 *ditto.*
45. *Brahat kalpa*—on the conduct of the followers of *Jaina*; 500 *ditto.*

Pancha kalpa—general observations on the whole of the preceding works; 1433 *ditto.*

The *Jainas* have also fourteen books of great antiquity not now in common use, but kept in a sort of sacred deposit in a few of their principal temples in *Guzerat*. These books are not written in the *Magadhi basha* as the rest of the *Jaina* books are, but in an ancient *Sanskrit* character, scarcely to be deciphered or understood by any of the learned *Jainas* of the present day.

Besides these the *Jainas* have many works on their religion, history, &c. A. W.

NOTE G.

Since this [1]paragraph was written I have had some conversation with an agent of FATTEH MAHOMED, and I annex a memorandum of what passed. His name is [*]KUBIRJI

[1] Paragraph 276. of Chap. III. p. 98.

[*] This name, in the MS. written KOOBARRGEE, and KUBEERJEE, is I apprehend correctly KUVERAJI; a cognomen from KUVERA, the *Hindu* deity of wealth. For particulars of the *Indian* PLUTUS the reader may consult the *Hindu Pantheon*. E. M.

MEHTA, and he is brother to FATTEH MAHOMED's *dewan*, the person who wrote the letter in the name of his master; whose circumstances, it will be seen, rendered it politically unadvisable to attempt any unpleasing innovation on the prejudices of the *Jarejahs*.

KUBIRJI, in reply to my question, as to the reason of the extraordinary answers returned by FATTEH MAHOMED to my letters,* on the subject of discontinuing the practice of Infanticide, said, that the peculiarity of FATTEH MAHOMED's situation with respect to the *Jarejahs*, obliged him to be extremely cautious and conciliatory in his conduct—he professes to be a servant of the RAO and acts accordingly, and never sits on the *gadi*, (or throne, or seat of state) without taking a young *Jarejah* in his arms. Until lately he never used a *palky*—he does not sleep on a cot, or bedstead, in camp; that being a privilege of the *Jarejahs*.

When he received a wound from an assassin, RAO gave him °permission to use a *palky*—were he to disgust any of the *Jarejahs*, he adds new strength to the cause of his rival HUNRAJ-SA.

The business of Infanticide concerns the *Jarejahs* alone, and the letter was written under their influence.—The *Jemadar* neither commits nor justifies the practice. A. W.

* No. 18 to 22. of Chap. IV. ° See the *Remarks*.

Remarks.

The indulgence of a *palky*, or *palanqueen*, as we sometimes see it written, is not, under some of the native governments of *India*, permitted indiscriminately. It is a mark of distinction; allowed, as I imagine, to many, perhaps most, families of rank, as a matter of course. To other individuals it is conceded as a mark of favour, purchased by services to the state; or probably by a pecuniary consideration. Certain offices too, I believe, convey the privilege of using this luxurious article. All *Europeans* in the service of the country powers, act, in this point, as they please; and their having so done has probably rendered such governments less particular in this sumptuary indulgence.

Under the *British* government there is not now, I believe, any restriction on the natives riding in *palkys*; but within my recollection there was, both in *Madras* and *Bombay*. Prior to General Sir WILLIAM MEDOWS' government (1788) no native was allowed to use a *palky* within the fort of *Bombay*, without the permission of the Governor; and I recollect that such permission used to be inserted in the order books of the fort gates in this form. "DADY NASSERWANJEE has obtained the leave of the Honourable the Governor to ride in a *palanqueen*, in consequence of his lameness—he is not, therefore, to be stopped at the gates." Not more than two or three natives were, at this time, thus indulged: the name of my worthy old friend DADY NASSERVANJI I well recollect as one. This name is a corruption of نوشیروان NUSHIRVAN, famous in the ancient annals of *Persia*. DADY, being a sort of familiar appellation like our *Father*, without meaning exactly a parent—the termination *ji*, (see page 119) has been almost universally adopted by the *Parsis* of *Bombay* and *Surat*, where most of these descendants of the ancient *Persians* reside. They affect the illustrious names of their ancestors, RUSTAM, KHUSRU, ARDSHIR, SURAB,[p] JAMSHID, HURMUZ, KURSHID, &c. Some of these, to be sure, appear rather in masquerade in their modern dress, ARDASEER, JIMSETJEE, HORMAJEE, CURSETJEE, &c.

On General MEDOWS' assuming the government of *Bombay*, I have heard that one or more of the respectable *Parsi* inhabitants waited on him to request the restriction might be taken off—his reply was characteristic—" So long as you do not force me to ride in this machine, he may who likes it." My gallant old friend never used a *palky*.

On another occasion, altogether unconnected with the subject of this note, the General exhibited his usual terseness, and disregard of precedent. The prohibition against foreigners walking on, or viewing or approaching the fortifications of *Bombay* is especially repeated and pointed. It was reported to him that a foreigner, an inhabitant of the settlement, was in the habit of forgetting the orders, and the officer inquired if it was the Governor's pleasure that they should, in this instance, be enforced. He replied, that he thought it of little moment: " friends walking on the works could do no harm; and as to enemies, the more they saw of them, the less they would like them." The fortifications of *Bombay*, are, to be sure, altogether a surprising work. To me it appears not unlikely, that the sum of labour and expense applied to their construction, would have raised one of the pyramids of *Egypt*. E. M.

[p] See page 144.

NOTE H.

Some detached memoranda on the subject of this portion of my letter (Chap. III. p. 105) have offered since it was written.—Respecting the *Karàda*, or *Karàra Brahmans*, it seems clearly established that they were heretofore, and probably still are, addicted to the superstitious notion that *The Goddess* is to be propitiated by the destruction of a human life.

This goddess is known under a variety of names; and may be worshipped by her devotees, sometimes as the dispenser of riches and blessings, and at other times as a deity whose wrath is to be deprecated, or as her worshippers may respectively be of the sect of SIVA or of [1]VISHNU.

It is already noticed in the text, that the *Karara Brahmans* are numerous in *Guzerat;* and they fully acknowledge the origin of their tribe, as well as that of the *Kokanastha*, described by Mr. WILFORD in Vol. IX. of the [2]*Asiatic Researches.* They deny, however, that they have destroyed or mutilated the second part of the *Skanda Purana*, as there stated, and assert that it is still extant.

The term *Karara*, or *Karada*, is derived from a village of the [3]*Kokan*, and comprehends a numerous tribe, who are divided into several sects: the difference in their tenets consist principally in their preference of the worship of a particular

[1] See *Remarks* (1.) at the end of this Note.

[2] See *Remarks* (2.) at the end of this Note.

[3] The low country between the sea and the western ghauts, or mountainous passes—sometimes written *Concan:* but *Kòkan*, or *Kùkan*, is the true spelling and pronunciation. E. M.

deity, and consequently in being guided by his institutions or dictates. They are supposed to be under the influence of the *Vishara boot*, or *spirit of poison*. This we may perceive to be either the cause, or the effect of the prejudice against them.

To appease the wrath of this wicked demon, they administer poison to their guests and friends—by this the spirit is gratified, and in return extends his protection to the offerer and his family. This character is probably exaggerated by ignorance or enmity: it is too horrid and extravagant to be wholly true; but it is given on such authority as admits not of its total rejection.

This prejudice against the *Karara Brahmans* has derived some credibility and weight, from a very general and popular opinion, that the *Kokan* is, in a particular degree, infested with evil spirits.

Although a *Karara*, aware of the prejudices against him and of the indignation of other tribes, unwillingly discusses this subject, yet they sometimes will admit that their tribe bear the odium of the practice: and if they should even be convinced of its spiritual expediency, they must at present be sensible of its danger:—the law and custom, humanity and reason, would now call for punishment on the perpetrator of so atrocious a deed. If therefore it be now practised, it certainly is done with all possible secrecy.

That this sect formerly yielded to their prejudices on this point to a considerable extent, there can be little doubt; though now, like many other customs of the *Hindus*, this has happily fallen into disuse: particularly, it is said, since the family of the *Peshwa* gained the ascendency in the *Mahratta*[1] empire.

[1] See *Remarks* (3.) at the end of this Note.

It deserves particular notice that the *Brahmans* of the sect of VISHNU, or the *Vaishnavas*, as well as the *Saivas*, or worshippers of SIVA, are equally implicated in the accusation of practising these savage rites.

The following anecdote is too vague to be received as any evidence; but it was related to me by several people:—

The wife of a certain *Karara Brahman* made a vow to her patron deity, that if she obtained a particular end, she would gratify him by a human sacrifice—she was favourably heard; and in searching for a fit subject, she found it necessary, from the danger of publicity, to select the victim from her own family. It was the destined husband of her infant daughter, to whom only, and that from necessity, as will appear in the sequel, she entrusted the fatal secret.

According to custom the young bridegroom was invited to a nuptial feast at the house of the bride's father; and the mother fixed on this opportunity for effecting her diabolical purpose. She mixed poison with the portion of food intended for the boy, which was put apart, as is usual, with that of his intended bride, who, entrusted with the secret, was instructed by her mother to lead her promised husband to his apportioned share. The child, however, terrified at the prospect of misfortune and her future misery, wilfully guided her young husband to another share, and saved his life, but at the expense of her father's: for the mother, observant of her daughter's conduct, was compelled to remain in silence, an agonized witness of her own approaching widowhood; as the guests indiscriminately sitting down to the repast, the fatal portion fell to the lot of her own husband.

There is another traditionary story relating to the origin

of human sacrifices, of a certain *Raja*, who having built a spacious and beautiful tank, found every effort to fill it with water impracticable. Greatly distressed, after having in vain exerted every expedient of devotion and labour, the *Rája* at length vowed to his patron deity, the immolation of his own child; if this precious offering were accepted by the grant of the boon which he solicited.

The *Raja* accordingly placed one of his children, with appropriate ceremonies, in the center of the tank, when the deity gave an undeniable testimony of his assent and gratification—the tank immediately filled with fine water, and the sacrifice was completed in the drowning of the child.

Although stories of this description are too wild for implicit belief, they yet show how generally certain impressions have been received. The following memorandum of a conversation with a *Karara Brahman* on this subject is more positive.

VISHNUPANT NAPRAI TATTIA, a *Karara Brahman*, a *gomasta* in the house of [a]HARI BHAGTY, acknowledges that his tribe bear the odium of offering human sacrifices—so he has heard, but is himself ignorant of the existence of the practice.

A *Brahman* of this sect being poor or childless, propitiates the goddess DURGA, but under another name, by killing a *Brahman* of any sect:—the more holy, learned, beautiful,

[a] HARI, is a name of SIVA. BHAGTY may be derived from BHAGA, another of his names, or from BHAGAVATI, a name of his consort PARVATI. The name of this respectable banker is usually written HURRY BHUGTY. VISHNUPANT, is an abbreviation of VISHNU PANDIT—the latter term meaning a learned *Brahman*, a philosopher—*Panditya*, philosophy. *Gomasta*, means an agent, or factor. E. M.

highly bred, rich and flourishing either in family or wealth, the more acceptable is the offering.

It is effected by treachery; and generally by an invitation to a feast, where the intended victim is treated with extraordinary respect, by being oiled, perfumed, flowers put about his neck, &c. and poison is given him in his food; which food must be presented to him by a widow. No man, or woman having a husband, will give it. VISHNU PANDIT in describing the victim, said that 'such a man as the [x]*Sastri* would be a very acceptable offering.'

Both the *Sastri* and VISHNU PANT enumerated some instances of sacrifices of this description, which have, according to common rumour, taken place. I record the three following:—

1. TRIMBAKBHAT DAVEKER, grand nephew of the *Sastri*, died at *Sattara*, from poison administered to him at the house of BABU RAO [y]TALWALKER, a *Karara Brahman*.

2. A *Telinga Brahman*, his name doth not occur, *is said* to have been poisoned at the house of BABU RAO KESU, a *Karara Brahman* of high respectability at *Poona*.

3. SEDBHAT THAKAR, a *Karara Brahman*, and *Guru*, or spiritual preceptor, of the *Sahu Rajah*, administered poison

[x] *Sastri*, means one deeply read in the *Sastras*. The person here, perhaps humorously, alluded to by VISHNU PANDIT, is his friend GANGADHER PATWERDHEN, a very learned and good man, long in habits of confidential intercourse with Colonel WALKER. The *Sastras*, usually written *Shasters*, are books of holy repute, of which the reader desirous of particulars will find some in the *Hindu Pantheon*, referred to from that word in the Index. See also note in page 8, preceding. E. M.

[y] See *Remarks* (4.) at the end of this Note.

to BIKUBA GOSAVI [a]WYNKER, a *Brahman.*—This likewise is only from report.

These or similar superstitious practices among the *Hindus,* must now, however, be considered as declining, or wholly abandoned; they have felt the progress of civilization and humanity in *India* as well as in *Europe,* and have disappeared in both countries as social manners have improved:—but there are still permitted some anomalies shocking to humanity, and strongly opposed to the benevolence generally characteristic of the *Hindu* religion. Widows burning with their husbands,[a] the practice of female Infanticide, and meritorious suicide, are of this description.

The unnatural practice also of a son supporting and exposing to the flood, a parent enfeebled by age, is perhaps to be found at this day in *India* only. It is not frequent; and if it admit of palliation, it may be found in the consideration that it is done at the desire of the [b]victim.

As more peculiarly connected with the subject of Infanticide, the custom of mothers, who have been long barren, offering their first-born as a sacrifice of gratitude to their gods, is deserving of notice. I have not, however, been able to

[a] *Wynker,* or, as I suppose, *Wyeker,* or *Wàhiker;* that is, of the town of *Wye,* or *Wahi,* in the *Kokan.* See page 153. E. M.

[a] This species of suicide is not permitted in the *British* territories in *India,* nor under the *Mahomedan* governments. At *Poona,* in ordinary and quiet times, it occurs annually about a dozen times on an average of as many years; but during the last year that I was there, it occurred but six times; it was a turbulent and revolutionary period, and the people were put out of their ordinary habits. Some of those that I attended are noticed in the *Hindu Pantheon;* where also the different kinds of meritorious suicide are enumerated. See in the Index, under *Sati,* and Suicide. E. M.

[b] This subject is discussed in the *Hindu Pantheon.* See Index under *Hindus.* E. M.

ascertain that this is done, as has been related, by leaving the child in woods to be devoured by wild beasts or birds of prey, or by throwing it into rivers. It has uniformly been described to me as most common, if not peculiar, to the fourth class, or *Sudra*,[c] and as an act of devotion. They leave the child to the service of the god, where it remains, unless redeemed by the parents, which is generally the case.

The circumstance of parents devoting their offspring to a particular deity is illustrated by the case of FATTEH SING GAIKAWAR, the presumptive heir to the *Gaikawar* dominions. GOVIND RAO GAIKAWAR, his father, married two ladies, second cousins, of the same family; GEHNA BHYE, and ANAPURNA BHYE—the former was the favourite wife; and she persuaded GOVIND RAO to dedicate his son by ANAPURNA to the service of KANDUBHA, an incarnation of SIVA, and the tutelary deity of the *Gaikawar* family. This was accordingly done, and FATTEH SING remained in the *Dekkan*, until through the interference of the *British* government he was brought into *Guzerat*, with the view of taking a share in the administration of his family concerns.[d]

Previously, however, to his entrance into business, and preparatory also to his marriage, it was deemed an indispensable act that he should be redeemed from the god, by distributing to *Brahmans*, or expending in pious acts, an equivalent to his weight in silver and gold.[e] This ceremony is called *Tula-dàn* (*tula*, weight; *dàn*, charity) and was performed at a temple of KANDUBHA's in the neighbourhood of

[c] See on the subject of the grand and subdivisions of the *Hindus*, *Ibid.* E. M.

[d] See *Remarks* (5.) at the end of this Note.

[e] See *Remarks* (6.) at the end of this Note.

Baroda, some short time before his marriage. Until this redemption be effected, the object is not deemed competent to the performance of any civil duty. A. W.

Remarks (1.)

The first perusal of the tenth paragraph of the Postscript to Colonel WALKER's Report, (page 105) whence reference is made to the preceding Note, rather staggered me—it runs thus: 'The object of their worship (*i. e.* of the *Karara Brahmans)* is MAHA LAKSHMI, to whom human sacrifices are acceptable; and the more so if the victim be a *Brahman* learned in the *Sastras.*'

I did not think it likely that human sacrifices were ever offered except to KALI, or to that terrific goddess under some of her avenging names and forms. On farther consideration, if I have not altered my opinion, I have, I think, gained a clue enabling me to account for dissonances on this point.

The principal goddesses of the *Hindu* mythological machinery are the active energies of their respective lords—their *Sakti*, as they are called: and differing from them only in sex, they are endued with coequality of potency, and are their might and glory; the executors of their divine will. To explain this fully would require the occupation of some pages, that are more appropriately devoted to it in the *Hindu Pantheon.*

PARVATI, under a variety of names and forms, KALI, DURGA, &c. among them, is the *Sakti* of SIVA, who is a personification of the *destroying* power of The Deity. LAKSHMI, in like manner under many names, is the *Sakti*, or consort, to the various forms of VISHNU, The Deity's *preserving* power. These two gods, or personifications of the justice and mercy of The Almighty, or BRAHM, being respectively symbols of *destruction* and *preservation*, we would expect to find them generally opposed to each other. And so we do; and their contests are physically represented by the poets with great fertility of genius, and splendour of imagery: "but," say the philosophers, "to *destroy* is only to *reproduce* in another form:" hence the *destructive* and *preservative*, as well as the *creative* powers of the Deity, are acting in unity of effect; and their attributes and characters occasionally coalesce. So, likewise, do the attributes and characters of their *Saktis*, or helpmates; and sometimes also their names and titles. DEVI, although more especially applicable to PARVATI as a *name* (it meaning *The Goddess*, by her own sectaries pre-eminently and exclusively so applied) is by the *Vaishnavas*, or worshippers of VISHNU, given as an *epithet* to his *Sakti* LAKSHMI, who is called LAKSHMI *Devi*; and sometimes it is likely that she will by her votaries, be designated by the epithet only: and if so, we see the authority on which Colonel WALKER may have received and written the passage, that I am now endeavouring to reconcile with my own preconceptions.

A *Vaishnava*, or votary of VISHNU, will clothe the object of his exclusive worship with the attributes of The Deity; although he might demur at calling him expressly by the name of BRAHM. A *Saiva*, or worshipper of SIVA, would do the same: this great sect have, indeed, and apparently with general assent, assumed as an appellative of their divinity, the title of MAHA DEVA; that is, The Great God; by which he is, in a manner rather anomalous, distinguished by other sects; who do not, as we might expect they would, give this sort of pre-eminent epithet to the more immediate power to whom they offer their praises. LAKSHMI and PARVATI, as the *Saktis* of the two great types of the *preservative* and *destructive* powers, are addressed by their votaries in the same strain of praise; such as is, in fact, due only to the Archetype of both their lords. The same may be said of the sectaries who adore VISHNU, not directly, but through the mediation of an *Avatara*, or manifestation. Those of KRISHNA, or RAMA, respectively called *Gokalast'ha* and *Ramanuj*, adore VISHNU in these *Avataras*, either singly or combined with their *Saktis* RADHA and SITA, who also have their exclusive worshippers, equally disposed to magnify them to the extent even of Omnipotence and Omnipresence. The same may be said of the *Sauras*, who address themselves only to SURYA, or the Sun, who shares largely also in the mixed adoration of many other sects. There are, besides, several other schisms, if we may so term them, distinct from all and from each other, who although agreeing in some important theological doctrines, attach themselves to one *Deva*, or *Devi*, male or female, or to two conjoined; as *Papists* do to one Saint, or to the Virgin, glorifying such object in language due only to GOD.

This natural arrogance, or proneness of sectaries to exalt the object of their particular adoration into the seat of Omnipotence, is, of necessity, amply discussed in the *Hindu Pantheon*, for it is of perpetual recurrence in researches into their mythology. And as each sectary is also naturally prone to teach his own doctrines, we may hence discover how liable

Remarks (2.)

Some curious particulars, connected with the present *Peshwa's* family, and other *Brahman* and *Mahratta* tribes, not very flattering to their pride of ancestry, are contained in Mr. WILFORD's chronological essay in Vol. IX. of the *Asiatic Researches*, art. iii. whence I extract the following:—

"According to the *Puranics*, PARASU RAMA, having extirpated the *Cshaitries*" (or *Kehtris*, the military class, see pages 2. 167. 207.) "and filled the earth with blood, wanted to perform a sacrifice, but could find no *Brahman* who would officiate, on account of his being defiled with so much human blood. As he was standing on the summit of the mountains of *Kokan*, he spied fourteen dead bodies stranded on the adjacent shores below: these were the corpses of so many *Mleck'chas*" (individuals of a strange or impure race) "who had been flung into the sea by their enemies in distant countries in the west. They had been wafted by the winds, and were then in a high state of putrefaction. RAMA recalled them to life, imparted knowledge to them, and conferred on them the *Brahmanical* ordination, and bade them perform the sacrifice. From these fourteen dead men is descended the *Kukanast'ha* tribe of *Mahrattas:* thus called, because, since that time, they have always *staid* and remained in the *Kùkan*.

"There were three other individuals whose corpses were similarly stranded, more to the northward, toward the gulf of *Cambay;* and these were brought to life again by a magician; and from them are descended three tribes: one of which is the *Chitpawana;* and the *Ranas* of *Udayapur*, with the *Peshwa's* family, belong to it."

From the same authority we learn that the *Karara* tribe of *Mahrattas* are descended from men who were formed of the ribs of a dead camel, by a magician, who could get no *Brahman* to assist at his nefarious rites. By his powerful spells he made men of the camel's ribs, and moreover conferred on them the *Brahmanical* ordination.

Another passage applicable to the subjects of this work, if not especially to those now under discussion, occurring near that just quoted, I will here extract it also.

"The *Mahrattas* are called *Maha-rashtra* in *Sanskrit*: *Maha*, is great and illustrious; and *Rashtra*, synonimous with *Raja-putra*, implies their royal descent; and their name also indicates that they were acknowledged to belong to the second class on their arrival in *India*, and, of course, that they were not *Brahmans*. When our new adventurers had obtained power and influence, they assumed the superior title of *Maha-rashtra*; and by striking out such letters as become useless when brought to the standard of the spoken dialects, we have *Maha-rata*, *Mahrata*, and sometimes *Mahrator*. Thus, also, we have *Surat* from *Surashtra;* and *Gujarat*, from *Gurja Rashtra*."

Concluding this item of *Remarks*, I will add that the above named PARASU RAMA, who, by extirpating the military class of *Kehtri*, one of the four grand divisions of the *Hindus*, had filled the earth with blood, was VISHNU, the *Preserving* power of the Deity, in one of his ten principal incarnations; an anomaly adverted to in the *Remarks* preceding this item. This incarnation, or *Avatara*, is detailed in the *Hindu Pantheon*, comprising also some other particulars connected with the subject of the Note to which these *Remarks* are appended.

E. M.

Remarks (3.)

The family of BAJI RAO, the present *Peshwa*, obtained a paramount ascendency over the western *Mahratta* empire in 1740; retaining their official designation of *Peshwa*, which means the first officer of the state. Being *Brahmans*, to whom an assumption of royalty is, on divine [f]authority, pointedly prohibited, they, by a political fiction, retain the title of prime minister to a nominal *Ràja*, or sovereign, who is kept in an honourable state of imprisonment at *Satara*, and to whom the semblance of homage is paid; the *Peshwa*, on succeeding to that dignity, being always duly invested with the insignia of office, by the patent of the royal pageant.

At the time of the assumption of the reins of empire by the *Peshwa*, the government and country appear to have suffered a violent partition: for the *Bakshi*, or paymaster, an office heretofore of very great dignity and power in native courts, a relation also, in this instance, of the deposed *Raja*, seized on *Berar*, the eastern portion of the empire; and being

[f] *Rajas*, or kings, must be of the *Kehtri*, or military tribe. See note in page 2. A learned *Brahman* is forbidden, in the Institutes of MENU, to accept any gift from a king not born in the military class—" With a slaughterer who employs ten thousand slaughter houses, a king, not a soldier by birth, is declared to be on a level: a gift from him is tremendous." Chap. IV. v. 84. See also page 167 preceding. In the miscellaneous section of the *Hindu Pantheon*, page 345, the reader will find some particulars, perhaps original, on the subjects of these Notes and *Remarks*. E. M.

a *Mahratta*, an inferior tribe of the military grand division of *Khetri*, he threw off altogether even the appearance of homage, by assuming the title of *Raja* of *Berar;* and fixed his chief residence at *Nagpùr;* leaving the *Peshwa* at *Poona*, the capital of the descendants of SIVAJI.

It may be thought a striking coincidence that BAJI RAO was the name of the first independent *Peshwa*, and RAGHUJI of the first *Raja* of *Berar*, the names also of the present *Peshwa* and *Raja:* the time is recent when such coincidence might have been looked upon as ominous likewise, for events portended that they were to be the last.

Bhùnsla is a patronymic retained by the *Berar Raja*, as well as by SIVAJI, the *Raja* of *Kolapore*, the head of the pirate states on the coast, as mentioned in Note B. of this Chapter. The said SIVAJI, being a lineal descendant of his namesake, the daring founder of the *Mahratta* empire, is said sometimes to speak, and even to act, on the presumption of his royal descent and claims. I have heard that in occasional effervescences of pride, the present *Raja* of *Kolapore* (I allude to him of 1798) speaks of 'the usurpers of his *Ràj*,' or government, 'at *Poona*,' with threats of reaction. But although in the present posture of affairs this may be mere bravado, ventured only when he feels himself strong, or the *Poona* government weak, yet in such shocks as that government hath of late years met with, such claims, generally believed legitimate although perhaps never severely scrutinized, backed by a man of talents and enterprize, might materially harass an unpopular or an embarrassed government.

We have lately seen what no very great portion of these qualifications have enabled an inferior member of the HOLKAR family to achieve—and we may now contemplate the growing power of one of the military adventurers under that individual. I allude to AMIR KHAN, a *Patan*, to whom JESWANT RAO HOLKAR was greatly indebted for his military successes against SINDEA and the *Peshwa*. Of all countries perhaps in the world, *India* is that where an enterprizing individual can easiest find adherents—it is redundant in a population of high spirited warrior tribes, who will follow any leader of address; he must, of all things, be active, and liberal of plunder or pay. This AMIR KHAN is perhaps the only man who now threatens to interrupt the tranquillity of *India*—but I will avoid dipping in the turbid waters of *Indian* politics. E. M.

Remarks (4.)

The penult of this name TALWALKER is, I apprehend, derived from *Talwàr*, which is a *sword*, very extensively, and in several dialects, in *India*. Its name may, I have fancied, be traced to *Tal*, or *Tala*, meaning *head*, and *awar*, a derivative from *awarden*, to bring.—*Talawar*, or *Talwar*, thus meaning *head-bringer*. I do not think it very unusual to see *Sanskrit*[*] and *Persian* words combined in names of persons and places. *Talwalker*, or *Talwarker*, or *Tarwarker*, (a sword is mostly called *Tarwar*, the *l* and *r* being convertible letters) means *he of the sword*, and was, perhaps, assumed consequent to some exertion of personal prowess. Such assumptions are not unusual; and seem generally recognized. Whether they be authorised by any patent or permission I am ignorant, but imagine not.

[*] DOWLAT RAO SINDIA, for instance, and FATTEH SING; see page 18. E. M.

A *Mahratta* friend of mine at *Poona* I recollect by no other name than that of Wagmari. He had killed a tiger.—*Bàg*, a tiger; *màrì*, an irregular derivative from *màrna*, to kill; the *b* and *w*, being, like *l* and *r*, convertible. This assumed or bestowed name, he was usually known and called by; and, if I ever heard them, I cannot call to mind what his real names were.

From *Tal*, sounding the *a* as in our *tar*, many words in eastern tongues may be derived, that have some reference to *head*. The village and place whence the river *Kàveri* flows through *Mysore*, is called *Tal-kàveri*. In the *Malabar* dialect, *Tal*, I believe, means *head*; but it is so many years since I was in the country where it is spoken, that I have forgotten what I once knew of the language. I recollect, however, that *Talamùri*, and *Taldòria*, are terms of abuse, equivalent to our *cut-throat*, but meaning rather *cut-head*. The town that we call *Tellicherry*, the natives call *Talchery*, which, or more correctly, perhaps, *Tálcheria*, means *little head*, to distinguish it from a greater promontory, or *head-land*, simply named *Tal*, or *the head* (land)—this latter we have called a *mount*, and have corrupted it to *Mount Dilly*. This is near *Tellicherry*. Farther northward, near *Bombay*, is a similar promontory, or head-land, that our navigators have rightly named after the native pronunciation—this is *Tal point*: in our charts it is spelled *Tull*. In former pages (21. 64.) *Talpurì*, and *Tilàt* occur; and both, I believe, refer to *head*, or superiority.

As well as in *Hindu* dialects, derived from their common parent, the *Sanskrit*, this vocable *Tal* may, I think, be found designative of the *head*, or bearing allusion to it, in *Arabic*, and its kindred tongues. Whence, for instance, is the word

Turban? It is, perhaps, most current in the *Turkish*, and is I conjecture spelled تربند or طربند *Terband*, literally *head-band.* Here, as in a former instance, I would suggest the *r* and the *l* to be convertible, and that authority may be adduced for reading تلبند or طلبند or perhaps طالبند *Talband*, for *Terband.* We have seen that *Tarwàr*, or *Talwàr* تروار or تلوار a compound derivative from تل اواردن *tal awardan*, *to bring a head*, is indiscriminately used as the common and extensive name of a *sword.* Again تلاب *Tal-àb* means an artificial lake, formed by a *head*, or *band*, carried from hill to hill across a valley, to retain water. *Talàb* literally is *waterhead;* and is a word in general use with both *Hindus* and *Mahomedans*, to signify a lake so formed. It is sometimes pronounced *Talào.*

Tàlà, or *Tàala*, an epithet of *The Deity*, in *Arabic* meaning the *Highest*, I would derive from the same root. Whether spelled تالا or تعلا or طالا is of little moment. I have no lexicon at hand. The same sense may be traced in *Hebrew*— תלה *Tààle*, to raise on high, elevate, lift up.

The word *band* used above as our similar word, has a similar sense in several eastern dialects. In *Persian*, and in other languages of *Mahomedan* usage, it is written بند *bnd*, and pronounced rather like the *u* in our *bun*, than our *a* in *band;* but it has very extensively the same meaning. It is applied as with us, to any thing that confines, or retains, or shuts, or encloses. A *dam*, for instance, that retains water— hence *bander*, or as it is usually spelled *bunder*, is an artificial harbour or bason, and has in time become applicable to any wharf, or place where vessels can unload: and at length to almost any sea-port. I will take this occasion to notice that

I have in the engraver's hands a chart or map from actual survey, the first perhaps that ever was made, of a great portion of the Peninsula of *Guzerat*. Not expecting to have a better opportunity, it is my intention to present it to my readers with this Tract; but at the time this sheet is sent to the press I am uncertain if it will be ready in time. Were I certain on this point, I should here refer to several places called *Bander* in it; all necessarily situated on the sea, or on a river. *Purbander*, for instance, a considerable town on the sea coast, usually written *Poorbunder*. See notes in pages 24 and 72. This town may have been named after PUR or PURU, one of three royal brothers, who appear by *Hindu* tradition to have founded empires and cities in *Guzerat*, and its neighbouring country *Kutch*. Another of them, as observed in Note C. of this Chapter, p. 163, founded *Bùj* in *Kutch*, which is still its capital, and is sometimes called *Katch-bùj*. My projected *Map* will, I believe, comprehend this city: my uncertainty respecting it has prevented me from making frequent reference to towns and districts mentioned in earlier pages of this little volume, whose locality would thereby have been more readily seen.

To conclude on the word *Bander*:—as well as extending it to a dam, a wharf, and to a harbour or seaport, we have given it also to buildings situated in the neighbourhood of such wharfs. In *Bombay* (as well as to several wharfs properly so termed) we have given the name of *The Bunder*, to a quadrangular series of barracks erected fifty or sixty years ago as a residence for the junior classes of the Company's civil servants;—it being situated close to the *bander*. These quarters were then and since reckoned very good; but they have, of late years, been found more convenient for public offices. In page 110 we find *Bandery*, for *bondsman*—and its root, as well as that of all its derivatives, is a verb equivalent to our *bind*, *close*, *shut*, &c. A prison is called *Banda-khana*, a house of *bondage*. E. M.

Remarks (5.)

In former pages I have hinted at my intention of saying something on the name and family of the present ruler of *Guzerat*. In page 94 his name and titles appear in this form (triflingly altered in point of orthography) ANANDA RAHU GAIKAWAR SENA KHAS KHIL SHAMSHIR BEHADUR. The first, ANANDA, means *happy;* and was the name of the foster father of the pastoral deity KRISHNA; another of whose names, GOVINDA, the name also of the father of ANAND RAO, has reference to his occupation of herdsman; *Go*, or *Gao*, or *Gai*, meaning a *cow*, or *kine*—hence, as I have supposed in the note in page 62, the patronymic of the *Gaikawar* family. It would perhaps be straining etymology too far to derive the termination of this name from the same verb as *Talawar*, *head bringer*, discussed in the preceding item of *Remarks*. If this were permitted, *Gai-ka* is, in the genitive case, *of kine*; *awar*, a *bringer*, from *awardan*, *to bring*, as before noticed. In composition, when two vowels meet, as final and initial, one is dropped, and we have *Gai-ka-war*. This style of compound is admitted by the idiom of several *Indian* dialects. *Ganjawar* گنجاور for instance, the *bringer* of [h] *treasure*—*Ganj* meaning a *magazine*, or *riches*, or *treasure*.

[h] Hence the usual *Indian* name of playing-cards—a little varied to *Gunjeefer*, as commonly pronounced. E. M.

This name is well applied to a lucky ship belonging to the port of *Bombay*, a little altered to *Gunjàva*. *Gai-ka-war-è*, may mean also the *place*, or *quarter* of kine—*war*—*warry*, or *war-è*; having that meaning. *Kattywàr*, the name of *Guzerat*, may thus be the country of the tribe of *Katty*, formerly the chief occupiers of that province. See note in page 23, and page 165.

RAHU, the medial of the three first names, is usually spelled RAO, or ROW; but I apprehend more correctly RAHU, from the hero of the Nodes. RAHU's head, being the *Dragon's* head, or ascending node, and his body, KETU, the tail, or descending node. As an instance of the wildness of *Hindu* science, and how blended every thing is with their extravagant mythology, hanging, or hinged, on it as it were, I refer the reader to a note containing the history of RAHU in page 282 of the *Hindu Pantheon*, descriptive of the eighty-eighth plate of that work, representing an ancient *Zodiac* and *Solar system* of the *Hindus*. From RAHU, as well as the names or titles, *Rao*, or *Row*, or *Rau*, as they are pronounced among the *Mahrattas* and other *Hindu* people, I am disposed to derive those also, locally pronounced *Rai* or *Rahi*, *Raya*, *Ruhi* or *Roi;* or as they are sometimes written *Raee* (p. 19) *Roee* (p. 32) &c. Most of these are, or have been, high titles, indicating independence, and almost royalty. Even now a chief is sometimes called, The *Ràhu*, or The *Ràhì*, The *Rùhì*, or The *Ràya*, or The *Ràja*, almost indiscriminately. The latter is the *Sanskrit* word; the others are popular. In some provinces *Ràna* and *Rànì*, designate the male and female personages of the first rank.

The three next names or titles of ANANDA RAHU GAIKAWAR, are SENA KHAS KHIL.—These I supposed were a part of the *alkàb*, or title, granted by the King, or *Great Moghul* as we call him, to princes on accession, or before, or at any time, to almost any person of rank who may choose to apply through the proper channel, and go to the expense of forty or fifty pounds in fees on taking out the patent. Of this something occurs in page 126. But the three names in question are said not to be part of the King's *alkàb;* but titles assumed by, or granted to, PILAJI, an ancestor of the *Gaikawar* family, and the founder of it in the *Gadi*, or *Raj*, or Government of *Guzerat*. This happened, as I learn from WARING'S *History of the Mahrattas*, in 1730, as will be noticed presently. He says, that PILAJI GAIKAWAR, received from the *Sahu Raja* of *Sattera*, "the title of *Sena Khas Khyl Shamsher Buhadur*," p. 142. The meaning of the three first names or titles I do not know; they are, I apprehend, *Mahratta*, or corrupt *Sanskrit* words—the next, which I spell *Shamshir Behàdur*, are *Persian* شمشیر بہادر, and mean the *Hero of the drawn sword*. This flaming title sounds largely in *English*, but is much tamer in *India*, where, although it may formerly have been a high and dignified title, it is now very common, being given not only as a title, but as proper names, singly and together. Of *Behadur* some notice is taken in a note in page 111. The word in strictness means of *pearl* (like) *value*. SHAMSHIR BEHADUR, is the name of a chieftain with whom we have had lately some discussions relative to the province of *Bandelkand*, ceded to us for a valuable consideration by the *Peshwa*. He is the son of ALLY BEHADUR; who in WARING'S History of the *Mahrattas*, p. 229, is stated to be the illegitimate offspring of the great BAJI RAO. Among some memoranda made at *Poona*,

I find a paragraph, at variance, in some points, with this. I will here give it; and crave indulgence while I digress to discuss a topic that arises out of it, bearing on the subjects of this work.

"ALLY BEHADUR is the natural son of a former *Peshwa*, (I believe of NARAYAN RAO, father of the late MADHU RAO) by a *Moghul* dancing girl. A *Brahman's* son, by so impure a mother, could not inherit the holiness of his father's class; and, rather than reduce him to a degraded tribe, the child was made a *Mussulman*, and has been educated in that religion. ALLY BEHADUR has ever been highly countenanced by the reigning family and party; considered by them, indeed, as a relative and friend. He is at present at the head of a considerable army in the north, on *Mùlkgìrì*, and SINDEA wishes his removal thence. His son, SHAMSHIR BEHADUR, is now at *Poona;* a very fine lad about sixteen. I have seen him in the *durbar* treated with great distinction; little short of that shewn to the *Peshwa's* family, of whom, indeed, he seems to be considered as one." This memorandum was written in 1798.

The term *Mulkgiri* used above, means plundering, or levying contribution. A native, especially a *Mahratta*, officer, at the head of a body of troops out of employ, if he have no other immediate object in view, will move about from town to town, demanding and receiving from such towns, a sum of money, clothes, provisions, &c. adequate, in the estimation of the officer, to their means, or to his wants. It is not unusual in *India* for partizans to collect a body of men, sometimes only a few hundreds, sometimes several thousands, and forming them into something of the appearance of soldiers, let them, and himself, out to any prince or adventurer in want of aid, at so much a month. The bargain generally is so much for himself, so much for every *European*, for every gun, and for each horse and man. Regular musters are admitted. Or sometimes the bargain is, to the Commander a certain sum, and a gross sum for so many battalions of a given strength in men and guns. The hired party furnishes every thing—pay, provisions, guns, arms, tents, bullocks, ammunition, repairs, &c. &c. and receives every month after muster, a gross sum. Some of these corps are commanded by *Europeans; English*, or *French*. One respectable corps of this description was commanded by my friend Mr. BOYD, an *American* gentleman, now a Colonel of militia, and a member of Congress in the United States. It was of the following strength, as near as I can recollect; but I do not pretend to be very exact. Three battalions, each of about 500 men, armed with firelocks, and clothed and disciplined like our Sepoys—a smaller irregular corps called *Najib*, who armed and clothed themselves as they pleased, with matchlocks, swords, targets, pistols, bows, &c. These were taught very little—they fire well in their own way, and are formidable troops, but do nothing very connectedly. He had six guns, four and six pounders, each attended by one or two *European* gunners. Three or four elephants, for state and for moving heavy baggage—and as many *English* officers. To his second in command he gave about 600 rupees a month—at the time I speak of, his second was my able friend Mr. TONE, who was since killed in an attack on a fort. To the other officers, one, two, or three hundred rupees each.

This corps, as far as regarded arms and every sort of

equipment was the sole property of Colonel BOYD; and he took service with any power or person in want of troops. In the course of a few months I have known it in several different services. He, with his corps, was once in the pay of TUKAJI HOLKAR, father of the present varied characters of that surname:—afterwards in the *Peshwa's* service:—disliking that, he quitted the *Mahratta* employ and territory, and marched to *Hyderabad*, where he was hired by the minister AZIM AL OMRA, for the service of NIZAM ALLY KHAN. After two or three months, on some supposed slight, he demanded his dismission, and marched with his corps back to *Poona*, where soon after, having no eligible offer of service, and being desirous of returning to *America*, he disposed of his elephants, guns, arms and equipment, to Colonel FILOSE, a *Neapolitan* partizan in the service of DOWLAT RAO SINDEA—paying all his adherents their arrears, and discharging them. At the time he was last out of employment at *Poona*, where such expenses and no income would soon ruin any individual, I have heard him express his apprehension that he should be forced to go on *Mulkgiri*. This shows the estimation in which such land piracy, for such it really is, is held in the *Mahratta* territories. Their idea of piracy by sea may be gathered in Note B. of this Chapter. It would have been a measure of necessity, and by no means of that moral enormity which at first attaches to the idea in the mind of western people. No man is more averse to immoral or ungentlemanly conduct than Colonel BOYD. When at *Paris*, in the year 1808, it was discovered that he had been in the service of some of the native powers of *India*. That vigilant Government did not overlook such a circumstance, but endeavoured to engage

Colonel BOYD's services in furtherance of the projects which BUONAPARTE was then supposed to have in contemplation against our eastern colonies.

The names and titles of ANANDA RAHU GAIKAWAR, have been sufficiently discussed. I request now, returning from the preceding digression, to be allowed to offer a few lines on the subject of his family.

After the death of that successful villain ALLAM GIR, in 1707, better known in *Europe* by his princely name of [i]AURANG ZEB, the other having been assumed with the throne of *India*, the mighty kingdom that his genius had united, fell to pieces from the contentions of his sons; and the other moral effects inevitably resulting from the political construction of such baseless fabrics as eastern empires mostly are.

Among the conquests of the *Moghul* arms by ALLAM GIR and his ancestors, was *Guzerat*, which province, in the form of a little kingdom, had till then been ruled by its native *Hindu Rajas;* who, it is probable, had been compelled by SIVAJI, the consolidator of the *Mahratta* empire, to a nominal subjection: to the extent perhaps of paying some tribute to the head of the state, and an engagement to support it with a certain contingent of troops in case of need.

A branch, or connection of the *Guzerat* family appears to have resided at *Talagaum*, a large town near *Poona*, expelled

i AURANG ZIB اورنک زیب means The *Ornament* of the *Throne*. ALLAM GIR, or AALAM GIR, عالم کیر was the name or title assumed by this prince on obtaining the empire. It means *Seizer* of the *World*. He was, however, after his accession, called by both names united. I have seen many, and have in my possession some coins of his impressed AURANG ZIB AALAM GIR. E. M.

probably by the conquerors; and to have been either distinguished by the title of *Dhabàry*, or *Dhabàrya*, or to have connected itself with a respectable family of that surname. TRIMBAK RAO *Dhabàry*, about the year 1724, quarrelled with the *Mahratta* Government, and taking the field was defeated and killed by the *Peshwa* BAJI RAO. His widow AMMA BHYE, remained at *Talagaum;* and ESWANT RAO her son fled to the *Moghuls* for safety and assistance. PILAJI GAIKAWAR was a general in the service of the *Dhabary*, and shortly after his death (1726) we find PILAJI leading an army in the name, and apparently under the authority, of AMMA BHYE, into *Guzerat*, at that time governed on the part of the King (or *Great Moghul)* by SHUJAET KHAN, who was defeated; and the province in the course of three or four years was in a great measure conquered by PILAJI. He compelled the *Mahomedans* to cede half *Guzerat* to AMMA BHYE; and she, having during these contests, although exactly how doth not appear, lost all her sons, adopted her victorious General PILAJI, who being thus raised to the *Gadi* was confirmed therein by the *Sahu Raja* of *Satara* (the head of the *Mahratta* empire) and received also the title, as before mentioned, of SENA KHAS KHIL SHAMSHIR BEHADUR. PILAJI was thus the founder of the *Gaikawar* dynasty in *Guzerat*.

Continuing his successes, he or his son DAMAJI, took *Baroda* in 1731; and he died in the following year, and was succeeded by DAMAJI.

In the troubles incident to newly acquired or recovered states, we find DAMAJI in arms against the *Peshwa;* and somehow in league with the *Dhabary* family of *Talagaum*, sustaining a defeat, in which both he and his ally were taken prisoners. This event, which took place in 1748, is differently related. The friends of the *Peshwa* state it as the result of a rebellious coalition between the *Gàikawar* and *Dhabarya* families; and the latter as an act of treachery on the part of the *Peshwa;* who, on a *banderry* (see page 110) of personal security, got DAMAJI into his power, and in violation of his promise, imprisoned him, and imposed on him very severe conditions as the price of his liberty. In these varied statements both parties probably tell the truth, but neither of them the whole truth.

The conditions are said to have been these: the payment, or engagements for the payment, of 1,500,000 *rupees;* about a million and a half sterling—the cession of the revenues of half his country; this amounted to six *lakhs* annually, or about 60,000*l.*, to the *Peshwa* in perpetuity; and in acknowledgment of the *Peshwa's* authority, to keep a contingent of 10,000 horse, in readiness for the service of the state when called for.

These conditions indicate that the wealth and means of the *Gaikawar* were estimated highly. *Guzerat* is certainly a very productive province, furnishing its own great population with abundance of the necessaries and comforts of life, and a great surplus that is exported. DAMAJI had, however, at this time annexed the rich city and province of *Cambay* to his other acquisitions; and in the restlessness of his disposition, carried his arms into the contiguous kingdom of *Kutch;* and, as it would appear, with success; for, as related in pages 18. 30. 70. he induced RAHU LAKPAT, the *Jarejah Rajah* of that country, to yield to him in marriage his daughter DANKUR

Bhye, who, contrary to the usage of that tribe, had, by her extraordinary beauty, elicited a maternal spark from the hard heart of her murderous parent. This concession we may suppose to have been the consequence of coercion; for the high minded *Jarejah*, exalted among the tribes of the second, or military grand division of *Khetri*, would deem it a derogation to match his daughter to a *Mahratta;* who, although of the same grand division, is of a tribe but just elevated above baseness. (See on this subject pages 2, 206; and Note D. of this Chapter.)

Damaji died in 1768. Four sons survived him—Sayaji, Fatteh Sing, Govind Rao, and Manaji. I am not sure which of the two last was the eldest. From some recollections I incline to the seniority of Govind Rao; although other points lead to the other conclusion. Very little, however, occurs of Manaji. Another of Damaji's sons died before him—his name was Devaji Rao. Sometimes he is called *Dewan* Devaji (see page 119) from having acted for many years in certain districts, as a sort of viceroy or deputy to his father, with whom, however, he was not always on good terms.

Sayaji and Fatteh Sing were the first born; but Govind Rao was by a superior wife; and this gave rise to family quarrels as to the succession. On reference to *Poona*, it was decided, conformably to the *Sastra*, that the first born should succeed. But the first born, Sayaji, was blind, and thereby incapacitated; and this afforded scope for the introduction of the ever-ready eastern engines of presents and bribes. In one or both of these shapes the *Peshwa* Madhu Rao received, or was promised, seventy *lakhs* of rupees from

FATTEH SING, for the *Sanads* (or *Sunnuds)* or patent, and the *Kheldt*, or dress of investiture, for the Government of *Guzerat*.

At this time, or soon after, the *Peshwa's* family was in as unsettled a state as that of the *Gaikawar:* for the *Peshwa* MADHU RAO, and his powerful and able uncle RAGHUVA, had for some time distracted the empire by their violent dissensions. A reconciliation took place; and the *Peshwa* dying in 1772, placed his young brother NARAYAN RAO under the especial care of his aspiring uncle, who, the following year, basely murdered him, and assuming the authority of *Peshwa*, issued *Sanads*, &c. for *Guzerat* to GOVIND RAO GAIKAWAR, who forthwith repaired to *Guzerat*, and levied troops to wrest the Government from his half brother FATTEH SING.

GOVIND RAO is said to have given RAGHUVA twenty-two *lakhs* of rupees for the *Sanads* of *Guzerat*. But the Regicide having been forced by the just indignation of his countrymen, as noticed in page 135, to flee from his usurped capital, took refuge in *Bombay*, where he was, from the mistaken policy of that Government, encouraged in his views; and thus supported, proceeded toward *Guzerat*, of course expecting GOVIND RAO to make common cause with him.

I will stop here for a moment to observe that the murdered NARAYAN RAO left a widow. The assassins were about to murder her also, but felt some "compunctious visitings" from her state of pregnancy, which, however, did not deter her from a vow of becoming *Sati*, or self-devoted to the flames, with her husband's corpse. But this was denied; in such a state, indeed, it is never allowed, and in this case, moreover,

radii from the lips of the base-born damsel. During this march, uncalled for in a military point of view, the army laid waste scores of towns and thousands of acres; indeed whole districts—we fought battles, stormed forts, destroyed a large army, and ran every military risk, at a time when our essential co-operation with the army of Lord CORNWALLIS (my kind and deeply regretted friend) at *Seringapatan*, was eagerly looked for. "What great effects arise from little things."

The *Bhao* was said to have been weighed against gold and silver, amounting to eight or ten thousand rupees (1200*l.*) A son held each scale. ORME (*Fragments*, p. 60. Note XXVIII.) notices the weighing of SIVAJI, in the year 1674. His weight was 16,000 *pagodas;* about 7000*l.* which was given to the *Brahmans.* He is said to have given to them, and in charity, a *lakh* of *pagodas* more (upwards of 40,000*l.*), and a like sum in rewards to officers. E. M.

NOTE I.

Extract from BRYANT'S *Analysis of Ancient Mythology.* Vol. VI. 8vo Edition.

One would think it scarce possible, that so unnatural a custom, as that of human sacrifices, should have existed in the world; but it is very certain that it did not only exist, but almost universally prevail. I have before taken notice, that the *Egyptians* of old brought no victims to their temples, nor shed any blood at their altars; but human victims and the blood of men must be here excepted, which at one period[l] they most certainly offered to their gods. The [m]*Cretans* had the same custom; and adhered to it a much longer time. The natives of *Arabia* did the same. The people of [n]*Dumah* in particular sacrificed every year a child, and buried it underneath an altar, which they made use of instead of an idol; for they did not admit of images. The *Persians* buried people alive. AMESTRIS,[o] the wife of XERXES, entombed twelve persons quick under ground for the good of her soul. It would be endless to enumerate every city, or every province, where these sad practices obtained. The [p]*Cyprians*, the *Rhodians*, the *Phoceans*, the *Ionians;* those of *Chios*, *Lesbos*, *Tenedos*, all had human sacrifices. The natives of the *Tauric Chersonesus* offered up to DIANA, every stranger whom chance threw upon their coast. Hence arose that just expostulation in EURIPEDES (IPHIG. in *Tauris)* upon the inconsistency of the proceeding, wherein much good reasoning is implied. IPHIGENIA wonders, as the goddess delighted in the blood of men, that every villain and murderer should be privileged to escape; nay, be driven from the threshold of the temple; whereas if an honest and virtuous man chanced to stray thither, he, only, was seized upon and put to death. The *Pelasgi*, in a time of scarcity, vowed the tenth of all that should be born to them, for a sacrifice in order to procure plenty. ARISTOMENES the [q]*Messenian* slew

[l] EUSEB. *Præp. Evan. lib.* 4. *cap.* 16. ARNOBIUS, *lib.* 2.

[m] ATHANAS. *Orat. ad Gentes.* HERODOTUS says the same of the *Scythians.* See also PORPH. *de abstinentiâ, lib.* 2.

[n] PORPHYRY, as above. These people are also mentioned in ISAIAH, chap. 21. "The burthen of the desert of the sea."—"The burthen of *Dumah.*"

[o] PLUTARCH.

[p] CLEM. ALEX. vol. I. See also PORPHYRY, as before.

[q] CLEM. ALEX. and PORPHYRY, as above.

three hundred noble *Lacedemonians;* among whom was THEOPOMPUS the king of *Sparta*, at the altar of JUPITER at *Ithome*. Without doubt the *Lacedemonians* made ample return; for they were a severe and revengeful people, and offered the like victims to MARS. Their festival of the [r]*Diamastigosis* is well known; when the *Spartan* boys were whipped in the sight of their parents with such severity before the altar of DIANA *Orthia*, that they often expired under the torture. PHYLARCHUS, as quoted by PORPHYRY (*de abstin.* lib. 2.) affirms that of old every *Grecian* state made it a rule, before they marched towards an enemy, to solicit a blessing on their undertakings by human victims.

The *Romans* were accustomed to the like sacrifices. They both devoted themselves to the infernal gods, and constrained others to submit to the same horrid doom. Hence we read in TITUS LIVIUS (lib. 22. cap. 57. *Zonaræ annales*, lib. 8. cap. 19.) that in the consulate of ÆMILIUS PAULUS and TERENTIUS VARRO, two *Gauls*, a man and a woman, and two in like manner of *Greece*, were buried alive at *Rome* in the Ox-market, where was a place under ground walled round to receive them, which had before been made use of for such cruel purposes. He says it was a sacrifice not properly *Roman;* that is, not originally of *Roman* institution: yet it was frequently practised there, and that too by public authority. PLUTARCH makes mention of a like instance a few years before, in the consulship of [s]FLAMINIUS and FURIUS. There is reason to think that for a long time, all the principal captives who graced the triumph of the *Romans*, were at the

[r] PLUTARCH, *Inst. Laconicæ.* He says that the cruelty lasted all day long.

[s] In *Marcello*, vol. IV. p. 547. Ed. H. STEPH. See DIONYSIUS *Hal. Hist. lib.* I.

close of that cruel pageantry put to death at the altar of JUPITER *Capitolinus*. CAIUS MARIUS offered up his own daughter for a victim to the *Dii Averrunci*, to procure success in a battle against the *Cimbri;* as we are informed by DOROTHEUS, quoted by CLEMENS. *(Cohort.)* It is likewise attested by [1]PLUTARCH *(paral. 20.mum)* who says that her name was CALPURNIA. MARIUS was a man of a sour and bloody disposition, and had probably heard of such sacrifices being offered in the enemy's camp, among whom they were very common: or he might have beheld them exhibited at a distance, and therefore murdered what was nearest, and should have been dearest, to him, to counteract their fearful spells, and outdo them in their wicked machinery. CICERO *(pro Fonteio,* § 10) making mention of this custom being common in *Gaul*, adds that it prevailed among that people, even at the time when he was speaking: whence we may be led to infer, that it was then discontinued among the *Romans*. And we are told by PLINY *(Nat. Hist.* lib. 30. cap. 1.) that it had then, and not very long, been discouraged; for a law was enacted, when LENTULUS and CRASSUS were consuls, so late as the 657th year of *Rome*, that there should be no more human sacrifices: till that time those horrible rites had

[1] The name of this person in PLUTARCH is MANIUS: whoever it may have been, the fact is the same: it takes not at all from the evidence of the history. BRYANT. CALPURNIA might be traced to a *Sanskrit* source—*Cal*, or *Kal, Time*—hence KALA, a name of SIVA in his *Saturnian* character; and KALI, his consort; another of whose names is ANA-PURNA; the latter word meaning *abundance, fulness*—if this epithet were appended to KALI, which however I never saw or heard, it would be pronounced very similarly to the name of the victim in PLUTARCH. See *Hindu Pantheon*, Index, under the above names. ANA-PURNA occurs as a proper name in page 199 preceding, and some comment offered thereon in *Remarks* (5.) after Note H. of this Chapter. E. M.

been celebrated in broad day, without any mask or controul; which, had we not the best evidence for the fact, would appear scarcely credible. And however discontinued they may have been for a time, we find that they were again renewed, though they became not so public nor so general: for not very long after this it is reported of AUGUSTUS CÆSAR, when *Perusia* surrendered in the time of the second *Triumvirate*, that besides multitudes executed in a military manner, he offered up upon the *Ides* of March, three hundred chosen persons both of the *Equestrian* and *Senatorian* order. (SUETONIUS, cap. 15.) Even at *Rome* itself this custom was revived, and PORPHYRY (*de abstin.* lib. 2. p. 226.) assures us, that in his time a man was every year sacrificed at the shrine of JUPITER *Latiaris*. HELIOGABALUS offered the like victims to the *Syrian*[u] deity, which he introduced among the *Romans*. The like is said of AURELIAN.

The *Gauls* and *Germans* were so devoted to this shocking custom, that no business of any moment was transacted among them, without being prefaced with the blood of men. They were offered up to various gods; but particularly to HESUS, TARANIS, THAUTATES. These deities are mentioned by LUCAN (*Phars.* lib. 1. v. 444.) where he enumerates the various nations who followed the fortunes of CÆSAR.

The altars of these gods were far removed from the common resort of men; being generally situated in the depth of woods, that the gloom might add to the horror of the operation, and

[u] XIPHILIN. *in* HELIOGAB. VOPISCUS *in* AUREL. These customs prevailed in most parts of the *Roman* empire till the time of ADRIAN, who took great pains to have them abolished, but could not entirely effect it. EUSEB. *Præp. Evang. lib.* 4. *cap.* 15. and PALLAS, quoted by PORPHYRY, as above.

give a reverence to the place and proceeding. The person s devoted were led thither by the *Druids*, who presided at the solemnity, and performed the cruel offices of the sacrifice. (CÆSAR, *de Bell. Gall.* lib. 6.) TACITUS takes notice of the cruelty of the *Hermunduri* in a war with the *Catti*, wherein they had greatly the advantage; at the close of which they made one general sacrifice of all that was taken in battle. (*Ann.* lib. 13. cap. 57.) The poor remains of the legions under VARUS suffered in some degree the same fate. (*Ibid.* lib. 1. cap. 61.) There were many places destined for this purpose all over *Gaul* and *Germany*; but especially in the mighty woods of *Arduenna*, and the great *Hircinian* forest; a wild that extended above thirty days' journey in length. The places set apart for this solemnity were held in the utmost reverence, and only approached at particular seasons. LUCAN (lib. 3. v. 399.) mentions a grove of this sort near *Massilia*, which even the *Roman* soldiers, though commanded by CÆSAR, were afraid to violate. CLAUDIAN compliments STILICO, that among other advantages accruing to the *Roman* armies through his conduct, they could now venture into the awful forest of *Hercinia*, and follow the chase in those much-dreaded woods, and otherwise make use of them.

These practices prevailed among all the people of the north of whatever denomination.[x] The *Massagetæ*, the *Scythians*, the *Getes*, the *Sarmatians*, all the various nations upon the *Baltic*, particularly the *Suevi* and *Scandinavians*,

[x] The learned author here quotes and refers to various works in proof of this assertion—these references, and the quotations, I omit—they show the existence of holy homicide among the *Goths*, the *Franks*, the *Sicambri*, the *Rugians*, the *Danes*, the *Norwegians*, the *Britons* in the island of *Mona*, and other nations. Numerous authorities are also cited for the facts stated in this and following paragraphs. E. M.

held it as a fixed principle, that their happiness and security could not be obtained, but at the expense of the lives of others. Their chief gods were THOR, and [y]WODEN, whom they thought they could never sufficiently glut with blood. They had many very celebrated places of worship; especially in the island *Rugen*, near the mouth of the *Oder;* and in *Zeeland:* some too very famous among the *Semnones*, and *Naharvalli*. But the most reverenced of all, and the most frequented, was at *Upsal*, where there was every year a grand celebrity, which continued for nine days. During this term they sacrificed animals of all sorts; but the most acceptable victims, and the most numerous, were men. Of these sacrifices none were esteemed so auspicious and salutary as a sacrifice of the prince of the country. When the lot fell for the king to die, it was received with universal acclamations, and every expression of joy; as it once happened in the time of a famine, when they cast lots, and it fell to king DOMALDER to be the people's victim; and he was accordingly put to death. Another prince was burnt alive to WODEN. They did not spare their own children. HARALD the son of GUNILD, the first of that name, slew two of his children to obtain a storm of wind—" He did not let," says VERSTEGAN in his *Antiquities*, " to sacrifice two of his sons unto his idols, to the end he might obtain of them such a tempest at sea, as should break and disperse the shipping of HARALD king of *Denmark*." A like fact is mentioned by another author, who speaks of the persons put to death as two very hopeful young princes.

[y] That the WODEN of the *Edda*, is the same deity as the BUDHA of the *Hindus*, might, I think, be shown with a great appearance of plausibility. But this is no place for the attempt. E. M.

Another king slew nine sons to prolong his own life; in hopes, I suppose, that what they were abridged of, would in great measure be added to himself. Such instances however occur not often; but the common victims were without end. The awful grove at *Upsal*, where these horrid rites were celebrated, is described as not having a single tree but what was reverenced, as if it were gifted with some portion of divinity: and all this, because they were stained with gore, and foul with human putrefaction.

The manner in which these victims were slaughtered were diverse in different places. Some of the *Gaulish* nations chined them with the stroke of an axe. The *Celtæ* placed the man who was to be offered as a sacrifice, upon a block, or an altar, with his breast upwards; and with a sword struck him forcibly across the *sternum:* then tumbling him to the ground, they, from his agonies and convulsions, as well as from the effusion of blood, formed a judgment of *future events. The *Cimbri* ripped open the bowels, and from them they pretended to divine. In *Norway* they beat men's brains out with an ox-yoke: in *Iceland*, by dashing them against a stone. In many places they transfixed them with arrows; suspending the bodies, after death, on trees, and there leaving them to putrefy. One of the writers above quoted, (ADAM *Bremensis*, who wrote in the tenth century) mentions that in his time, seventy carcases of this sort were found in a wood of the *Suevi*. Another author of nearly the same age (A.D. 976) speaks of a place called *Ledur* in *Zeeland*, where every year there were ninety and nine persons sacrificed to the god SWANTOWITE. During these bloody festivals a general joy

* In the *Hindu* ritual, similar sources of augury are pointed out. E.M.

prevailed, and banquets were most royally served. They fed, and caroused, and gave a loose to indulgence, which at other times was not permitted. They imagined that there was something mysterious in the number nine: for which reason these feasts were in some places celebrated every ninth year; in others every ninth month; and continued for nine days.[a] When all was ended they washed the image of the deity in a pool, on account of its being stained with blood, and then dismissed the assembly. Many servants attended, who partook of the banquet; at the close of which they were smothered in the same pool, or otherwise made away with. On which TACITUS remarks, how great an awe this circumstance must infuse into those who were not admitted to these mysteries.

These accounts are handed down from a variety of authors in different ages; many of whom were natives of the countries which they describe, and to which they seem strongly [b]attached; and they would not therefore have brought so foul an imputation on the part of the world in favour of which they were each writing; nor could there be that concurrence of testimony were not the history generally true.

[a] These strongly remind one of similar rites at the *Hindu* festival of *Dasera*, or *Durgotsava*; in honour of the sanguinary DEVI, to whom human sacrifices were formerly offered in *India*. The festival continues *nine* days—is a period of much merriment and joy—the image of the deity is, at the conclusion, consigned to the water: groves are deemed fit places for the observance of these rites, and one of the names of this deity is ARANYA DEVI, the *Goddess of the Forest*, other coincidences might be enumerated. See *Hindu Pantheon*. E. M.

[b] Such was ARNGRIM JONAS, born amid the snows of *Iceland*, yet as much prejudiced in favour of his country as natives of a happier clime. In his *Crymogæa*, written in defence of his country against the invectives of another author, he is obliged to acknowledge that human sacrifices were offered up in *Iceland*; but he tries at all rates to extenuate the fact, and to make it appear not a general practice. BRYANT.

The like custom prevailed to a great degree at [c]*Mexico*, and even under the mild government of the *Peruvians*; and in most parts of *America*. In *Africa* it is still kept up; where in the inland parts they sacrifice some of the captives taken in war to their *Fetiches*, in order to secure their favour. SNELGRAVE was in the King of *Dahoome's* camp, after his inroad into the countries of *Adra* and *Whidaw*, and witnessed the cruelty of this prince, whom he saw sacrifice multitudes to the deity of his nation. He mentions four thousand *Whidaws* being sacrificed, besides people of other nations. To part of the tragedy he was an eye-witness. Voyage to *Guinea*, pp. 31. 34.

The sacrifices, of which I have been treating, if we except some few instances, consisted of persons doomed by the chance of war, or assigned by lot to be offered. But among the nations of *Canaan*, of whom I first spoke, the victims were peculiarly chosen. Their own children, and whatever was nearest and dearest [d]to them, were deemed the most worthy offering to their god. The *Carthaginians*, who were a colony from *Tyre*, carried with them the religion of their mother country, and instituted the same worship in the parts where they settled. It consisted in the adoration of several deities, but particularly of KRONUS, to whom they offered human sacrifices; and especially the blood of children. If the parents were not at hand to make an immediate offer, the magistrates did not fail to make choice of what was most fair and pro-

[c] JOANNES ACOSTA, lib. 5. of the *Mexicans*, and the sacrificing children in *Peru*. Another author says that the *Incas* put a stop to all such sacrifices.

[d] This has been remarked as an idea among *Hindus*, see page 196; and will be noticed again hereafter. E.M.

mising, that the god might not be defrauded of his dues. Upon a check being received in *Sicily*, and some other alarming circumstances occurring, HIMILCAR without any hesitation seized upon a boy and offered him on the spot to KRONUS; and at the same time drowned a number of priests to appease the deity of the sea. The *Carthaginians* another time, upon a great defeat of their army by AGATHOCLES, imputed their miscarriages to the anger of this god, whose services had been neglected. Touched with this, and seeing the enemy at their gates, they seized at once two hundred children of the prime nobility, and offered them in public for a sacrifice. Three hundred more, who were somehow obnoxious, yielded themselves voluntarily, and were put to death with the others. The neglect of which they accused themselves, consisted in sacrificing children purchased of parents among the poorer sort, who reared them for that purpose; and not selecting the most promising and the most honourable, as had been the custom of old. In short, there were particular children brought up for the altar, as sheep are fattened for the shambles; and they were bought and butchered in the same manner. But this indiscriminate way of proceeding was thought to have given offence. It is remarkable that the *Egyptians* looked out for the most specious and handsome person to be sacrificed. The *Albanians* pitched upon the best man of the community, and made him pay for the wickedness of the rest. The *Carthaginians* chose what they thought the most excellent, and at the same time the most dear to them; which made the lot fall heavy on their children.

KRONUS, to whom these sacrifices were exhibited, was

an *oriental deity, the god of light and fire, called by the *Greeks* KORONUS; and therefore always worshipped with some reference to that element. The *Carthaginians*, as I have observed, first introduced him into *Africa*. He was the same as the ORUS of the *Egyptians*, and the ALORUS of the eastern nations...........

...........The *Greeks*, we find called the deity, to whom these offerings were made, AGRAULOS; and feigned that she was a woman, and the daughter of CECROPS: but how came CECROPS to have any connexion with *Cyprus?* AGRAULOS is a corruption, and transposition of the original name, which should have been rendered UK-EL-AUR, or UK-EL-AURUS; but has, like many other oriental titles and names, been strangely sophisticated, and is here changed to AGRAULOS. It was in reality the god of light; the ORUS and ALORUS, of whom I have said so much, who was always worshipped with fire. This deity was the MOLOCH of the *Tyrians* and *Canaanites*, and the MELECH of the east; that is the great and principal god, the god of light, of whom fire was esteemed a symbol; and at whose shrine, instead of viler victims, they offered the blood of men.

Such was the KRONUS of the *Greeks*, and the MOLOCH of the *Phenicians:* and nothing can appear more shocking, than the sacrifices of the *Tyrians* and *Carthaginians*, which they performed to this idol. In all emergencies of state, and times of general calamity, they devoted what was most necessary and valuable to them, for an offering to the gods; and par-

* In *India*, the human victims were immolated to KRONOS, or Time, (through the intervention of his *Sakti)* personified in SIVA, who also is Fire and the Sun. See *Hindu Pantheon*, p. 306, and Index under SIVA. E. M.

ticularly to MOLOCH. But besides these undetermined times of bloodshed, they had particular and prescribed seasons every year, when children were chosen out of the most noble and reputable families, as hath been before mentioned. If a person had an only child, it was the more liable to be put to death, as being esteemed more acceptable to the deity, and more efficacious of the general good. Those who were sacrificed to KRONUS, were thrown into the arms of a molten idol, which stood in the midst of a large fire, and was red with heat. The arms of it were stretched out; with the hands turned upwards, as it were to receive them; yet sloping downwards, so that they dropped from thence into a glowing furnace. To other gods they were otherwise slaughtered; and, as it is implied, by the very hands of their parents. What can be more horrid to the imagination, than to suppose a father leading the dearest of his sons to such an infernal shrine? or a mother, the most engaging and affectionate of her daughters, just rising to maturity, to be slaughtered at the altar of [f]ASHTEROTH or [g]BAAL? Such was their blind zeal that this was continually practised; and so much of natural affection still left unextinguished as to render the scene ten times more shocking, from the tenderness which they seemed to express. They embraced their children with great fondness; encouraged them in the gentlest terms, that they might not be

[f] This is a name of DEVI, the sanguinary goddess of the *Hindus*. See *Hindu Pantheon*, p. 155. E. M.

[g] JUSTIN and EUSEBIUS describe this custom very pathetically. *Hist.* lib. 18. cap. 6. *Præp. Evang.* lib. 3. cap. 15. There is no accounting for the infatuation of these nations, and the inconsistency of their practices. The *Phenicians*, who were so liberal of man's blood, would not hurt a cow; and the *Carthaginians* held it worse than sacrilege to maim an ape! BRYANT. So the *Hindus*: see page 48. E. M.

appalled at the sight of the hellish process, and exhorted them to submit with cheerfulness to this fearful operation. If there was any appearance of a tear rising, or a cry unawares escaping, the mother smothered it with her kisses, that there might not be any show of backwardness or constraint; but the whole be a freewill offering. These cruel endearments over, they stabbed them to the heart, or otherwise opened the sluices of life; and with the blood, warm as it ran, besmeared the [h]altar, and the grim visage of the idol. These were the customs, which the *Israelites* learned of the people of *Canaan*, and for which they are upbraided by the *Psalmist*—"They did not destroy the nations concerning whom the Lord commanded them; but were mingled among the heathen and learned their works. Yea, they sacrificed their sons and their daughters unto devils, and shed innocent blood, even the blood of their sons and of their daughters, whom they sacrificed unto the idols of *Canaan*: and the land was polluted with blood. Thus were they defiled with their own works, and went a whoring with their own inventions." Psalm 106.

These cruel rites, practised in so many nations, made PLUTARCH debate with himself, whether it would not have been better for the *Galatæ*, or for the *Scythians*, to have had no tradition, or conception of any superior beings, than to have formed to themselves notions of gods, who delighted in the blood of men; of gods who esteemed human victims the most acceptable and perfect sacrifice. "Would it not," says he, "have been more eligible for the *Carthaginians* to have

[h] The *Scythians* and *Germans* received the blood in a vessel. BRYANT. So did the *Hindus*; the vessel called *patra* is seen in many plates of the *Hindu Pantheon*, and described in the pages referred to from the Index. E. M.

had the atheist CRITIAS, or DIAGOROS, their lawgiver at the commencement of their polity, and to have been taught that there was neither god nor dæmon, than to have sacrificed, in the manner they were wont, to the god which they adored? wherein they acted, not as the person did, whom EMPEDOCLES describes in some poetry, where he details this unnatural custom. The sire there with many idle vows offers up unwittingly his son for a sacrifice; but the youth was so changed in feature and figure, that his father did not know him—these people used, knowingly and wilfully, to go through this bloody work, and slaughter their own offspring. Even they who were childless would not be exempted from this cursed tribute; but purchased children of the poorer sort, and put them to death with as little remorse as one would kill a lamb or a chicken. The mother who sacrificed her child, stood by without any seeming sense of what she was losing, and without uttering a groan. If a sigh did by chance escape, she lost all the honour which she proposed to herself in the offering; and the child was notwithstanding slain. All the time of this celebrity, while the children were murdering, there was a noise of clarions and tabors sounding before the idol, that the shrieks of the victims might not be heard."—"Tell me now," says PLUTARCH, "if the monsters of old, the *Typhons* and the giants, were to expel the gods, and to rule the world in their stead, could they require a service more horrid than these infernal rites and sacrifices?"

(In the "Observations on the dispersion of mankind" added to the last volume of the *Analysis*, is a passage applicable to the topic discussed more at length, in that portion of the "Additional Remarks" whence I have made such a copious extract.)—"From the foregoing account we may see good reason for the severities shown towards the *Canaanites*; whom if it had pleased God to have swallowed up quick by an earthquake, or extirpated by fire from heaven, nobody could have arraigned his justice. But as he was pleased to make use of an arm of flesh, and to employ the *Israelites* as ministers of his vengeance, many have presumed to call in question the equity of the proceeding, and to represent it as an instance of injustice and cruelty; whereas the intention of Providence, in the instruments it made use of, is apparent. It was to make the *Israelites* detest these nations and their horrid customs, and to be detested by them; and to render them inexcusable, if, after such severities exercised upon this people, they should themselves thereafter relapse into the same apostacy and disobedience. To question whether God could in justice act thus in respect of the *Canaanites*, and whether he did right in choosing such implements of his vengeance, is a doubt as idle as it is impious. How the rebellion of the *Canaanites* was aggravated, and what were their crying sins, may be gathered from many parts of the Scriptures; but especially from the book of *Wisdom*, chap. 12. where they are particularly displayed—"For it was thy will (O Lord) to destroy by the hands of our fathers, both those old inhabitants of thy holy land; whom thou hatest for doing most odious works of witchcrafts, and wicked sacrifices.—And also those merciless murderers of children, and devourers of man's flesh, and the feasts of blood: With their priests out of the midst of their idolatrous crew, and the parents that killed with their own hands, souls destitute of help: For it was a cursed seed from the beginning."—"This," says Bryant, "may serve to vindicate the dispensations of Providence in this particular; and its just retributions on a rebellious and wicked people."

To these quotations Colonel WALKER has annexed the following:—

N.B. The accompanying extract from the Preliminary Discourse to SALE's *Koran*, contains farther evidence of the practice of Infanticide, assimilating more than in any other case, with the custom of the *Jarejahs* of *Kutch* and *Kattywar*.

This barbarity among the Pagan *Arabs*, as related by SALE, seems to have been confined to the female infants as with the *Jarejah Rajputs;* and it is remarkable that the difficulty of providing for them in marriage, or the apprehension of their conduct disgracing their parents, is assigned in both cases as the cause of this inhuman custom.

Extract from SALE's *Koran, Prel. Disc.* page 174.

"The law of MAHOMMED also put a stop to the inhuman custom, which had been long practised by the Pagan *Arabs*, of burying their daughters alive, lest they should be reduced to poverty by providing for them; or else to avoid the displeasure and disgrace which would follow, if they should happen to be made captives, or to become scandalous by their behaviour; the birth of a daughter being, for these reasons, reckoned a great misfortune, and the death of one, as great a happiness. The manner of destroying the infants is differently related. Some say, that when an *Arab* had a daughter born, and he intended to bring her up, he sent her clothed in a garment of wool or hair to keep camels or sheep in the desert; but if he designed to put her to death, he let her live till she became six years old, and then said to her mother, "Perfume her and adorn her that I may carry her to her mothers"—which being done, the father led her to a well or pit dug for that purpose, and bidding her look down, pushed her into it headlong, as he stood behind her; and then, filling up the pit, levelled it with the rest of the ground. But others say, that when a woman was ready to fall in labour, a pit was dug, and she was delivered on its brink—if of a daughter, it was thrown into the pit; if a son, it was preserved. This custom, although not observed by all the *Arabs*, was yet very common among several of their tribes, and particularly by those of *Koreish* and *Kundeh;* the former using to bury their daughters alive in mount *Abu Dalama*, near *Mecca*. In the time of ignorance, while they used this method to get rid of their daughters, SASAA, grandfather to the celebrated poet AL FARASDAK, frequently redeemed female children from death, giving for each child two pregnant camels and a he camel; and hereto AL FARASDAK alluded when vaunting before one of the *Khalifs* of the family of OMEYAH, he said, "I am the son of the giver of life to the dead;"—being censured for the expression, he excused himself by quoting these words of the *Koran*—"He who saveth a soul alive, shall be as if he had saved the lives of all mankind." The *Arabs*, in the murder of their children, were far from being singular; the practice of exposing infants and putting them to death, being so common among the ancients, that it is remarked as a thing very extraordinary in the *Egyptians*, that they brought up all their children; and by the laws of LYCURGUS, no child was allowed to be brought up without the approbation of public officers. At this day it is said, that in *China* the poorer sort of people frequently put their children, the females especially, to death with impunity.

"This wicked practice is condemned by the *Koran* in several passages; one of which, as some commentators judge, may also condemn another custom of the *Arabians*, altogether as wicked and as common among other nations of old, viz. the sacrificing of their children to their idols—as was frequently done in pursuance of a vow made to offer one child in sacrifice, in return for a certain number of sons."

Colonel WALKER concludes this portion of his [1]Report with the following observation:—

The existence of the custom of Infanticide has now been traced to almost every nation; scarcely any appearing to be exempt from the reproach of having practised it; and one benefit which has resulted to mankind from the success of MAHOMED's imposture is the abolition of so inhuman a usage amongst his numerous followers. A. W.

[1] In reference to Note [b] in page 98, where I express uncertainty as to which, if any, of the papers or Notes of this Chapter, accompanied the *Report* forming Chap. III., I might evidently have recollected this Note I., as having made one of its accompaniments. As Colonel WALKER's MS. had been copied by a native writer, I found it necessary to refer to BRYANT's work, whence I have, indeed, re-written the preceding Note, and added some of the references of that learned author:—with some other additions, and, perhaps, some omissions. I am now enabled, by a communication received just as this sheet was going to the press, to state that all the Notes of this Chapter, marked, (to distinguish them from my interpolations) A. W. accompanied Colonel WALKER's Report of 15th March, 1808. forming Chap. III. E. M.

Remarks.

It might be tedious, but would not be very difficult, to show that Infanticide, and the exposure of children, have been, more or less, practised by almost every nation of antiquity, of whose history many particulars have descended to these times: and, indeed, although a doubt of the general fact of the existence of these practices can by some be scarcely shaken off, it is yet too true that even in the present day these crimes have a lamentable prevalence.

BRYANT's work, from which so copious an extract precedes these *Remarks*, necessarily restricted him to the usages of antiquity; and the question of Infanticide was with him casual, forming no part of the subjects to which he particularly directed his attention. A degree of research trifling compared to that exhibited by BRYANT, would develope the existence of the usage under our consideration, in times both past and present, to an extent that is, perhaps, imagined by very few.

If *data* were afforded for tracing in every instance the origin of this custom, it is probable that it would be found in every instance to have originated in one cause; that is, in *necessity*, resulting from extreme poverty. In morals, as well as in physics, every effect must have an adequate cause: and what less strong than necessity, to the extreme of hunger and the dread of starvation, can be supposed adequate to produce an effect so violently opposed to the feelings universally operating throughout animated nature, for the preservation of offspring? Some societies and tribes are found to retain the usage after the supposed necessity hath ceased to exist: in these instances, the origin is, I conclude, too remote for research to deduce any argument from. Once established, a practice, however atrocious, may be perpetuated by the operation of feelings, of pride or convenience, for example, by no means sufficiently potent to have called it originally into existence.

This reasoning is applicable to the *Jarejahs* and the other Infanticides of *India;* among whom I am not aware of any present pressure of extreme poverty. But they live in countries, which, however happy in the enjoyment of many of nature's bounties, have been frequently cursed by war and famine; and subjected, farther, to inundations, that may be well supposed to have occasionally reduced a redundant population to the deepest distress. Under these calamities, Infanticide must have originated: their frequent recurrence, blunting the feelings, rendered the act less and less acute; until at length an experience of its convenience was found sufficiently strong to induce its continuance.

The instances that I am now about to adduce, chiefly from MALTHUS's essay on the Principles of Population, of the prevalence of Infanticide, refer mostly to modern times. They will be found, I believe, to confirm the above line of reasoning, which seeks the cause of every case of Infanticide originally in necessity.

"The condition of these women" (of *New South Wales)* "is so wretched, that I have often, on seeing a female child, anticipated the miseries to which it was born, and thought it would be a mercy to destroy it." COLLINS's *New S. Wales*, Ap. p. 583, cited by MALTHUS, b. I. c. 3. This author gives many affecting instances of the miseries of the females, subject to the barbarians of this colony.

"If the mother of a sucking child die, the helpless infant is buried alive in the same grave with its mother. The father himself places his living child on the body of his deceased wife, and having thrown a large stone upon it, the grave is instantly filled. This dreadful act was performed by Co-LE-BE, a native well known to our colonists; and who, on being talked to on the subject, justified the proceeding by declaring that no woman could be found who would undertake to nurse the child, and that therefore it must have died a much worse death than that which he had given it. Mr. COLLINS had reason to believe that this custom was generally prevalent; and observes that it may in some measure account for the thinness of the population." *Ib.* b. 1. c. 3.

"This places in a strong point of view, the difficulty of rearing children in savage life. Women obliged by their habits of living to a constant change of place, and compelled to an unremitting drudgery for their husbands, appear to be absolutely incapable of bringing up two or three children of nearly the same age. If another child be born before the one above it can shift for itself, and follow its mother on foot, one of the two must necessarily perish for want of care. The task of rearing even one infant in such a wandering and laborious life, must be so troublesome and painful, that we are not to be surprised that no woman can be found to undertake it, who is not prompted by the powerful feelings of a mother." *Ibid.*

"It is finely observed by Dr. ROBERTSON, that, 'whether man has been improved by the progress of arts and civilization, is a question which, in the wantonness of disputation, has been agitated among philosophers. That women are indebted to the refinement of polished manners for a happy change in their state, is a point which can admit of no doubt.' In every part of the world, one of the most general characteristics of the savage is to despise and degrade the female sex. Among most of the tribes of *America*, their condition is so peculiarly grievous that servitude is a name too mild to describe their wretched state. A wife is no better than a beast of burden. While the man passes his days in idleness or amusement, the woman is condemned to incessant toil. Tasks are imposed upon her without mercy, and her services are received without complacence or gratitude. There are some districts in *America* where this state of degradation has been so severely felt, that mothers have destroyed their female infants, to deliver them at once from a life in which they were doomed to such a miserable slavery." *Ib.* b. I. c. 4.

" Among some of the ruder tribes of *America*, it is a maxim not to burden themselves with rearing more than two of their offspring. When twins are born, one of them is commonly abandoned, as the mother cannot rear them both; and when the mother dies during the period of suckling her child, no chance of preserving its life remains; and, as in *New Holland*, it is buried in the same grave with the breast that nourished it.

" As the parents are frequently exposed to want themselves, the difficulty of supporting their children becomes at times so great, that they are reduced to the necessity of abandoning or destroying them. Deformed children are very generally exposed; and among some of the tribes of *South America*, the children of mothers who do not bear their labours well, experience a similar fate, from a fear that the offspring may inherit the weakness of its parent." *Ib.*

The above instances of habitual Infanticide refer to *America* and *New Holland.* I shall now quote, from the same respectable authority, a few more cases taken from authentic accounts of *Otaheite*, *China*, &c. In every one Mr. MALTHUS refers to his authorities: this I shall generally omit, as the reader desirous of examining them can consult the Essay on Population.

"The successive accounts that we have received of *Otaheite* and the neighbouring Islands, leave us no room to doubt the existence of the *Eareeoie* societies, which have justly occasioned so much surprise among civilized nations. They have been so often described, that little more need be said of them, than that promiscuous intercourse and Infanticide appear to be their fundamental laws. They consist exclusively of the higher classes; and, according to Mr. ANDERSON, so agreeable is this licentious plan of life to their disposition, that the most beautiful of both sexes thus commonly spend their youthful days, habituated to the practice of enormities that would disgrace the most savage tribes. When an *Eareeoie* woman is delivered of a child, a piece of cloth dipped in water is applied to its mouth and nose, which suffocates it. Captain COOK observes, 'It is certain that these societies greatly prevent the increase of the superior classes of people, of which they are composed.' Of the truth of this observation there can," Mr. MALTHUS observes, "be no doubt."

"Though no particular institutions of the same nature have been found among the lower classes, yet the vices which form their most prominent features are but too generally spread. Infanticide is not confined to the *Eareeoies.* It is permitted to all; and as its prevalence, among the higher classes of the people, has removed from it all odium, or imputation of poverty, it is probably adopted rather as a fashion than a resort of necessity, and appears to be practised familiarly and without reserve.[k]

"It is a very just observation of HUME (Ess. vol. I.) that the permission of Infanticide generally contributes to increase the population of a country. By removing the fears of too numerous a family, it encourages marriage; and the powerful yearnings of nature prevent parents from resorting to so cruel an expedient, except in extreme cases. The fashion of the *Eareeoie* societies in *Otaheite* and its neighbouring islands, may have made them an exception to this observation; and the custom has probably there a contrary tendency.

"The common marriages in *Otaheite* are without any other ceremony than a present from the man to the parents of the girl. And this seems to be rather a bargain with them for permission to try their daughter, than an absolute contract for a wife. If the father should think that he has not been sufficiently paid for his daughter, he makes no scruple of forcing her to leave her friend, and to cohabit with another person who may be more liberal. The man is always at liberty to make a new choice. Should his consort be pregnant, he may kill the child; and may continue the

[k] To vindicate the maternal character of the *Otaheitans,* from a universal willing concurrence in this lamentable custom, I will notice that I have heard Sir JOSEPH BANKS relate, that he was never more affected than by the sorrow expressed by a woman of that island, when reciting the sad necessity she was under of destroying her child. A similar feeling was evinced on the part of the *Raj Kumar* females, in their gratitude to Mr. DUNCAN for relieving them from the recurrence of so severe a pang. See note in page 56. E. M.

connexion with the mother, or leave her, according to his pleasure." *Ib.* b. I. c. 5.

"In *Easter Island*, from the great disproportion of the males to the females, it can scarcely be doubted that Infanticide prevails, though the fact may not have come to the knowledge of any of our navigators. From the description of PEROUSE it appeared, at the time of his visit, to be recovering its population, which had been in a very low state, probably from drought, civil dissensions, or the prevalence in an extreme degree, of Infanticide and promiscuous intercourse..........

"In the *Marianne* Islands, according to *Pere* GOBIEN, a very great number of the young men remained unmarried, lived like the members of the *Eareeoie* society in *Otaheite*, and were distinguished by a similar name. In the island of *Formosa*, it is said that the women were not allowed to bring children into the world before the age of thirty-five. When with child prior to that period, an abortion was effected by the [1]priestess.

"Sir JOHN CHARDIN relates that among the *Mahomedan Tartars* they justify it as lawful to have many wives, because they bring many children, which they can sell for ready money, or exchange for necessary conveniences; yet when they have not wherewithal to maintain them, they hold it a piece of charity to murder infants newly born; as also they

[1] The most positive evidence is required to induce a belief of a custom so strange as this. It is related by MANDESLOE, who is thought by Mr. MALTHUS to have taken it from the *Dutch* writers quoted by MONTESQUIEU (*Esp. des Loix*, l. 23. c. 27.) It is, I think, also stated by OLEARIUS, but I have not his work to consult, and is said to be attended by such dangerous and painful operations, as render the fact still less credible. E. M.

do such as are sick and past recovery; because, they say, they free them from a great deal of misery." *Ib.* b. I. c. 7.

Sir GEORGE STAUNTON in his Embassy to *China*, Vol. II. countenances the idea of permitted Infanticide tending to encourage population. He says, "That whatever is strongly recommended, and generally practised, is at length considered as a religious duty; and that the marriage union as such takes place in *China* wherever there is the least prospect of subsistence for a future family. This prospect, however, is not always realized, and the children are then abandoned by the wretched authors of their being. But even this permission given to parents thus to expose their offspring tends undoubtedly to facilitate marriage, and encourage population. Contemplating this extreme resource beforehand, less fears are entertained of entering into the married state; and the parental feelings will always step forwards to prevent a recurrence to it, except under the most dire [m]necessity." *Ib.* b. I. c. 12.

DU HALDE says, "That the prodigious population of *China* causes a great deal of misery. There are some so poor, that, being unable to supply their children with common

m The prevalence of this custom, continued rather as a fashion than from the pressure of necessity, both in *India* and in *Otaheite*, and in other parts of the world, furnish sufficient exceptions to this dangerous theory of HUME's, however plausibly it be supported. How far it may have tended to the increase or decrease of the population of *Guzerat*, I am not prepared to state. I have always understood it to be a very well-peopled country. Be it as it may, it is still dangerous to encourage mankind to view with complacency the first steps of sin; depending upon "natural," or even on "parental feelings," to discourage its approach. The idea of an author, not always to be quoted to advantage, expressed in these lines, are more safely to be applauded:—

> "To avoid the first offence is in man's choice,
> But having sinned, to stop exceeds his power." ADELGITHA. E. M.

necessaries, they expose them in the streets. In the great cities, such as *Pekin* and *Canton*, this shocking sight is very common." *Ibid.*

The *Jesuit* PREMARE says, "A spectator in *China* who examines things closely, will not be surprised that mothers destroy or expose their children." *Ibid.*

Another of the *Jesuits*, speaking of the number of infants whom the poverty of their parents condemns to death the moment they are born, writes thus—"There is seldom a year, in which the churches at *Pekin* do not reckon five or six thousand of these children purified by the waters of baptism. This harvest is more or less abundant, according to the number of catechists which we can maintain. If we had a sufficiency, their cares need not be confined alone to the dying infants that are exposed. There would be other occasions for them to exercise their zeal; particularly at certain times of the year, when the small pox, or epidemic disorders carry [n] off an incredible number of children." *Ib.* b. I. c. 12.

[n] The advantages derived from this "abundant harvest" of "dying infants" may not perhaps at once appear; or why the "zealous cares" of these laborious *Jesuits* should be extended to those "carried off" by small pox, &c. An incident related by one of them will explain it. He was called in to prescribe for an infant, which he perceived was at the extreme point of life, and requesting to be left alone with it, he seized with necessary and pious haste, the opportunity of administering to it the sacrament of baptism. He exultingly writes to his superior, that had no other benefit resulted from his voyage to *China*, his having been thus the means of saving one soul from perdition would have amply rewarded him. We hence see that heaven exclusively benefited by these zealous labours of the active fraternity, who from such successes, perhaps, entitled the Letters composing the volumes of their transactions, *Edifiante et Curieuse*, a work that I quote from memory, not having seen it for many years. The preceding passage left a lasting impression. However the sincere exercise of religious zeal ought at all times to command respect, one may be allowed to regret, at least, such an erroneous application of it. E. M.

"Respecting the number of infants which are actually exposed it would be difficult to form any accurate estimate; but if we believe the *Chinese* writers themselves, the practice must be very common. Attempts have been made at different times by the government to put a stop to it, but always without success. In a book of instructions written by a *Mandarin* celebrated for his humanity and wisdom, a proposal is made for the establishment of a foundling hospital in his district; and an account is given of some ancient establishment of that kind, which appears to have fallen into disuse. In this book the frequency of the exposure of children, and the dreadful poverty which prompts it, are particularly described. "We see," he says, "people so poor, that they cannot furnish the nourishment necessary for their own children. It is on this account that they expose so great a number. In the metropolis, in the capitals of the provinces, and in the places of the greatest commerce, the number is the most considerable; but many are found in parts that are less frequented, and even in the country. As the houses in towns are more crouded together, the practice is there more obvious, but every where these poor unfortunate infants have need of assistance."

"In the same work part of an edict to prevent the drowning of children, runs thus:—'When the tender offspring just produced is thrown without pity into the waves, can it be said that the mother has given, or that the child has received life, when it is lost as soon as it is begun to be enjoyed? The poverty of the parents is the cause of this crime. They have hardly enough to support themselves, much less are they able to pay a nurse, and provide for the expenses necessary for the support of their children. This drives them to despair; and not being able to bring themselves to suffer two people to die that one may live, the mother to preserve the life of her husband, consents to sacrifice her child. It costs much however to the parental feelings; but the resolution is ultimately taken, and they think themselves justified in disposing of that life to prolong their own. If they exposed their children in a secret place, the babe might work upon their compassion by its cries. What do they then?—They throw it into the current of the river, that they may lose sight of it immediately, and take from it all chance of life.'

"Such writings," Mr. MALTHUS observes, "appear to be most authentic documents respecting the general practice of Infanticide." *Ib.* b. I. c. 12.

"Sir GEORGE STAUNTON has stated from the best information which he could collect, that the number of children exposed annually at *Pekin*, is about two thousand; but it is highly probable that the number varies extremely from year to year, and depends very much upon seasons of plenty and seasons of scarcity." *Ibid.*

"It is probable that the practice of Infanticide prevailed from the earliest ages of *Greece*. In the parts of *America* where it was found to exist, it appears to have originated from the extreme difficulty of rearing many children in a savage and wandering life, exposed to frequent famine and perpetual war. We may easily conceive that it had a similar origin among the ancestors of the *Greeks*, or the native inhabitants of the country. And when SOLON permitted the exposure of children, it is probable that he only gave the sanction of law to a custom already prevalent." *Ib.* b. I. c. 13.

"PLATO, in his philosophical Republic, proposes that the most excellent among the men should be joined in marriage to the most excellent among the women, and the inferior citizens matched with the inferior females; and that the offspring of the first should be brought up, of the others, not; but, together with those of the other class which are imperfect in their limbs, to be buried in some obscure and unknown place............When both sexes have passed the age for presenting children to the state, PLATO allows a great latitude of intercourse; but no child is to be brought to light. Should any infant by accident be born alive, it is to be exposed in the same manner as if the parents could not support it." *Ibid.*

Mr. MALTHUS justly reprobates these execrable expedients, and those similar of ARISTOTLE; who, in his similar work *(de Repub.)* limits the number of children allowed to each marriage; and if any woman be pregnant after she have produced the prescribed number, abortion is to be procured. And after a certain age, sexuál intercourse is permitted; but, as in PLATO's Republic, no child which may be the result is to be brought to light.

"There is reason," Mr. MALTHUS continues, "to believe that the practice of Infanticide prevailed in *Italy*, as well as in *Greece*, from the earliest times. A law of ROMULUS forbad the exposing of children before they were three years old, which implies that the custom of exposing them as soon as they were born had before *prevailed." *Ib.* b. I. c. 14.

* PLUTARCH and TACITUS allude to this custom in *Rome*; and so common was it, that even PLINY attempts to excuse it; '*Quoniam aliquarum fecunditas plena liberis tali veniâ indigit.*' Lib. XXIX. ch. 4.

I will make one more extract from the valuable work of this humane author, referring to some of the preceding passages.

" Mr. GODWIN does not acknowledge the justice of Mr. HUME's observation respecting Infanticide: and yet the extreme population and poverty of *China*, where this custom prevails, tends strongly to confirm the observation. It is still, however true, as Mr. GODWIN observes, that the expedient is, in its own nature, adequate to the end for which it was cited; but to make it so in fact, it must be done by the magistrates, and not left to the parents. The almost invariable tendency of this custom to increase population, when it depends entirely on the parents, shows the extreme pain which they must feel in making such a sacrifice, even when the distress arising from excessive poverty may be supposed to have deadened, in a great measure, their sensibility. What then must this pain be, upon the supposition of an interference of a magistrate, or of a positive law, to make parents destroy a child which they feel the desire, and think they have the power of supporting?

Infanticide had arisen to so common a pitch among the *Greeks*, that, as we learn from BRYANT on the authority of LYCOPHRON, the deity to whom the offerings were made "was styled INFANTICIDA, on account of the number of children which were offered at his shrine." *Anal.* III. 338.

Parents in extreme poverty, wavering between the horrors of murdering their offspring and starving, may have found in the extravagant theogonies of *Greece*, an example to guide their determination; touching, also, directly on the question of defective formation. VULCAN was born a cripple; his mother hence detesting him ejected him from heaven. In HOMER's hymn to APOLLO, JUNO is made (in the rendering of BRYANT, *An.* IV. 62.) to exclaim

" My crippled offspring VULCAN, I produced:
But soon I seized the miscreant in my hands,
And hurl'd him headlong downward to the sea." E. M.

The permission of Infanticide is bad enough, and cannot but have a bad effect on the moral sensibility of a nation; but I cannot conceive any thing much more detestable, or more shocking to the feelings, than any direct regulation of this kind, although sanctioned by the names of PLATO and ARISTOTLE." *Ib.* b. III. c. 3.

The present Sir GEORGE STAUNTON in his recent work, *Ta Tsing Leu Li*, touches tenderly on the practice of Infanticide undeniably existing among the *Chinese*. As the imputation of such a crime cannot fail of exciting, in *Christian* countries, feelings deeply unfavourable to the national character of the perpetrators, it may be but fair to hear the sentiments thereon of those best informed on the subject.

"The virtues of the *Chinese*," this respectable author observes, "although very inferior no doubt to their professions, and of a lower order than those which *Christianity* has happily implanted, or invigorated, in the *European* world, may perhaps be found as little alloyed either with the sanguinary or the selfish vices, as those of any other people, for whose guidance the salutary light of revelation has not yet penetrated.

"Even the crime of Infanticide, for instance, which has been considered such an indelible stain upon the *Chinese* character, might be found to admit of some extenuation, if it were discovered to be rarely, if ever, practised, except in the anguish of hopeless poverty, or in cases of such unhappy and defective formation, as might be conceived to render life a painful burden. The criminality of the *Chinese*, in this respect, might also be safely contrasted with the legalized cruelty and unnatural indifference of *Roman* fathers under similar circumstances. Passing from the people to the government, the obvious and undeniable defects of the latter, might justly be compared with the acknowledged corruptions and imperfections of those of *Europe;* and it might perhaps be found, upon a general view, that the happiness of the people was not more frequently neglected or interrupted, upon the one system, than upon the other." *Preface.*

I will here interpose a remark that may perhaps tend to strengthen the soothing supposition that Infanticide is practised in *China* only in the cases of hopeless poverty or of defective formation; as is several times adverted to in the preceding extracts. During a residence of several months in *Canton* I never witnessed, or even heard of a case of Infanticide. Many thousands of the poorest classes live entirely on the water; among these it is that the instances are supposed to be most frequent. Their situation offers the greatest facilities, and their poverty the strongest inducements; and such instances would be oftenest seen by strangers. Yet I never saw one, and I have been much on the water about *Canton*, among the most thronged parts of the floating population: nor do I know of any other person having seen one; nor did I, to the best of my recollection, ever hear of any well-authenticated case, although, like me, every body has heard of the supposed frequency of the fact. I should not deem the evidence of a drowned child an exception. Out of so many thousands crawling about such embarkations as float for miles above and below *Canton*, many children must doubtless be drowned accidentally; and I have heard a case related as a proof of exposure or of Infanticide, that conveyed, to my mind, a contrary impression. It was of a child seen floating tied to a hollowed gourd. The appendage argued care, rather than neglect or criminality; but it was retorted as a proof of exposure, and of some maternal feeling, viewing with hope the child's chance of a humane deliverance. It is not very unusual to see in the *Canton* boats, infants crawling about with a calabash on their backs; so that when one falls overboard, it can easily, and without alarm or anxiety, be picked up.

On the whole I am inclined to the belief that Infanticide in *China* is practised only in seasons of severe pressure. Denied the relief of emigration, the distresses of such a redundant population, aggravated by the encouragement of early marriage, renders some check almost necessary; and accounts for, although nothing can excuse, the practice even of Infanticide.

The *Portugueze* have endowed a foundling hospital at *Macao*, where many exposed children are carefully nourished; and their number may be fairly quoted in proof of the frequency of exposure. But although the existence of such an establishment may prove the prior existence of the crime that rendered its institution expedient, it would not, in every instance, be just to estimate the number of infants received as the uniform measure of the utility of such establishments. It may reasonably be doubted, allowing unqualified praise to the benevolence that "bade the heaven-directed spires arise," if their effects be, on the whole, ever beneficial to society. They tend to encourage the desertion of offspring, by taking from parents the strongest impulse of protection. In *China*, where the poorer classes live so wretchedly and with such difficulty, the certainty of a child being so much better provided for, in the Foundling hospital, than it could be at home, must, under the pressure of poverty, operate as an inducement to exposure. The same argument holds good elsewhere: and if we imagine a country where Infanticide and the exposure of children are unknown, it may be difficult, however, to name such a country, the erection of a Foundling hospital (admitting for argument's sake such a solecism) would in all probability soon call such crimes into existence. But this is no place for such a discussion. The subject is ably handled in the Essay on Population. Be this as it may; it is grateful to find *Christianity*, both in *China* and in *India*, interposing to soften the enormities of heathens; and, in both cases, mitigating, what it has not yet obtained sufficient influence to suppress.

The *Chinese* are not found to have any sanction in their law for Infanticide; and it is no accusation to say they have no express law against it. A code is not thence peculiarly defective. In their penal code, indeed, a father killing his child by excessive chastisement is punishable. But such laws are not intended to meet the crime under consideration. It is, of course, invariably perpetrated under the shade of darkness and in the silence of solitude; and it may perhaps be wise in legislators to refrain from the attempt to check by penal denunciations, a custom existing in opposition to feelings of a nature beyond the scope of temporal controul.

It is certain that parental feelings are in the East very extensively and essentially different, in reference to sons and daughters. In *India*, *China*, *Persia*, *Arabia*, &c. there exists a decided preference to male children. The birth of a boy is a subject of gratulation; of a girl, not. If not deemed a misfortune, it is rarely, with the exception of certain tribes of peculiar habits, regarded in a light more favourable than indifference. In the works on *Hindu* law or literature that have appeared in *English*, I do not recollect a passage indicating an increase of happiness on the birth of a daughter. The birth of a son among the *Hindus* is almost essential for the relief of the father from eventual purgatory. It is on a variety of accounts an event of much joy; but of a daughter, very rarely, if ever. This different feeling respecting daughters, this continued contemplation of their relative unimportance, may, combined with the anguish of poverty, have led, or smoothed, the way to their neglect and destruction.

Many texts might be cited from MENU, as to the importance of a son; but not where a daughter is looked on as a welcome increment. In Chapter IX. of the Institutes, it is laid down:—

Ver. 45. Then only is a man perfect, when he consists of three persons united; himself, his wife, and his son.

81. A wife bringing forth only daughters for eleven years may be superceded.

137. By a son a man obtains victory over all people; by a son's son he enjoys immortality; and, afterward, by the son of that grandson, he reaches the solar abode.

138. Since the son delivers his father from the hell named *put*,[p] he was therefore called *putra* by BRAHMA himself.

161. Such advantage as a man would gain, who should attempt to pass deep water in a boat made of woven reeds,

[p] There is no such hell, however, in MENU's own list of receptacles for sinners. The twentieth of the one and twenty hells that he enumerates in Chap. IV. v. 88. of his *Institutes*, called *Asi-patra-vana*, meaning *sword-leaved-forest*, may be that here alluded to. A son may have been called *putra* from the allegory of a tree being in most languages likened to a father or the converse, and a son to a leaf or branch. The fifteenth hell is named *Putimrittika*, which means *stinking dirt*. No other of the list given by MENU (see *Hin. Pan.* p. 297.) contains the root of the word whence reference is made to this note. E. M.

the father obtains who passes the gloom of death, leaving only contemptible sons.

Nothing affectionate occurs of daughters. This difference of feeling may be very extensively traced. Both JOB and JEREMIAH make the distinction in nearly the same words:— "Cursed be the man," exclaims the latter in the bitter absence of comfort and charity, "who brought tidings to my father, saying, a *man-child* is born unto thee, making him very glad." XX. 15. In both the *Hebrew* and the *Arabic* languages the word for a male implies *remembrance:* for a female, *oblivion*. See JONES' *Commentary on* ISÆUS.

In the penal code of *China*, murdering father, mother, son, uncle, &c. is duly denounced, p. 322. but a daughter seems to be overlooked.

We may thus fancy a clue to guide us to some of the reasons why daughters are, by many nations, less esteemed than sons; and why, in cases of distress, or prompted by other causes, daughters perish first. In some predicaments, however, sons have the melancholy preference; but this arises from their superiority, and the notion that the deeper the pang self inflicted by the sacrifice of the most beloved object, the more grateful is the victim to the deity thus propitiated.

This notion is found to have existed among many people. In the quotation from BRYANT, forming so great a portion of the preceding NOTE I. to which these *Remarks* are annexed, many instances are given of divers and distant nations fancying that their own children, and whatever was nearest and dearest to them were the offering most suitable to their (infernal) deities. The same idea is found to have existed formerly, at least, whatever may now be the fact, among *Hindus*. In NOTE H. of this Chapter, Colonel

Walker has noticed some instances strikingly in point:— "A *Brahmin;*" even, "and the more holy, learned, beautiful, highly bred, rich and flourishing either in family or wealth, the more acceptable is the offering." (p. 196. 244.) We may find in our Scriptures several examples of this feeling:—"Will the Lord be pleased with thousands of rams, or with ten thousands of rivers of oil? Shall I give my first-born for my transgression; the fruit of my body for the sin of my soul?" Micah, vi. 7.

"This," says Burder, *Oriental Customs*, No. 1146, "was actually the practice of the inhabitants of *Florida.* The ceremony was always performed in the presence of one of those princes or *caciques,* whom they call *paraoustis.* The victim must always be a male infant. Its mother covers her face, and weeps and groans over the stone, against which her child is to be dashed in pieces. The women who accompany her sing and dance in a circle, while another woman stands up in the middle of the ring, holding the child in her arms, and showing it at a distance to the *paraousti;* who probably is esteemed a representation of the sun, or deity to which the victim is offered: after which the sacrifice is made. 'The *Peruvians* of quality, and those too of mean sort, would sacrifice their first-born to redeem their own life, when the priest pronounced that they were mortally sick.' More's *Explanation of Grand Mystery.*"

Mesha the King of *Moab,* a sheepmaster, as he is called in Scripture, unable to prevail against the *Edomites,* "took his eldest son that should have reigned in his stead, and offered him for a burnt-offering upon the wall." 2 Kings, iii. 27. "Nor," says Burder, *Or. Cus.* No. 2. "was the belief that the gods were rendered propitious by this mode of sacrifice confined to the nations contiguous more immediately to the territories of *Israel*. We learn from HOMER, that a whole *Hecatomb* of firstling lambs was no uncommon offering among his countrymen. And the ancient *Goths*, having 'laid it down as a principle, that the effusion of the blood of animals appeased the anger of the gods, and that their justice turned aside upon the victims those strokes which were destined for men,' soon proceeded to greater lengths, and adopted the horrid practice of devoting human victims. In honor of the mystical number three, a number deemed particularly dear to heaven, every ninth month witnessed the groans and dying struggles of nine unfortunate victims. The fatal blow being struck, the lifeless bodies were consumed in the sacred fire, which was kept perpetually burning; while the blood, in singular conformity with the levitical ordinances, was sprinkled partly upon the surrounding multitude, partly upon the trees of the hallowed grove, and partly upon the images of their idols. MALLET's *Northern Antiquities*, Vol. I. Chap. 7. "HACON, King of *Norway*, offered his son in sacrifice, to obtain of ODIN the victory over his enemy HARALD. AUNE, King of *Sweden*, devoted to ODIN the blood of his nine sons; to prevail on that god to prolong his life." *Ib.*

In a former page the *Sacæ*, mentioned by ancient authors, have been deemed the same people who still inhabit the coasts between the *Indus* and the gulf of *Cambay*. BRYANT, enumerating many nations of *anthropophagi*, exclusive of what are extracted in NOTE I. has this passage :—" I am sensible, that many people cannot be brought to believe what is reported of those nations. They think, that the disposition of man can never be so depraved, as to turn to its own species, and indulge in human carnage." *Anal.* V. 215. He leaves the facts which he quotes from various authors to remove the comfortable doubts of his readers. Among these he states the *Sacæ*, *Indi*, and *Indo-Scythæ*, to be of the same family as the *Scythæ Androphagi* spoken of by HERODOTUS and PLINY; and to be represented by MELA as indulging in these horrid repasts. " The *Scythæ* are cannibals, and so are the *Sacæ*. Some of the *Indi* will not kill any animal, nor feed at all upon flesh. Others make it a rule, before their friends are emaciated by years, or illness, to put them to death, like so many victims: and they think it not only a lawful thing, but a matter of duty and affection to feed upon their inward parts." These *Indo-Sacæ* we have noticed in p. 162, as renowned for piracy, both in ancient and modern days. They cannot now perhaps be accused either of homicide or cannibalism; but as few professions can render female infants a greater incumbrance than piracy, we may reasonably suspect them of Infanticide, and that it was this custom which caused women to be, as noticed in p. 163, one of their principal demands, when they levied their piratical contributions on the shores.

The care of animal life and abstinence from flesh meat, is, as has been frequently noticed, a striking characteristic of an extensive sect in *Guzerat*. That the humane sects of *Jaina* or *Baudha* can ever have been cannibals it is difficult to imagine. Man is, however, so contradictory an animal, that no speculation is to be hastily rejected on the grounds merely of its improbability. Who, for instance, till now could have believed or suspected the facts revealed in this volume, of the "innocent *Hindus*" murdering children, even their own children? But the fact is now so established that, however grateful it may be to indulge the consoling error of its non-existence, it is the wantonness of scepticism to doubt. On the question of the credibility of *Hindu* cannibalism, only one passage occurs to me as tending to fix that imputation on any sect among them, save that described in p. 352. of the *Hindu Pantheon;* and whether in that instance it be an individual extravaganza occasionally exhibited, or a sectarial propensity, I know not. The passage alluded to is somewhat equivocal; but if it will bear the interpretation that seems the most obvious, it imputes cannibalism to the *Baudhas*. It occurs in Vol. IX. of the *As. Res.* in Major MACKENZIE's account of the *Jainas*, Art. iv. and is quoted in the *Hin. Pan.* with this introduction:—'In that volume is a passage referring to the followers of the doctrines of BUDHA that countenances the idea that they are also cannibals; but it is so repugnant to the generally received notions of the humanity of that sect, that I shall, without laying any stress on it, merely quote the passage:'—"The *Jains* generally account modestly for all their tenets, and conduct themselves with propriety: and never assert that their bodies are eternal, and that there is *no God;* nor do they, like the *Baudhists*, say, 'After death there is no pain in the flesh or feeling: since it feels not pain, nor death, what harm is there in feeding upon it, when it is necessary to procure health and strength."

This character of the *Baudhists* seems to have been given them by the kindred sect of *Jainas*, and is thence to be received with increased suspicion. It is, probably, no new remark that the faintness of the shades of difference between the faith of religious sects, is in the inverse proportion to the degree of rancour and hatred usually subsisting between the individuals composing them.

The apparent incredibility of a relation must not cause a too great degree of scepticism. The customs and prejudices of distant nations we find as opposite as their geographical positions, and they are mutually astonished at each other's acts. That parents destroy or expose their children we at first find some difficulty in believing; although that it often takes place in our own and neighbouring countries, the existence of Foundling Hospitals in almost every capital in *Europe*, is alone, were there no other, sufficient evidence. That children kill and eat their parents, is perhaps still more difficult to believe; and yet it is a custom said to exist on *Sumatra*. The cannibalism of these *Anthropophagi*, Mr. MARSDEN deems confined to prisoners of war, or to condemned criminals; but a later writer differs in this point from my greatly respected friend, whose *History of Sumatra*, a new edition of which is recently announced, is justly considered as a model for that species of composition. Dr. LEYDEN in his dissertation on the language and literature of the *Indo-Chinese* nations, in Vol. X. of the *Asiatic Researches*, relates, that "when a man becomes infirm and weary of the world, he is said to invite his own children to eat him. In the season when salt and limes are cheapest, he ascends a tree, around which his offspring and friends assemble; and, shaking the tree, they join in a dirge, the burthen of which is this,—'The season is come;—the fruit is ripe, and it must descend.'—The victim descends; and those that are nearest and dearest to him deprive him of life, and devour his remains in a solemn banquet."

Dr. LEYDEN received this account from men of the tribe, the *Batta*, among whom this custom prevailed on *Sumatra*. The similarity of name reminded him of a like custom among the *Padaioi*, as related by HERODOTUS, who, about five hundred years before our era, were addicted not only to eating raw flesh, but to devouring, killing them for that purpose, their aged relations.

But enough of this, or I shall render my book a chronicle of human atrocities. That the direct causes of the miseries of mankind are diminishing, may, I think, be inferred from the discontinuance of many of those above enumerated, and the mitigation of others; without, I should hope, the substitution of more novel enormities in their place, equally inimical to human happiness. When alluding to a diminution of the causes of the miseries of man, it is impossible to avoid casting a triumphant glance on their late fruitful sources, the Inquisition and the Slave-trade. What, respecting the unenlightened people of antiquity can now be more incredible than it will seem to our remote posterity, that neighbouring nations who call themselves *Christians*, offered human victims to appease the anger of the God of Mercy. Half a century has scarcely elapsed, perhaps a much shorter space, since the *Portugueze* and *Spaniards* burned their brethren alive in vindication of the honor and glory of God! Nor can we exult in our entire exemption; for within how few years is it that similar outrages were committed even in *England*, by only a few wretched fanatics it is true, in the insulted name of religion. These are happily spoken of as things that were. —Still is the exclamation of the poet too just,

> " ————— (hear it not ye stars!
> And thou, pale Moon! turn paler at the sound—)
> MAN IS TO MAN THE SOREST, SUREST ILL.—
> Heaven's Sovereign saves all beings but himself
> That hideous sight, a naked human heart. YOUNG.

Nor among the unhappy causes of the increase of human misery, whatever it may ultimately lead to, can we avoid feeling the pouring out of that vial of wrath, the French revolution.

" Amid the calamities," as is remarked in a popular publication, " which this scourge of *Europe* (BUONAPARTE) has lately inflicted on the people of *Spain*, it is some consolation to contemplate the destruction of one of the most terrible instruments of hostility to the interests of human nature, which the enemies of human nature ever set up. If BUONAPARTE succeed in rendering himself master of *Spain* and *Portugal*, the Inquisition will cease to pollute the soil of *Europe*. It will never be forgotten in the annals of human happiness and misery, that such an act was left for such a man to perform. The *Romans*, says MONTESQUIEU, deserved well of human nature, for making it an article in their treaty with the *Carthaginians*, that they should abstain from sacrificing their children to their gods." *Edin. Rev.* No. XXXII.

Let us, however, congratulate ourselves, as well as on the general fact of the suppression of that accursed tribunal in *Spain* and *Portugal*, that it was not left for such a man to perform. Wretched indeed must that people be, beyond all names of wretchedness, who look for relief in the advent of NAPOLEON. Our own country has some claim to participate in the honor of the happy fact, that the Inquisition has ceased to pollute the soil of *Europe;* and the whole merit of abolishing from *Africa* its kindred curse. To have lived in an age wherein the abolition of the traffic in, and the torture of human flesh hath been effected, may repay a philanthropic mind for some of the pangs incident to its coeval atrocities. E. M.

We now proceed to the conclusion of the correspondence on the subject of *Hindu Infanticide*, including a detail of the proceedings that led to its abolition in *Guzerat*.

CHAP. VI.

Conclusion of the Correspondence between the HONOURABLE COURT *of* DIRECTORS, *the* GOVERNMENT *of* BOMBAY, *and* LIEUTENANT-COLONEL WALKER; *including a Detail of the Proceedings that led to the Abolition of* INFANTICIDE *in* GUZERAT.

THE Narrative, if it may be so termed, of the proceedings, having for their object the abolition of female Infanticide in *Guzerat* and the neighbouring countries, has been brought down to March 1808, by Colonel WALKER's copious Report, dated the fifteenth of that month; forming, with its accompaniments, Chap. III. and (with some additional matter, duly distinguished as such, by the editor) Chapters IV. and V. of this volume. We now proceed to the continuation and conclusion of the correspondence connected with the main subject of our work; inserting, however, first, an extract of a letter of an earlier date than that to which the narrative has, as just noticed, been brought: premising, introductorily, that the *Bombay* Government had brought the interesting project of the suppression of *Hindu* Infanticide, in its earlier stages, before the Honourable Court of Directors; who, as may be inferred from the known character of the Gentlemen who have of late years so ably filled the Chairs of that respectable body, received the project with much expectancy, and promoted its progress by the frequency and warmth of their commendations.

I shall, therefore, commence my extracts with the earliest paper that I deemed it necessary to take from the records at the India-House; access to which I was so fortunate as to obtain through the channel mentioned in another place, in terms adequate, I hope, to a proper sense of the attention thereby extended to [a] me. As well as the extract in question (No. 1.), the following papers of this Chapter were likewise so obtained—Nos. 3. 6, 7. 10, 11, and 12: my necessities extended no farther; but the liberality of the Honourable Court was unlimited. Should some of these papers seem to have a disjointed appearance, it will be recollected that they are extracts from the records in chiefly the *Political* and *Secret Departments*, that could not with propriety have been given in a more connected form.

[a] Having thus (in an author's coin) endeavoured to pay the literary debt incurred on this occasion to the Honourable Court, to whom my literary debt is, on other occasions, great; I still feel another, due to several individuals in less exalted stations of the same vast establishment.

Those who have occasion to transact business at the India-House, will find, in a greater degree, perhaps, than in any other extensive establishment in *London*, the most ready and obliging attention among its junior servants; even when, as hath sometimes been my case, his researches might be supposed troublesome and tedious. On such occasions it is indeed pleasant, when, expecting to find mere clerks, we meet with gentlemen. This remark is not applicable to the heads of departments—we then, of course, expect to find, in such responsible and lucrative situations, men of superior talents, and of corresponding deportment—but in gradations downward, there are, in every department, young men of highly respectable education, talents, and families, laudably looking up to the head of their respective offices, and striving to deserve success by emulating the example of those who have profitably ran the earlier race of dutiful industry. To several of these gentlemen I feel indebted for their attentions; and as it would be improper, perhaps, to mention names, I will here generally offer them my thanks, and best wishes for their deserved success in life. E. M.

No. 1.

Extract of a Letter from the GOVERNMENT *of* BOMBAY, *to the* HONOURABLE COURT *of* DIRECTORS, *dated* 31*st July*, 1807.

Para. 52............We refer to our proceedings for the particulars of our instructions (since approved by the Supreme Government) to that [b] officer, whose appearance in that sequestered [c] region, hitherto so rarely visited by Europeans, we have also incidentally in view, to render conducive to the abolition of the horrid practice of female Infanticide; such as is acknowledged to prevail in several families of some classes of the *Kattywar* chieftains, in the manner particularly set forth in the information from SUNDERJI SIVAJI, and other creditable and corroborative notices, recorded on our consultations of the 20th May and 30th December,[d] 1806. For which purpose the Resident has been authorised to urge, among the arguments to this prejudiced class of society, the similar abandonment which has happily been obtained from tribes of similarly misguided subjects of your government, under the immediate administration of the Presidency of *Fort William*, their knowledge of which may materially contribute to facilitate their acquiescence in a like amelioration, in as far as respects their own lamentable habits.

[b] Colonel WALKER. [c] *Kattywâr.*

[d] These have not been given in the form of the records referred to, as their substance is included among later and more matured communications. E. M.

No. 2.

From the Bombay Government *to Major* Alexander Walker, Resident *at* Baroda.

Sir,

I have the honour to acknowledge the receipt of your letter, dated the fifteenth of this month, and of its several accompaniments. I am directed by the Honourable the Governor in Council to inform you that, in addition to the approbation already expressed, under date the *7th instant, of the success of your exertions in putting (it is hoped) an effectual end to the horrid practice of Infanticide, in, and throughout the Peninsula of *Guzerat;* government have perused, with an interest commensurate to the extraordinary nature, and great importance of the subject; the more particular details furnished by your present address, of the probable rise and progress, and the too certain prevalence of this nefarious system among the *Jarejahs;* and, in one instance at least, among the *Jaitwa Rajputs.* And while the Governor in Council cannot sufficiently commend that solicitude, perseverance, and ability, to which is to be ascribed the procuring of the obligations entered into by the several chieftains to abandon it, he is sensible that it must require the vigilant and concurrent attention of both the governments of the *Gaikawar* and of the Honourable Company to ensure, especi-

* From which an extract is given in p. 40. E. M.

ally during the first years, the faithful adherence of the several parties to the salutary stipulations to which they have thus been brought to subscribe:—but the Honourable the Governor in Council relies on your zeal; and feels assured, that you will not fail to stimulate the native administration at *Baroda*, and through it, their officers in *Kattywàr*, to attend to, and make periodical returns of, the effects of the new system thus happily introduced; which if allowed to operate must become manifest in the number of female children that every *Jarejah's* house may soon be known to contain; whilst, on the other hand, the want of such indication will constitute proof sufficient of the influence of the old prejudice, and of the disregard to engagements; which, in the present instance, ought not to be treated with much indulgence, but rather punished by a moderate fine, to be always imposed, with the privity of the British government, through you; and the amount of which is to be applied to the relief of those among the more indigent classes of the *Jarejahs*, who shall be known to fulfil and adhere to the letter and spirit of their engagements or otherwise; by the infliction of such different description of penalty as the local authorities may deem the most impressive, and likely to ensure the attainment of an object so highly salutary, and indispensable in all respects, as is the extirpation of the baneful practice of Infanticide from all the districts of *Kattywàr*, with an ultimate view to the same humane object in *Kutch*.

2. You are accordingly desired to concert with the *Gaikawar* government the best means for obtaining periodical notices of the operation of the obligations; making it also a rule to submit (exclusive of such intermediate reports as

may become necessary) one general statement on the last day of each year, how far the amended system has been acted on and observed; what deviations are known or suspected to have been made from its rules; and what means pursued for their enforcement. The whole to be accompanied with an estimate of the number of lives that may, under the blessing of Divine Providence, be thus ultimately saved to the community.

I have the honor, &c.

(Signed) FRANCIS WARDEN,
Ch. Sec. to Gov.

Bombay Castle,
31*st March,* 1808.

No. 3.

Extract of a Letter from the GOVERNMENT *of* BOMBAY *to the* HONOURABLE COURT *of* DIRECTORS, *dated* 14*th October*, 1808.

Para. 76. .... A motive that might, with a view to the interests of humanity, conduce to the British government's seeking to improve your connection with [f] *Kutch*, is

[f] The connections either political or commercial, between the English and the rulers of *Kutch*, have hitherto been by no means close. We have occasionally had an officer residing at *Buj*, its capital, (see pages 18. 25. 163.) in a political capacity, with the object, chiefly, of extending our commercial intercourse with *Kutch*; as we have had also, but not of late years, in *Sind*. The piratical habits of these people occasionally interrupt the friendship, not very ardent, between the states. In the event of certain political contingencies, which, while their possibility must be still confessed, seem removing farther and farther from a probability of occurrence, it will become an object of more importance,

the opportunity, thence perhaps derivable, of extirpating from the habits of the tribe of *Jarejahs* in that country the practice that so generally prevails among them, of causing their female legitimate children to perish immediately after their birth; having in this respect the same manners as were found in the year 1789 to prevail among the RAJ KHUMARS of *Benares;* and which those people were then induced to renounce in the manner reported in the correspondence of our President (then the Resident of that province) with the Government of *Bengal.* That previous knowledge, combined with the information he brought round with him, as to similar customs having prevailed, or still obtaining, in *Guzerat,* led to those researches that have, through the able agency of Major WALKER, the Resident at *Baroda,* effected a similar renunciation of a system so abhorrent to every natural feeling among all the *Jarejahs* throughout the *Kattawâr,* or Peninsula of *Guzerat;* for the particulars of which we beg leave to refer to the Major's interesting report of the 15th of March, recorded on the proceedings marked in the margin; which will also show that for want of a similar influence in *Kutch* as we possess in *Kattawâr,* the abominable practice of female Infanticide still continues in a country, which boasts at the same time with justice, of observing greater tenderness [g] towards the brute creation than any other division of *India.*

importance, and will doubtless be sedulously kept in view, the improvement of our connection with the governments of *Kutch* and *Sind*; thereby giving us greater influence than we could otherwise have in the navigation and other events on the *Indus.* E. M.

[g] This anomaly is remarked of the *Jarejahs* of *Kutch* by Mr. DUNCAN in p. 48. It is boasted of by FATTEH MAHOMED, in p. 124. And is noticed as a trait of the *Egyptian* character by BRYANT in p. 235. and of the *Phenicians* and *Carthaginians,* in p. 247. E. M.

88. ....This little state of [h] *Poorbunder* is become subject to the cognizance of your government, as one of those who, having (although the ruling family be of the *Jaitwa*, and not of the *Jarejah* tribe of *Raj-puts*) allowed the force of example to habituate them also, of late years, to the killing of their female offspring, have in consequence executed the renunciatory obligation against that abominable practice; their failure in the future observance of which renders them, in the terms of that deed, obnoxious to the animadversion of the British government: as to the mode of proceeding in respect to which we refer to our instructions to Major WALKER of the 31st of March [i] last.

89. ....The exercise of that correctional power will be in every instance conducted in the same spirit of tenderness, that excited originally the solicitude to effectuate this reform; which may, we hope, prove in its object and consequences, creditable to the government of *Great Britain* in *India;* by its having thus undertaken, and so far, we trust, accomplished, what will be found in the letters on this subject from [k] FATTEH MAHOMED the principal ruler of *Kutch*, to have never been thought of by any of the successive rulers in this quarter of the world, during a lengthened series of ages; and as to which, although himself a *Mahomedan*, he attempts to justify the great majority of his *Jarejah* countrymen, at the head of whom is the *Rajah's* own family, for having thus continued, and still persevering, within that province, in the observance.

96. ....These several dispatches having been in due

[h] In *Guzerat*. See pages 72. 212.

[i] No. 2. of this Chapter.

[k] Nos. 20 and 22. of Chapter IV.

course communicated to the Supreme Government, have been honoured by its decided and distinguished approbation; such as they cannot probably fail to be farther honoured with, by the final sanction of the superior authority, to whose judgement their merits are now respectfully submitted; introductory, as we hope they will prove, to a new æra of civilization and tranquillity among this turbulent race; to the improvement of whose morals and worldly circumstances, all the efforts of this Government, and so well qualified an agency as that of Major WALKER, have been thus sedulously directed. Nor can these efforts ever prove otherwise than grateful to our remembrance, in their having, under the blessing of Divine Providence, led the *Jarejah* and *Jaitwa* part of that community, to stipulate to abstain in future from the horrid, and almost incredible, crime of being the habitual executioners of their own innocent offspring.

No. 4.

From the Resident at Baroda, *to the Honourable* JONATHAN DUNCAN, *Governor, &c. &c. &c. Bombay.*

HONOURABLE SIR,

1. Adverting to the chief secretary's letter of 31st March 1808, I have great satisfaction in submitting for your information the accompanying copy of a letter with its enclosure, from [l]SEWRAM SADASHEO, the native agent in [m]*Kattywar*.

[l] This is the current pronunciation of the name of this gentleman—it would be

[m] Vide Nos. i. and ii. at the end of this letter.

2. It is little more than a month since that I desired SEWRAM to direct his inquiries to ascertain the number of females which he might learn had been preserved in the *Jarejah* families in consequence of their engagements for refraining from Infanticide; and the satisfactory nature of the information which he communicates from a very limited portion of the *Jarejah* territory, seems to promise that the humane expectations of the Honourable Company's government will not be disappointed in the result.

3. I have also the honour to transmit another memorandum (No. iii.) from the verbal communication of a *Jarejah* who came from *Murvi* to *Baroda* some time since; and I have no doubt that subsequent inquiries will greatly extend the list of those lives, which the influence of the Honourable Company's government have saved from the early death to which a barbarous superstition had doomed them.

4. When it be recollected that with a very strict inquiry during my early progress in *Kattywar*, not more than four or five instances of the preservation of daughters could be traced for years past; the importance of this reform will be estimated by the number which have been saved within the few months that have elapsed since the engagements were executed.

5. The number of lives thus, by a very limited inquiry, ascertained to have been saved, is a decisive proof of the beneficial nature of those engagements; but the effect which

classically written SIVA-RAMA SIDA-SIVA. In this instance the name of RAMA doth not, as might at first sight be supposed, refer to either of the *Avataras*, or incarnations, of VISHNU under that name; but to the husband of RAMI, a name of PARVATI—the feminine of RAMA. SIDA is also a name of SIVA—SIDI of his consort. See hereon *Hindu Pantheon*. E. M.

they have had on the minds of the *Jarejahs* is probably shown in a prominent light by this circumstance—that one of the *Jarejahs* mentioned in the enclosure No. ii. under the *bhyaud* of *Dherole*, is the same *Jarejah* JUSSAJI of *Jallia*, noticed in the 92d paragraph of my [a] Report of the 15th March last, who had already destroyed three daughters.

6. It is now difficult to prove the fact of any female children being put to death; but in a country where this act has never been considered criminal or disgraceful, and where indeed every one avowed it without scruple or compunction, the circumstances of three Infanticides only appearing to have been committed since the date of the engagements of relinquishment, and one of these resting on report, deserves notice; as tending to prove the rapid decrease of the practice, and that it is viewed by the public in a different light from formerly.

7. For those that have been ascertained, I have suggested to the *Gaikawar* government the mode of punishment which Mr. Secretary WARDEN's letter recommends.

8. I trust the information that I have now the honour to forward will prove satisfactory, and afford you, Honourable Sir, the pleasing hope that the horrid practice of female Infanticide may be eradicated from *Kattywar*.

I have the honour, &c.

Baroda,
16th December, 1808.

(Signed) ALEXANDER WALKER.

[a] Page 58. See also page 69.

No. i.—*enclosure of the preceding letter.*

From SIVARAMA SIDASIVA, *to Lieutenant-Colonel* WALKER, *dated Camp at* Sanuserra, *8th December* 1808.

(After compliments) ....It is certain that the *Gondal* man has put his daughter to death, though no one will come forward to prove it against him. I am using my endeavours on this point, and when we shall have actually detected him, the *Dewanji* will according to his orders take measures to fine him. I shall have the honour hereafter to send you a particular list of those persons who have respectively preserved and sacrificed their female offspring.

No. ii.—*of the enclosures.*

Memorandum from °WITTOBA, Dewanji—*of those* Jarejah Rajputs, *who, according to their agreement, have preserved their daughters; and of those who, it has been ascertained, or, as is suspected, have put them to death.*

Of the *Taluka* of *Rajkut*, and the *Bhyaad.*

1. *Jarejah* DADAJI, has preserved his daughter, and had done so previous to the agreement on this head—she is now two years old.[p]

° This name of WITTOBA is taken from one of VISHNU's subordinate *avataras,* or incarnations. Its history is detailed in the *Hindu Pantheon,* p. 417. and plate 11. contains a representation of this form of the incarnate preserving power, with his *Sakti,* or consort. *Diwan,* is a title equivalent to *Deputy,* or *Agent—ji,* a respectful termination, as noticed in page 119, and other places. E. M.

p See pages 67, and 142. preceding, and the note after enclosure No. i. of No. 8. of this Chapter. E. M.

2. *Jarejah* [q]Dosaji of the village of *Kotari*, has had a daughter since the agreement—she is now nine months old—he has named her Jijiba.

1. *Jarejah* Raduji has a daughter four months old.
2. .... Bapuji has a daughter four months old.
3. .... Desulji of *Rahdur* has a daughter three months old.

Of *Dherole*, and the *Bhyaad*.

1. *Jarejah* Jusaji of *Jallia*, preserved a daughter, but it died naturally after a month.
2. .... Waktaji of *Dherole*, has a daughter ten weeks old.
3. .... Makji of *Sanusura*, has a daughter nine months old, and his brother has also a daughter twelve months old.
4. .... Sagaramji of *ditto*, has a daughter five months old.
5. .... Barraji has a daughter four months old.
6. .... Nathuji of *Sia*, has a daughter eight months old.
7. .... Kanterji of *ditto*, has a daughter seven months old.
8. .... Karsanji of *Rajpur*, has a daughter ten months old.
9. .... Dahji of *ditto*, has a daughter nine months old.

[q] In p. 146, this person is called Dosaji of *Kotaria*; in enclosure i. of No. 8. of this Chapter, *Koer* Dosaji of *Kotaria Murvi*. E. M.

10. *Jarejah* DESAJI of *Jabiru*, has a daughter seven months old.
11. .... JETTAJI of *Jaiwojara*, has a daughter ten months old.
12. .... PATABAHI of *Radka*, has a daughter six months old.
13. .... VIRAJI of *Dirakder*, has a daughter five months old.
14. .... TOGAJI of *Dangar*, has a daughter three months old.
15. .... WAZUBAHI of *ditto*, has a daughter three months old.

1. *Jarejah* KHANJI of *Worali*, has put his female infant to death.
2. .... [1]NATHUJI of *Gondal*, the legitimate son of DIVAJI the *Raja* of *Gondal*, has also destroyed a daughter—this is affirmed by a number of people, but hitherto no one has come forward to substantiate the fact.

[1] This person now styled *Jarejah* NATHUJI, the legitimate son of DIVAJI the *Raja* of *Gondal*, appears to be the same person who, with his father, set the example of renouncing Infanticide by first signing the deed to that effect, as recorded in page 94, paragraph 262, wherein, however, we see him called *Koer* NATHU. We here find a member of the *Gondal* family relapsing into the crime, that some individuals of it had the merit (see page 92, paragraph 250) of having spontaneously discontinued. Adverting to the prefixture of *Koer* to this name, the reader is referred to pages 117, and 147, where I have noticed it as, probably, a family or familiar appellation, or as designating a relationship to a *Raja*. Here it is applied to the legitimate son of a *Raja*, as the chief of *Gondal* is above styled, although both he and his son NATHU, or NATHUJI (in reference to *ji*, see pages 119, 152.) are in pages 26 and 95, called *Zemindars* only. In page 146, their names are *Jarejah* DIVAJI, and *Koer* NATHUJI. E. M.

3. Another *Rajput* is said to have put his daughter to death—but this is only report.

Recapitulation—Female infants preserved 20
died 2
put to death 3
Total . . . 25

The above information has been obtained by an inquiry of one month—but these people are great vagabonds, and it is with difficulty that they can be detected in putting their female issue to death.

No. iii.—*enclosed in Colonel* WALKER'*s letter of* 16*th Dec.* 1808.

According to the information of the *Jarejah* JEYTAJI of *Murvi*, the following families have saved their daughters since the agreements for abolishing Infanticide.

Jarejah MURGI of *Dherole*.
. . . . JANAJI of *Nagrawar*.
. . . . RAMABAY of *Rajkut*.
. . . . SHITANY of *Dherole*.

These four, JEYTAJI observes, are of his acquaintance; and says that there are many others who have reared their daughters, and that the practice is becoming general. This information was given on the 10th of August 1808. A. W.

No. 5.

From the GOVERNMENT *of* BOMBAY *to Lieutenant-Colonel* WALKER, *Resident at* Baroda.

SIR,

In acknowledging the receipt of your letter dated 16th of this [*] month, I am directed to advise you that the Honourable the Governor in Council experiences a sensible satisfaction at the prospect afforded of extirpating, from the Peninsula of *Guzerat*, the horrid and so long prevalent practice of female Infanticide; such as a vigilant attention in encouraging an adherence to the engagements lately entered into for renouncing it, and an enforcement of the recommended mode of punishment against those who may still be detected in its commission, cannot fail, under the blessing of Divine Providence, to achieve; and thus, as is trusted, to stamp an era in the history of *Guzerat* lastingly creditable to the *English* name and influence.

I have the honour to be, &c.

(Signed) FRANCIS WARDEN,
Ch. Sec. to Gov.

Bombay Castle,
24th December, 1808.

[*] No. 4. of this Chapter.

No. 6.

Extract of a Letter from the GOVERNMENT *of* BOMBAY *to the* HONOURABLE COURT *of* DIRECTORS, *dated 20th January*, 1809.

Para. 46. ……….In continuation of the subject of the 76th, 88th, and 96th paragraphs of our letter of 14th October[1] last, we have much pleasure in referring to a letter recently received from the Resident at *Baroda*, as containing a satisfactory account of the success that has already attended our endeavours to repress, among the *Jarejah* families in *Kattawar*, the horrid practice of female Infanticide. We congratulate your Honourable Court on the prospect thus afforded of extirpating from the Peninsula of *Guzerat*, a custom so long prevalent, and so outrageous to humanity. This object will not be lost sight of; and, trusting to the aid of Divine Providence, we look with confidence to its gradual but certain accomplishment, to such a degree as may form an era in the history of *Guzerat*, lastingly creditable to the *English* name and influence.

[1] No. 3. of this Chapter. It is usual in official correspondence in *India* to number the paragraphs of public letters. This is a very convenient and useful custom; affording, among other advantages, a ready reference to any desired subject, and rendering subjects so divided, less liable to misapprehension than when connected multifariously, and the paragraphs be lengthened by such connection. Series of instructions, for instance, are more clearly laid down, and are easiest adverted to in short numbered paragraphs. I have noticed this (aware at the same time, that some ridicule has of late attached to the high numbers to which the paragraphs of certain Eastern compositions have reached) in view to the remark that it is not, as I have been informed, usual to number the paragraphs in the communications of our public offices at home; and to hint the probability that its adoption would be found convenient and useful. E. M.

No. 7.

Extract of a Letter from the HONOURABLE COURT *of* DIRECTORS *to the* GOVERNMENT *of* BOMBAY, *dated 30th August* 1809.

Para. 6. ....We cannot quit this subject, without expressing our entire approbation of your having instructed Major WALKER to prevail upon the several chieftains in that district[w] to renounce the horrid practice of destroying their female children. We have the consolation to observe, that, in consequence of Major[x] WALKER's interference, several of these chieftains have by the execution of a most solemn deed, renounced this shocking custom in future.

No. 8.

From the Resident at Baroda *to the Honourable* JONATHAN DUNCAN, *Governor, &c. &c. Bombay.*

HONOURABLE SIR,

1. During the recent [y]expedition into *Kattawar*, I was not unmindful of inquiring into the success of the humane

[w] *Kattawar.*

[x] This officer being sometimes styled *Major*, and sometimes *Colonel*, is accounted for in a former page. E. M.

[y] Colonel WALKER, the reader will have observed, was Political Resident at the *Gaikawar durbar*, or the Court of GOVIND RAO GAIKAWAR, the sovereign of *Guzerat.*

In

arrangements introduced under the Honourable Company's Government, for the abolishment of female Infanticide among the *Jarejah Rajputs;* and I am happy to report, that this reform has completely taken root.

2. I have the honour to enclose a list of those *Jarejahs*, who have preserved their female children, which fell under my own direct observance. On my halt at *Dherole*, I had all those in the immediate neighbourhood, who were capable of attending, brought to my tent; and many were too young to be brought to any distance. It was extremely gratifying on this occasion to observe the triumph of nature, feeling, and

In *Europe*, this situation would be called that of an ambassador, but in *India* all our diplomatic ministers are styled *Residents*. In addition to this appointment, Colonel WALKER was also Commercial agent on the part of the *Bombay* Government, and Collector of the Revenue—each of them, in the infancy of our close intercourse with that court and country, an office of great labour and responsibility; and requiring in the execution of its complicated and delicate duties great talent and address. This friendly intercourse between the two governments has been productive of very important benefits to us; and is a blessing to the country of the *Gaikawar*—still, there were many turbulent and intriguing spirits who ill brooked the interference of the *English*; and every engine of intrigue, in a country proverbial for it, was set at work to prevent the introduction of our influence, forecasting therefrom the downfall of the system of corruption and oppression and injustice under which both court and country were, and had long been, cruelly suffering. Nor was intrigue alone resorted to—it enlisted under its banner the armed force of a country of warriors, and large bands of foreign auxiliaries, whose ill-directed efforts were with great energy aimed at preventing the introduction of the *British* power and influence; and at their expulsion after they had commenced their operation. We have in consequence, been engaged, first and last, in an extensive series of warfare in *Kattawar*; in which have been displayed as much valour, skill, and perseverance, as in any of our more brilliant and better known campaigns. In several of these Colonel WALKER commanded the *Bombay* army; and (I do not say established, for it was before established, but) confirmed a character in all military points, equal to that which he has on so many occasions evinced with such national benefit, in the line of a Civilian. This is no place to dilate on the campaigns in *Kattywar*, but they would form a volume of great interest. E. M.

parental affection, over prejudice, and a horrid superstition; and that those, who, but a short period before, would, as many of them had done, have doomed their infants to destruction without compunction, should now glory in their preservation, and doat on them with fondness.

3. The whole of the instances submitted in the accompanying lists have occurred since the execution of the engagements, renouncing the practice of Infanticide. Among these, the Honourable the Governor in Council will observe the name of the *Raja* of *Murvi*, *Kooer* DADAJI of *Rajkote*, and *Kooer* WAKTAJI of *Dherole;* and of several other men of rank and influence; whose example must have a most beneficial effect.

4. The list of lives which have been saved to the community, by the humane interference of the Company's Government, might be very considerably increased, by extending the inquiry into the *Jarejah* villages; but this will be sufficient to shew that the preservation of female children has now become general; and I trust that there is no reason to doubt of the final abolishment of this inhuman practice:—when once the natural emotions of parental affection have resumed their sway, it may reasonably be expected, that this cruel and barbarous prejudice will be condemned by those who formerly most strongly supported it.

5. As every anecdote relative to Infanticide is deserving of notice, it may be worthy of remark, that, in *Kutch*, there is a village inhabited by *Jarejahs*, who have for many generations abstained from the general custom of the *caste*, and preserved their female offspring.

6. This reformation has been produced in their manners,

by the influence of religion, and the presence of a Temple of VISHNU in their neighbourhood; it is well known that the tenets of this sect inculcate a regard to animal life, and which have in this case extended their influence to the support of humanity.

7. I respectfully beg leave to submit to the consideration of the Honourable the Governor in Council a memorandum of disbursements made in presents, to those *Jarejahs* who had preserved their daughters, and who visited me at *Dherole.*— The fund whence this disbursement is to be defrayed, is from the [*]*Nazzerdna*, exacted from the chieftain of *Gondal*, and of which the Honourable the Governor in Council is already apprised.

8. This arrangement is in conformity to the instruction of the Honourable the Governor in Council; and I respectfully trust it will be honoured with their approval and sanction.

I have the honour to be, &c.

Baroda, (Signed) ALEXANDER WALKER,
25th December, 1809. *Resident.*

[*] It has been remarked in a former note, that many of the revenue terms, even under some *Hindu* governments, in *India*, as well as under our own, are taken from the languages of the *Mahomedans*. *Nazar*, or *nezzar*, written sometimes *nuzzur*, is a *Persian* word, meaning a present, or gift, or offering, from an inferior: hence *nazaràna* is an amplification of that sense, applied to some kinds of the produce of governmental ways and means. From a superior, a *gift* is called *bakshish*, from the verb *baksh—(idan,* to) *give*—hence probably is our Christmas *box*; for the *Persian* word has, when vulgarly pronounced, nearly the same sound: in *Bengal* especially, where, at *Christmas*, and at other times, natives of the lower degree solicit *boxes*, or *buxies* as it is sometimes expressed, from the *Europeans*. The word *baksh* occurs often in composition. KAMBAKSH, the *Granter of Desires*

No. i.

Translate of a Memorandum specifying those Jarejahs *who have preserved their female children.*

	Names.	*Taluk*, or village.
1.	*Koer* WAKTAJI, ...	*Dherole.*
2.	DADA ABUJI, ...	*Ditto.*
3.	DADA JETAJI, ...	*Dherole Byaad.*
4.	*Jarejah* JETAJI, ...	*Jywah.*
5.	. . . . PUNZAJI, ...	*Lealah.*
6.	. . . . MAKENDJI, ...	*Sansora.*
7.	. . . . MAILAJI, ...	*Ditto.*
8.	. . . . MULOJI, ...	*Rufi-anna.*
9.	. . . . HOLAJI, ...	*Dàngar.*
10.	. . . . MARUJI, ...	*Waguder.*
11.	. . . . BHANJI, ...	*Guletan.*
12.	. . . . PUCHANJI, ...	*Lealah.*
13.	. . . . DOSAJI, ...	*Ditto.*
14.	. . . . JAYMALJI, ...	*Razpura.*
15.	. . . . JAGUJI, ...	*Maigpur.*

Desires, was the name of AURANG ZIB's favourite son, and is a royal name in ancient *Persian* history; but having an unmusical termination in the fastidious organs of the *Greeks*, they harmonized it into KAMBYSES, or CAMBYSES. *Kam*, both in *Sanskrit* and *Persian*, has thus the same meaning, and the god of desire is appropriately named KAMA in the language of *Hindu* mythology. Besides *nazar* and *bakshish*, there are several other words expressive of a *gift*; distinguishing also the relative rank of the giver and receiver, and the nature of the service on account of which the operation has arisen. The *nazeràna* exacted on this occasion from the *Gondal* defaulter, was, I have heard, twenty thousand *rupees*; about £2500. E. M.

	Names.	Taluk, or village.
16.	*Jarejah* Byji, ...	*Veperdi.*
17.	. . . . Bharaji, ...	*Ditto.*
18.	. . . . Ajobaji, ...	*Anendpur.*
19.	. . . . Halaji, ...	*Ajamchera.*
20.	. . . . Dosaji, ...	*Bajorka.*
21.	. . . . Khandaji, ...	*Babara.*
22.	. . . . Dhulji, ...	*Tanole.*
23.	. . . . Jataji, ...	*Dagara.*
24.	. . . . Muluji, ...	*Sanosura.*
25.	. . . . Togaji, ...	*Dangra.*
26.	. . . . Haldore Mareji.	
27.	. . . . Juitaji.	
28.	. . . . Jehaji, ...	*Rajkut.*
29.	*Koer* Dadaji, ...	*Rajkut Byaad.*
30.	. . . Dosaji, ...	*Kotaria*[a] *Murvi.*
31.	*Jarejah* Jehaji, . . *Raja* of	*Murvi,* a daughter just born.
32.	. . . . Jalerajah[b] Jusaji,	*Jallia.*

(Signed) Alexander Walker,
Resident.

[a] See enclosure ii. of No. 4. of this Chapter.

[b] This is the same person noticed in paragraph 5. of Colonel Walker's letter forming No. 4. of this Chapter. *Jalerajah* I imagine to be a convenient and harmonious manner of distinguishing the *Rajah* of *Jallia*; as Ralakaji occurs in page 30, as a mode of pronouncing Rao, or *Raja* Lakpat. The *Raja* of *Murvi*, No. 31. of the above list has often appeared in earlier pages of this work, (39. 87. 108, 109, &c.) as a great stickler for the custom that we happily see he has practically renounced. This person is in this work variously styled *Raja*, *Koer*, *Thakur*, and *Jarejah*. Others of the above list, have appeared in the lists given in page 146, and in enclosure ii. of No. 4. of this Chapter; and in other pages. E. M.

No. ii.

List of presents to the daughters of the Jarejahs *of the* Taluk Dherole, *and* Bhyaad.

Jarejah WAKTAJI, ...	300 *rupees.*
.... BAWAJI's niece, ...	250
.... WALOJI, ...	150
.... JETAJI, ...	150
.... MAILAJI, ...	150
.... PONZAJI, ...	200
.... JETTAJI, ...	200
Total, ...	1400

No. 9.

Extract from the Minutes of Council of the Bombay *Government, of the 6th January* 1810.

We have read with interest and sympathy the preceding Report of the successful progress made in the abolition of female Infanticide; and we entirely approve of the measures which Colonel WALKER has adopted with a view to the advancement of that salutary and desirable object.

The acting *Resident at *Baroda* is to be also advised of these sentiments for his future guidance, in respect to the

* Colonel WALKER had now vacated his appointments in *Guzerat*. E. M.

measures to be hereafter adopted, with reference to the future repression, and ultimate extinction, of this horrid practice among the *Jarejah* tribe in *Kattywar*.

No. 10.

Extract of a Letter from the BOMBAY GOVERNMENT *to the* HONOURABLE COURT *of* DIRECTORS, *dated 14th April* 1810.

Letter to —— dated 30th Aug. 1809.

Para. 6. Satisfaction expressed at the abolition of the practice of female Infanticide in *Kattywar*.

Para. 10. ....It will afford your Honourable Court increased satisfaction to observe by the Report from Colonel WALKER, under date 25th December[d] last, that the measures pursued by that officer, under our instructions on his first circuit of *Kattywar*, have had all the effect that could perhaps be reasonably expected from them, in so short a period; but as long as this horrid practice is allowed, and even cherished and extolled, in the adjoining and independent country of *Kutch*, we fear it may prove the more difficult to eradicate it entirely from *Kattywar;* to which effect, however, no efforts on our part shall be wanting.

[d] No. 8. of this Chapter.

No. 11.

Extract of a Letter from the HONOURABLE COURT of DIRECTORS *to the* GOVERNMENT *of* BOMBAY, *dated 29th August* 1810.

Letter from —— dated 14th October 1808.

Para. 88. 89. Relative to the success which has attended the endeavours to effect the abolition of female Infanticide in the Peninsula of *Guzerat*.

Para. 26. In the 6th paragraph of our dispatch in this Department (the *Political)* dated[e] 30th August 1809, we noticed with the highest satisfaction the measures which were in progress for putting an end to the horrid practice among the chieftains in the *Kattawar* districts, of destroying their female infants. We have the additional satisfaction to observe from Lieutenant-Colonel WALKER's Report of the 15th March 1808, containing the origin and history of this barbarous practice; and by his letter of the 16th December, referred to in the 46th paragraph of your subsequent dispatch of the 20th January[f] 1809, that he has been so far happily successful towards the accomplishment of this humane object, as to afford a prospect of completely extirpating from the Peninsula of *Guzerat*, a custom that has been so long prevalent, to the disgrace of humanity. Lieutenant-Colonel WALKER's perseverance herein is entitled to our highest commendations.

[e] No. 7. of this Chapter.

[f] No. 6. of this Chapter.

No. 12.

Extract of a Public Letter from the HONOURABLE COURT *of* DIRECTORS *to the* BOMBAY GOVERNMENT, *dated 26th October* 1810.

Para. 4. We perfectly accord with you that Lieutenant-Colonel WALKER, during his residence at the court of ANUND ROW, has rendered eminent services to the state by the restoration of order and regularity into the affairs of the *Gaikawar* government, and the establishment of the Company's influence in that country.

5. Your instructions to Lieutenant-Colonel WALKER to endeavour to prevail upon the several chieftains of *Kattywar* to renounce the horrid practice of female Infanticide, have already had our entire approbation, as expressed in the 6th paragraph of our Political Letter to you of the 30th August[g] 1809; and it is with the deepest interest that we have perused Lieutenant-Colonel WALKER's Report of the 25th December[h] 1809, referred to in the 40th paragraph of your Political Letter of the 31st January[i] 1810, wherein we find that the arrangements adopted by Lieutenant-Colonel WALKER for the prevention of this barbarous custom have been attended with success, and that the reform in the habits of the people among whom the practice obtained had completely taken root: and that natural affection and parental feelings had so far began to take place of prejudice and superstition, as to leave no doubt of the abolition of this inhuman practice being

[g] No. 7. of this Chapter. [h] No. 8. of Ditto. [i] Not extracted.

finally[k] effected:—and we cheerfully acknowledge Lieutenant-Colonel WALKER's merits in having so successfully exerted himself in the general interests of humanity.

6. We are also ready to admit that the successful result of Lieutenant-Colonel WALKER's political negociations at the *Gaikawar Durbar* and with the chiefs of the states bordering upon the *Gaikawar* dominions, and of the expeditions under his command, is to be attributed to the wisdom and prudence that suggested them, and to the ability and zeal with which they have been executed.

[k] In reference to the gratifying visit made to Colonel WALKER, in the neighbourhood of *Dherole*, where, as mentioned in page 299, many of the children preserved through his interference were brought to his tent, I omitted, in its properest place, to add, that, as the visit was premeditated, several officers and gentlemen assembled to witness so extraordinary a scene. The *Jarejah* fathers, who a short time back would not have listened to the preservation of their daughters, now exhibited them with pride and fondness. Their mothers and nurses also attended on this interesting occasion. True to the feelings that in other countries were found by Mr. DUNCAN and Sir JOSEPH BANKS (pages 56, 259) to prevail so forcibly, the emotions of nature here exhibited, were extremely moving. The mothers placed their infants in the hands of Colonel WALKER, calling on him and their gods to protect, what he alone had taught them to preserve. These infants they emphatically called "his children." And it is likely that this distinction will continue to exist for some years in *Guzerat*. Scenes like this, however impressive, are not easily described. E.M.

FINIS.

INDEX.

T. Bensley, Printer,
Bolt Court, Fleet Street, London.